KRISTIN WEIDENBACH

MAILMAN
OF THE BIRDSVILLE
TRACK THE STORY OF TOM KRUSE

 hachette
AUSTRALIA

hachette
AUSTRALIA

First published in Australia and New Zealand in 2003
by Hodder Australia
(an imprint of Hachette Australia Pty Limited)
Level 17, 207 Kent Street, Sydney NSW 2000
www.hachette.com.au

Reprinted 2003 (six times), 2004, 2005 (four times), 2006 (three times),
2007 (twice), 2008, 2009, 2010, 2012 (twice), 2014

This edition published in 2015

10 9 8 7 6 5 4 3 2 1

National Library of Australia
Cataloguing-in-Publication data:

Weidenbach, Kristin, author.
Mailman of the Birdsville Track: the story of Tom Kruse/Kristin Weidenbach.

978 0 7336 3328 7 (paperback)

Kruse, Tom.
Letter carriers – Birdsville Track (S. Aust. and Qld.) – Biography.
Postal service – Birdsville Track (S. Aust. and Qld.) – Employees – Biography.
Country life – Birdsville Track (S. Aust. and Qld.).
Birdsville Track (S. Aust and Qld.) – Description and travel.

383.49092

Map illustration by Ian Faulkner
Cover design by Christabella Designs
Cover photographs courtesy of Shutterstock and author's collection
Text design and typesetting by Bookhouse, Sydney
Typeset in Stempel Garamond
Printed and bound in Australia by Griffin Press, Adelaide, an Accredited ISO
AS/NZS 14001:2009 Environmental Management System printer

MIX
Paper from
responsible sources
FSC
www.fsc.org   FSC® C009448

The paper this book is printed on is certified against the
Forest Stewardship Council® Standards. Griffin Press holds
FSC chain of custody certification SGS-COC-005088. FSC
promotes environmentally responsible, socially beneficial
and economically viable management of the world's forests.

*To my father, Neil Weidenbach, for bringing
Tom into our lives*

ACKNOWLEDGEMENTS

The most common remarks I received upon approaching a new source and telling them I was writing a book about Tom Kruse were: 'It's about time' and 'Thank you for recording the history of our pioneers'. I would like to say thank you to Tom and Valma, in return. It has been a privilege and an honour for me to write this book and my life has been changed and enriched by the experience.

I am indebted to Valma for sharing her carefully maintained collection of photos, letters and newspaper clippings, and for graciously allowing my tape recorder into her home; and to Tom for willingly sitting for hours and yarning about old times and places. He generously laid his life before me, with very few instances of, '... Er, wouldn't like to see that on paper ...' or 'Ah ... better turn your whatsaname off ...' Whenever I checked an obscure detail that served as a memory time-peg for him, such as the year Delta won the Melbourne Cup or when Redditch won the Steeple, it was always spot-on, which gave me confidence in the accuracy of the remainder of his stories and anecdotes. For added reassurance, Valma was always ready to confirm or dispute crucial details when necessary.

Cross-referencing Tom's recollections with those of his peers, such as George Williams and Monty Scobie, also confirmed authenticity and helped fill in details. Each of these men has a deep-rooted knowledge of the Birdsville Track country and memories that are as extensive as they are impressive. The generous help of George, Monty and others such as Hans Mincham, Bob Bilton and Celia Teague have enhanced the book and made the writing of it a more enjoyable exercise for me, and for this I am extremely grateful. In particular, I would like to thank Monty; I am pleased to now count him as a friend.

I am grateful to Roger Clarke, Keith Webb and Ian Doyle for general assistance, and to Des Thompson, David Donaldson, Dave Burge, Aynsley Rowe, Helen Hamp, Charlie Stevenson, Colin Need, Peter Rogers, Jill Ford and others too numerous to mention for interview material and photographs. My thanks goes also to those who gave permission for their letters to be published, whether they were ultimately included or not, especially Margo Wilson's class of year four students at South Australia's Highgate Primary School and Margie Dawson's class of year three students at Burnside Primary School, also in South Australia.

Mark Metzger, Elizabeth Heyer, Film Australia, *The Advertiser* and the State Library of South Australia provided permission to reprint photographs and for this I am grateful. I also wish to acknowledge the reference works listed, which

Acknowledgements

I relied on for background information, and to thank my editors, Matthew Kelly and Jacquie Brown.

On a personal level I'd like to acknowledge my family for their interest and encouragement throughout the writing of this book. My father, Neil Weidenbach, in particular, assisted with fact checking, obliged me by acquiescing to several formal interviews and took immense pleasure in helping out however he could. If not for his involvement in the Badger's restoration I would never have conceived the idea for this book. And, finally, I'd like to thank Christoph Brockel, Melodie Jackson and Weber Hoen, who each appreciated the value of my endeavour and, together, created a steadfast support team for me in Boston, USA, where most of this book was written.

Contents

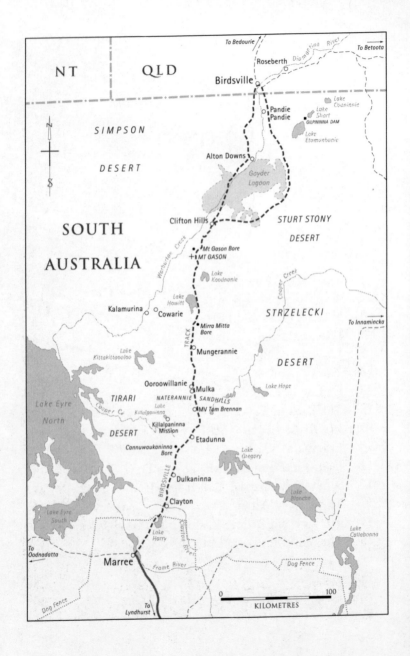

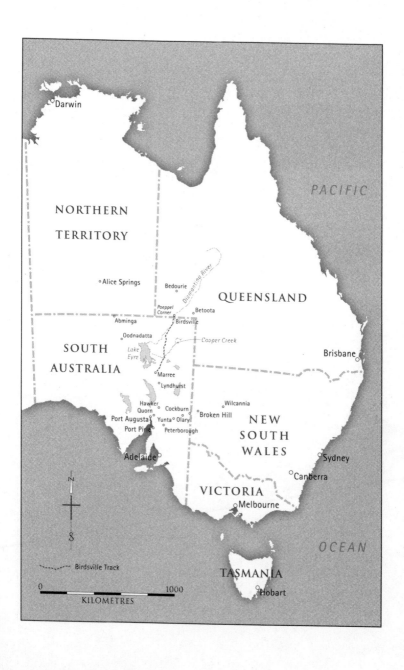

PACIFIC

NORTHERN
TERRITORY

°Darwin

°Alice Springs

Bedourie°

QUEENSLAND

Diamantina River

Poeppel
Corner   °Betoota
Abminga   °Birdsville

°Oodnadatta

Cooper Creek

SOUTH
AUSTRALIA

*Lake
Eyre*

°Brisbane

°Marree
°Lyndhurst

Hawker°   °Wilcannia
Quorn°   °Cockburn
Port Augusta°   Yunta° °Olary   °Broken Hill
Port Pirie°   °Peterborough

NEW
SOUTH
WALES

Adelaide°   °Sydney

°Canberra

VICTORIA
°Melbourne

OCEAN

- - - - Birdsville Track

0   1000
KILOMETRES

TASMANIA
°Hobart

Preface

For a storyteller in his eighties nothing beats whiling away the hours with yarns of the bush and reminiscences of outback faces from the past. For Tom Kruse, the quintessential mailman of the Birdsville Track, there is no better way to spend an afternoon.

Tom drove the Birdsville mail for twenty years. This is his story.

Tom is not a man of letters. He'd rather chop a load of wood with a blunt axe and load it on a high truck than write a letter, he says. But all of his tales are recorded nevertheless; written in detail on the pages of his mind. He can remember the name of a train guard on the Ghan in the 1940s and what a fine head of hair he had; he can tell you the name of one of the eminent families of the town in which he grew up in the 1920s and reel off the names of the family's three children and their children after that; he can give you coordinates for Potato Tin sandhill or Dead Men's sandhill—named for the four well-sinkers who perished there long ago in the agonies of thirst—Lover's Nook crossing on the Diamantina River, the Letterbox Claypan, or Kidman Swamp; and in the next breath tell you what he did last weekend and who came over yesterday. Everything is quietly stored away and neatly filed. His memory is like a web spread over the Corner Country of far northern South Australia, south-western Queensland and north-western New South Wales.

Tom's stories can be difficult to untangle at first because of the enormity of his recollections. He has an anecdote for everyone and each is filled with references and cross-references to other characters and places. He'll stop mid-sentence with an '. . . Ah George. Well, you wouldn't know George, he was . . .' or a '. . . now Mrs Willis, she was the Birdsville policeman's wife, actually she was Johnson the boring contractor's daughter, actually funny thing about old Johnson . . .' And there you go . . . you're off onto a completely different story. With time and patience, however, the stories run into one. The individual streams trickle together to fill up empty waterholes and dry creekbeds and eventually create a flow of tales that form the inland sea of Tom's life in the outback—his years as the Birdsville mailman, his career as an earthmoving contractor, and his life as a steady and constant provider and family figurehead.

I was lucky enough to know Tom and his wife, Valma, as friends before I ever considered writing their story. My father, Neil Weidenbach, and Tom had spent four years together, toiling side by side to bring Tom's old Leyland Badger mail truck back to life. It was a labour of love that nurtured a mutual admiration and respect between the two men who are nineteen years apart in age. When the Badger was complete Tom drove it one more time down the Birdsville Track and

Australians from around the country celebrated the man they hailed as a true outback hero. People regarded him as a living treasure, a fount of inspiration.

'He's a wonderful man,' my father says, trying to define the essence of the undeniable aura that surrounds Tom Kruse. His caring warmth and gentle humour create a halo about him akin to a swarm of sticky bush flies that a man invariably carries with him from sun-up to sundown in the dry desert country that belongs to Tom.

This book began as a personal project; collating all the material surrounding the restoration of the Badger for Tom and my father and perhaps for some of the other restorers who might be interested. I would transcribe the letters and logbooks documenting each day's mechanical advances, add other pertinent details to have the story make sense, and distribute them among Tom's friends. But as I began sorting through letters to Tom in which people had poured out their admiration for him and shared memories of their encounters with him stretching back 50 and 60 years, and while I was researching the broadest details of Tom's life for a short story of the 1999 re-enactment mail run I was writing for *Australian Geographic*, I soon realised that the restoration and re-enactment were merely small chunks of the larger story. The journal article barely scraped the surface of the Tom Kruse mythology, and my efforts to document the Badger's resurrection would be only another incomplete effort. The one person who could put everything in context and explain all the unanswered questions—What did Tom do before and after the film *The Back of Beyond*? What was the Birdsville mail run really like? Why was the Badger abandoned in the desert and how did it come to be rescued?—

was, naturally, Tom himself. But writing is anathema to Tom and no one else had stepped forward to write the full story of his life. Many Australians have some inkling of Tom Kruse and the Birdsville mail service but the complete story of the country's legendary postman remained untold. I felt that someone should do it before it was too late.

I would do it. And with Tom and Valma's blessing, *Mailman of the Birdsville Track: The Story of Tom Kruse*, was born.

He and Valma invited me into their home, and for a day each week I sat before him like a sponge, soaking up his history. Valma served me morning tea, afternoon tea and lunch while I asked question after question about Tom's life of 87 years. In September I let him wander, spooling out story after story at his own pace. Then, as my time with him grew short and October turned to November and eased into December, I tried to take charge, steering Tom toward the tiny outback community of Marree in the '40s, the Adelaide suburb of Cumberland Park in the '80s, the Cooper Creek in the '50s or the slow-moving country town of Waterloo in the '20s; filling in the gaps, checking how 'old Jack' or 'old So-and-so' fitted into the story; verifying sequences of events; and attempting to nail down dates pegged to the winner of a long-ago horse race or that year's footy champions. Each day was spent recording tales told in Tom's uniquely distinctive style—that soft, halting, slightly throaty voice spinning out narratives littered with 'ers' and 'ahs' and, 'Well, look, from my side . . .' and, 'Hey it's rather queer . . .'— liberally sprinkled with quirky metaphors, bushmen's quotes, antediluvian phrases and what I came to recognise as one-of-a-kind 'Tomisms'.

PREFACE

I had arrived with the outline, the skeleton—Tom Kruse, mailman of the Birdsville Track, star of *The Back of Beyond*, outback road builder, dam scraper; big, strong, barefoot Tom, that funny, gentle, warm-hearted gentleman of the bush. By the end of the year, I had the flesh—the behind-the-scenes film stories from *The Back of Beyond*; tales of life on the edge of civilisation—the endless dust storms, the heat, the flies, the self-sufficiency; anecdotes of memorable mail passengers and of drovers' antics in the Birdsville Hotel; encounters with the Track—broken clutch plates and axles, improvisation and long walks; the travails of the Cooper Creek—coping with a river that explodes its banks after laying dry for 30 years; stories of simply existing in the outback—death and tragedy, neighbourliness and mateship.

Tom's life story reflects the character of outback Australia in the mid-1900s—it was not a place for the timid or weak, but it was a place where this charming and humble man thrived and conquered. Tom Kruse is an inspiration and I feel lucky to have the honour of telling his story.

Kristin Weidenbach
November 2002

THE EARLY YEARS

The Birdsville mailman lays down his hammer and chisel and emerges from his backyard toolshed. He casually steps around the cloud of bees swarming to and from the hive he has graciously allowed them to construct directly in front of the doorway—he admires the insects' zeal and industry— and ambles through the vines and shade trees to the house. He walks with a measured tread, slow but deliberate, even graceful; free of the shuffling or tottering common among others of his age. His legs are sturdy. After decades of trudging through sandhills, of bending and kneeling to dig out bogged truck tyres, of climbing cat-like into and out of high truck cabins, of springing his thick frame up onto the backs of truck trays, and of bearing twice his body weight when lifting 44-gallon drums filled with petrol weighing close to 200 kilograms, they still support him.

He pulls back the screen door at the rear of the house and makes his way through the sunroom to the laundry. He places his cloth hat on the countertop near the sink and washes up. His hair is short and smooth. The thick mop of short dark tufts that once covered his head is now a dignified covering of straight, grey strands. Without the Birdsville Track dust, sweat and axle grease that once enlivened it with unnatural body and verve it lies neatly and obediently against his head.

His hands are broad and weathered, the skin extending up his forearms brown and tough and the fingers thick and able. The left ring-finger ends in a stump at the knuckle, the result of an accident in his father's blacksmith shop more than half a century ago. He doesn't miss it. 'Look, from my side . . . one less finger to wash,' he remarks.

For a total of twenty years, intermittently, throughout the 1930s, '40s, '50s and '60s, the carrier called Kruse had ferried the mail up the Birdsville Track, coaxing overloaded, ill-equipped, clapped-out old bangers the 1000 kilometres from Marree to Birdsville and back.

Tom had had a parade of trucks during the years he was on the mail run, but one stood out as a favourite: the 1936 Leyland Badger that had starred with him in the film *The Back of Beyond*. In 1952, when the film's director, John Heyer, was charged with producing a documentary that would reflect the spirit of outback Australia, he chose Tom Kruse as his leading man, and together they made an internationally award-winning movie that captured hearts and imaginations across the country. Since the film's premiere in 1954, a generation of Australians forever pictured him driving the battered old truck in a wide circle, generating speed to attack the flank of a far northern sandhill or slapping the sides of the old girl, urging her forward with the words, 'Come on! come on!' as she struggled to make the crest.

Off-camera, Tom had driven the Badger year after year over sandhills, through flooded watercourses and across stony desert plains when the Birdsville Track was only a track—two thin wheel ruts that all but disappeared when dust storms blew and the sandhills moved leeward, or when the contrary Cooper or Diamantina spilled their banks and drowned tyre marks and drovers' tracks under tens of kilometres of water. This was the Birdsville Track of the '30s, '40s and '50s—before the advent of four-wheel-drive, roadside assistance service, satellite phones and the Global Positioning System, before the Track grew into the wide, graded, gravel roadway it is today.

In the same way that the Birdsville Track embodied the isolated stock routes of central Australia, Tom Kruse epitomised the hard-working people of the bush. He was dogged, loyal and resourceful; strong and dependable. Once a fortnight—ostensibly—he would load up with mail and freight and steer his vehicle into the desert. When conditions were bad it would often take him much longer than the planned five or seven days to make the round trip, vehicle breakdowns, dust storms, floods or bogs conspiring to keep him on the 'road' for weeks at a time on some occasions.

It was in 1936 that Tom's then employer, outback transport pioneer 'Harry' (Henry) Edgar Ding, purchased the brand-new Leyland Badger from Crawfords in Adelaide (which later became Commercial Motor Vehicles), the local Leyland agent. In those days, trucks were sold as a chassis and frame only, with the cab and body built and fitted locally. The Badger's chassis was shipped from England and delivered to JA Lawton and Son in Adelaide for finishing. There, the Lawton's tradesmen built a cab and tray for the Badger alongside their usual milk floats, fire engines and baker's vans. One of Harry's drivers then took delivery of the Badger and drove it to Yunta in the mid-north of South Australia, where it became the newest addition to the Ding fleet.

Harry had set up a carting business in 1921. Aged fourteen, he had left school and begun using the family horse and cart to deliver supplies to the sheep stations surrounding the town of Olary in South Australia's mid-north. By the time the Badger came along, Harry's thriving business already owned two Leyland trucks—both Cubs—the first of which he had bought in 1932 for 1000 pounds, the sum of which included 300 pounds loaned to him by his father. The early 1930s being the last years of the Great Depression, big British trucks like Harry's new Leyland were a rarity on the roads. His truck was the best about and the residents of the railway centre of Peterborough came to gaze at the Cub in admiration when it pulled up at the wheat stacks with a full load.

A couple of years later young Tom Kruse, one of Harry's drivers, was sent to Adelaide to collect the second Cub.

'Don't be in a hurry to come home, drive it around for a day or two,' Harry told Tom before he left, figuring that the freshly painted truck with his trademark nameplate, 'HE Ding, Yunta' adorning both doors and running across the top of the cab would garner some free advertising.

The two Leyland Cubs earned their keep adequately hauling wheat and wool for northern pastoralists, but Harry's new Leyland Badger was a significant improvement over the Cubs. At six tons the Badger was heavier than the Cub and ran on diesel, which was almost half the price of petrol. This, combined with the fact that vehicles ran further on a gallon of diesel than a gallon of petrol, made it an attractive addition to the fold. The single-axle truck usually hauled 18 bales of wool and towed a trailer carrying the same number.

'Thirty-six or thirty-eight bales of wool used to be a full load. Harry kept it working 'round the clock,' says Tom. 'It was the first old diesel he ever had and it never used to stop. There was no sitting down. If one of his trucks came in at two o'clock in the morning with a load of wool, he'd say, "C'mon you tigers, on your feet." Then the driver'd go back and have a bit of a sleep while the others unloaded. Refuel, and you'd be on your way again.'

The Badger was originally assigned to Ding driver Wally Blucher, who took great pride in his new ride.

No one was allowed to take liberties with the Badger when Wally was around, not even Tom, his childhood friend who'd first got him the job with Ding's operation. 'Look, you could rest your elbow on the mudguard or lean against the side: He'd say, "For Christ's sake stand back! If you want a rest, go to bed and rest."

'It was Depression days. Wally Blucher was working for ten shillings a week and was pleased to get it. People were honestly pleased to even work for tucker. It was really rough. I tell you what, there were more dinnertimes than dinners in the little town of Waterloo.

'I asked Wally if he wanted a job working for HE Ding for 30 shillings a week. He was glad to be paid three times the money . . . didn't realise it would be three times the work.'

Born on 28 August 1914, Tom Kruse was tenth in the line-up of twelve born to 'Harry' (Henry) and Ida Kruse; the third youngest in a family of nine boys and three girls. Besides Tom, there was 'Joe' (Walter), the eldest, followed by Charlie; Ben; Adelaide; fair-haired 'Snow' (Arthur); Herb; Hilda; big, burly 'Skin' (Henry); Vera; wavy-haired 'Curly' (Norman); and Reg.

Tom had left school in 1927 at the age of thirteen and was doing odd jobs wherever he could find them close to home in the small town of Waterloo, 119 kilometres north of Adelaide. He helped out in the family blacksmith shop, gaining a valuable education in bush repairs and mechanical improvisation—and losing half a finger to the cogs of a drilling machine. He did day work harnessing horses, sewing wheat bags and milking cows at a nearby farm, in addition to a stint on a local council road-building team.

'Back in the Depression days the Council gave everyone in the district two days' work. We were cracking bluestone for the road. You'd crush them and stack them—very neatly, too, 'cause you were paid by the yard, and a yard of stones—there might be 10 000 stones in it. Hey, look, it's amazing how those old fellas took a lot of pride in their stone cracking.'

'Ray' (Sam) Durant, three years older than Tom and a boyhood friend from Waterloo, remembers all the Kruses as hard workers. 'Charlie and Herb used to go from farm to farm cold-shoeing horses,' he reminisces. 'They had a big blacksmith shop and serviced a large area. The boys used to have some old trucks and they'd cart grain into the sidings to the wheat stacks.

'They were all hard workers. The father—Harry Kruse—besides being a blacksmith, was the local undertaker—two horses and an old hearse. Very versatile lot, the Kruses.'

For a family of fourteen in the late 1920s money was tight and luxuries rare. Harry and Ida Kruse kept their flock clothed and fed but it was struggle that only deepened as the Depression rolled in and business at the blacksmith shop declined. Motor cars and trucks were the next new thing and demand for cartwheels, wagons and buggies was steadily decreasing. Mrs Kruse, abiding by her motto for life—hard work and religous faith—turned to her Bible for daily guidance and inspiration. She ensured that all the children were confirmed into the Lutheran Church at the tiny parish church down the road at Carlsruhe and she insisted that the Sabbath be a day of rest. In return, the Lord saw fit to keep the fruit trees growing and the hens laying, but He also served up a few lean days when 'a man could eat a horse and chase the rider'.

For Tom, though, it was a happy life. One of the purchases on which he spent some of his meagre savings was a puppy he bought at Saddleworth—the small town about 15 kilometres south of Waterloo that served as the hub of the area. Saddleworth held a monthly cattle market and Tom and the other local lads were irresistibly drawn to the action and excitement of market day.

'I went to a sale once down there—a mob of Kelpie pups was being sold and I got one for a shilling. I christened him "Swifty".

'He was amazing. At home—at Waterloo—we used to have about 75 ration sheep. We used to kill our own meat. I had Swifty really trained. No one else could handle him. Honestly . . . a finger and a whistle and, look, I tell you what, that dog . . . 75 sheep there and I'd pick out three sheep and he'd cut them out. No worries. I could get him to do anything. He'd be alert and watching . . . And he'd always wait to be told . . . even if the sheep were running past him. I was very attached to old Swifty.

'Then the butcher at Saddleworth said he'd give me three pounds for him and I reluctantly sold him. That was a lot of money, then. Queer thing, though, they couldn't get that dog to do a single thing. They couldn't get him to do anything . . . no one else could handle him. I happened to go down there once and Swifty spotted me, and I tell you what . . . that dog came running. He was desperate to hop on the back of the old truck and come back.

'Look, it's amazing how you can become attached to a dog. In those days everyone had sheep dogs and everyone was trying to sell them or give them away or so and so . . . try and get a few dollars. Well, it was part of a person's life. But he was the only one . . . ' Tom tails off. There was never another like Swifty.

Ray Durant eventually moved to the Riverland, the Murray area near the Victoria–New South Wales border, chasing elusive work during the Depression. On visits back to Waterloo he would sometimes run into Tom. 'Tom was sewing bags for a neighbour on one of my visits home and I went in to have a yarn. He said to me, "There has to be an easier way than this to earn a living." And next thing I know he's on the mail run in the north of the State—not a tougher job in the world!'

Tom had first moved 200 kilometres from the family home at Waterloo to the township of Yunta in the northeast of the State to work in a small garage owned by his older brother, Snow. The boys' maternal uncle, Arthur Stremple, had a place at Waukaringa—about 30 kilometres north of Yunta—and fair-haired Snow was a frequent visitor there. With his uncle's encouragement and support, Snow eventually opened a small garage-cum-service station in one of Stremple's premises in Yunta. Since the Depression had depleted business at the family blacksmith shop, the Kruse boys were all anxiously seeking work. Grateful for the opportunity, Snow was determined to make his small business a success.

He was a good mechanic and his garage in Yunta prospered. One day a message from Snow arrived at the Kruse family home in Waterloo: 'Chev truck going cheap, 120 pounds.' A local timber-cutter in the area had forfeited his truck to the hotel to settle his bill and the publican was now looking to recoup his losses. Tom's mother and father decided the bargain was too good to pass by and sent Tom to Yunta to close the deal and drive the truck back to Waterloo. It was his first excursion into the northeast. From then on, young Tom Kruse became one of the regulars around Yunta—occasionally working for his uncle loading and carting timber, and filling in for Snow if he was called away, serving petrol and keeping the garage doors open.

Like the rest of the Kruse boys, Tom was a hard worker. He was strong, dependable and likeable. It wasn't long before John Penna, the local storekeeper and Yunta postmaster offered him a job. Thus Tom's career as a truck driver began in 1932, at the age of eighteen, when he signed on as a driver for John Penna, who also operated a carting business that included the three mail delivery services out of the town. Tom took over the mail run from the previous driver, Jack O'Loughlin. Jack was unloading a drum of petrol at Lilydale station, a 12 000-square-kilometre sheep grazing property 66 kilometres south of Yunta, when the drum slipped and severed his thumb. He never drove the mail again.

In Tom's mind, the first year he spent in Penna's employ is inextricably linked to a pair of interstate horse races that occurred about six months after he started work. Yunta was a great betting town in those days and when the Grand National Hurdle and the Grand National Steeplechase came up at Flemington in the winter of 1933, one of Penna's customers asked Tom to lay a bet on his behalf. The amount of money entrusted to Tom for the wager has fallen from his mind but he hasn't forgotten the consequences that the races had for him.

'Look, I remember it clear as mud,' he says. 'This chappie said to me, "When you go back to Yunta, I want you to get Mr Penna to put this money on the horse called Belar and any money coming, put it all up on Redditch on the steeple." Belar was a cat jumper in the hurdles and he was a good price. Redditch was only even. He was a really good hurdler.

'Now, this is how dopey a man was. I didn't do it . . . forgot all about it. It wasn't that I did it purposely, but I did forget. Well, Belar won and Redditch won and John Penna paid up and I worked for three months to pay the money owed. And that's the year that I first started working for John Penna.'

Tom earned his nickname when he was just a lad. As a child in Waterloo he would hang around with an old man by the name of Tom Poole, who used to roam the town buying steel and bits of scrap metal—whatever he could resell to make a living.

'I was commonly known as Tom Poole because I was

always giving Tom Poole a hand and riding his old cart. And that's how I got the name of Tom,' he says. It would become the name that defined the man.

Working for John Penna, Tom was enjoying his first regular paid employment. In addition to driving the mail out to Lilydale, he was carting stores and supplies to the surrounding farms and stations and backloading with wool. He was making enough to be able to send some of his wages back to the family at Waterloo; he had his brother and uncle nearby, and he got along well with his boss. Boarding in the Penna home, Tom soon came to feel like one of the family.

But after about eighteen months in Penna's employ changes were afoot. Snow was getting itchy feet and was keen to move south to a new garage site at Meningie, on the coast east of Adelaide. John Penna was also thinking about getting out. He would see the big, heavy Ding trucks passing through town and knew that a new era of transport was on the way. He began to think about selling up rather than seeing his business submerged by the competition.

With his purchase of the Leyland Cub in 1932, Harry Ding, then still based at his hometown of Olary, had made a big step up from American Ford, Chevrolet and Dodge trucks and utilities to the larger, heavier, more robust and more reliable Leylands. In the wheat and wool carting seasons Harry made good money with his large-capacity truck, which carried 4620-kilogram loads—about 60 bags of wheat. But he knew that steady, year-round work would have to be found for the truck to make his investment profitable. He decided that mail runs were the answer, and began his first postal service with the Olary-to-Kalabity route, which ran twice a week, via Bimbowrie—a 110-kilometre return trip. Next came a contract for the Cockburn–Mulyungarie service—130 kilometres return.

In 1934, Harry swept into Yunta, buying Snow's garage and Penna's business, and relocating his entire operation. Yunta was only 81 kilometres southwest of Olary down the Barrier Highway from Broken Hill, but it was a three-hour drive away at the speed of travel of the time. The larger town provided a more central base. Tom and the other Penna drivers were folded into the package deal. Harry's fleet now consisted of the two Leyland Cubs, a Thornycroft, a Dodge buckboard and a new Ford buckboard, plus an elderly Albion and an old Brockway that had originally belonged to John Penna. His trucks and drivers were hauling wool, petrol, ore, mail and groceries throughout the north-eastern areas of the State.

Tom's nickname was well entrenched by that time and only those close to him knew that his real name was Esmond Gerald.

'Look, I might say, the only one that never, ever called me Tom, is my mother. No, she always referred to me by my Christian name—Esmond,' he says.

He recalls the day in August 1935 when Harry Ding sent him and fellow driver Don McRae up to a job at Murnpeowie station—'Mumpy' as the locals called it—cementing a water storage tank. Harry was keen to keep his employees busy, so if carting assignments were scarce the men were farmed out on various labouring jobs. Tom was the lackey that time and spent the whole day unloading, carrying, mixing and pouring bags of cement while Don, the builder, formed the tank lining.

At sundown, the manager, Mr Newland, came over, waving an envelope at them.

'He said, "Who's this EG Kruse?"' Tom recounts. '"There's a bit of mail here. I was going to send it back but . . . well, EG Kruse, who's he?"'

'Well, I'm EG,' Tom said with some surprise, taking the envelope and studying the handwriting. It was a letter from his mother. *Dear Esmond, I do hope this arrives on the 28th,* she'd written. *It will be your 21st birthday.*

'Here I am, 21 today, and I feel my arms are two inches longer, carrying that bloody concrete around,' Tom mused to himself. 'Look here,' he said, turning to Don. 'Let's have one of those bottles of beer that Mrs Dunn sent over.'

Emily Dunn, the hotelkeeper at Lyndhurst, had given Tom one dozen bottles of beer with which to celebrate his 21st birthday. Of course it was warm—no refrigeration in the workers' camp—but it would be a treat nevertheless.

On the way to Murnpeowie, Tom and Don had picked up a young Afghan lad on the side of the road. There'd been some kind of family dispute and the fellow was in tears, looking for a way out. He was only a weak little thing, no help with the manual labouring task at hand, but he was eager to pitch in and saw Tom's birthday as a way to express his gratitude.

'Can I help? What can I do?' he chanted, hopping around the two men.

'Look, there's some chops over there, turn them into a curry,' Don directed him.

'Well, anyhow, we had this meal,' Tom recalls. 'And the little Afghan lad—he was only about fourteen I s'pose—he started going round to Don and me:

'"Well," he said, "how'd you enjoy that stew?"

'Actually, bloody beautiful.'

'"Good. 'Cause I had a hell of a job scratching all those little white things off the meat."

'Oh, no! That's the maggots of course.' Tom chuckles, leaning back in his chair and snorting merrily at the memory.

'Look, eating them raw I don't like 'em. But if they're boiled . . . ah, nothing wrong with 'em. You scoop 'em off. Don't worry about the damn things.'

He divulged that a culinary trick used by one of his nephews was to boil the meat with some spaghetti or pasta to disguise their presence. 'Put a little more macaroni in, Uncle,' he'd tell Tom. 'That'll be all the white things floating in the water.'

By 1936, when the Badger first came on the scene, Tom had been driving for Harry Ding for two years, hauling livestock, wheat and wool from the big sheep runs along the Port Pirie-to-Broken Hill railway line to the train sidings at Yunta and Peterborough. He and the other Ding drivers mostly delivered stores and supplies to stations within a 150-kilometre radius of the Yunta base and backloaded with 200-kilogram bales of wool and 200-kilogram bags of wheat.

In the shearing season, from February to September, each of Harry's trucks carried its own loading pole and winch to help with the loading of the wool bales. With one man standing on the tray grabbing and manoeuvring the huge cubes with a short grappling hook and two helpers on the ground feeding the bales onto the winch, three men could load and tie down 110 bales in an hour. Wheat sacks, in contrast, were usually loaded by hand. Each sack was hoisted from the ground about one metre onto the tray of the truck and lugged into position by heaving and tugging at the ears of the heavy hessian bags. Then the back-breaking process was repeated in reverse at the railway yard. In the hot, dry conditions of the harvest season it was a job only for men who could toil like Trojans—men like Tom Kruse and his younger brother, Curly.

In August 1936, two days before Tom's 22nd birthday, nineteen-year-old Curly was killed in a trucking accident while working for Harry Ding. It happened when he was helping two Ding drivers transport a load of wool from Frome Downs, a remote sheep and cattle property 160 kilometres north of Yunta. Curly jumped out to open a gate. The two trucks kept moving. The wool was loaded wide. The track was narrow. 'He stumbled on a saltbush and rolled under the wheels,' Harry Ding recounted years later to John Maddock, author of *Mail for the Back of Beyond*. 'It was a terrible shock to everyone.' In his memoir, *Thirty Years with Men*, Ding reserves a special mention for Curly, 'whose splendid young life was cut short by an accident in my service—Curly was a lot of man'.

A couple of days passed before word reached Tom that tragedy had befallen Curly. He dropped everything and raced home. It wasn't until he arrived in Waterloo that he learnt that his brother had died in the accident. Despite being a family of fourteen, the Kruses were close-knit. To have Joe return to them from the War, yet have another son taken in a senseless accident was hard for the family to bear. It was even more so for Tom, who had to swallow his sorrow and anger and continue service for their shared employer.

•

By the end of 1935, HE Ding had successfully taken over five mail runs, having added the Yunta routes out to Lilydale and Waukaringa to his roster, in addition to a service from Waukaringa north to Frome Downs, calling on Koonamore, Curnamona and Erudina stations on the way. When the contract for the Marree-to-Birdsville mail route came up for tender that year, Harry made a bid for it. By then he was a specialist at providing mail and freight services to remote areas and felt that he understood the demands of the desert country well enough. Besides, the Track had an aura of romance about it that appealed to 28-year-old Harry's sense of adventure, and he was eager to expand his business into the untapped north of South Australia. At that time, Frome Downs station, near the southern tip of Lake Frome, was the top end of his mail runs.

The Birdsville Track was a dry, lonely cattle trail through the centre of Australia. A meandering path of hoofprints and camelpads with nary a tyre-mark to be seen. It was 500 kilometres of blinding sunlight glinting off orange gibber stones, eerie desert darkness and palpable silence. Five hundred kilometres of flies, choking dust storms and sand that would suffocate mouths and clog up vehicle air filters. Five hundred kilometres of searing heat that lay upon you like a thick wad of insulation, where walking from a disabled vehicle could mean walking to your death. Five hundred kilometres of mind-numbing monotony and mind-shattering isolation, where a person might not meet another living soul from one end to the other. The Birdsville Track.

It was a region on the cusp of change and Harry wanted to be a part of it. The camels that had carried freight up the Track for the past 60 years were gradually being replaced by a parade of optimistic motor mailmen who struggled up to Birdsville in overloaded light utilities—buckboards—and clapped-out wire-wheeled cars hopelessly inadequate for the desert conditions. Harry knew that with his big, sturdy truck running well within its load capacity he could replace car and beast in one fell swoop.

He won the contract for the Marree-to-Birdsville mail run with a quote of 300 pounds for 26 trips per year—125 pounds per annum less than the sum received by either of the previous two contractors. He would charge two pence per pound to cart goods to Birdsville and charge passengers a five-pound fare for the ride. With his superior vehicles and experienced drivers Harry was determined to make the Marree-to-Birdsville mail run the flagship route of the HE Ding enterprise.

2

TOM'S FIRST MAIL RUN

When Harry Ding won the Marree-to-Birdsville mail contract in 1936 it was natural that he would send Tom Kruse, his most competent driver, to establish the service. The HE Ding contract with the Postmaster-General's Department called for 26 trips a year—once a fortnight. Harry proposed a one-week schedule for Tom for the 1000-kilometre round trip—three days for the journey from Marree, one day in Birdsville, and three days back again. He would operate from a new Ding outpost at Lyndhurst, on the railway line 80 kilometres south of Marree, which Harry had established in December the previous year. During the Birdsville 'off' week Harry planned to keep Tom busy doing local carting trips from Lyndhurst to Murnpeowie, Beltana and Mt Lyndhurst stations.

The movement of cattle established the Birdsville Track, or the Queensland Road, as it was originally known. It was a stock route that had its heyday in the 1880s, in the days before Federation, when Birdsville was a thriving border town collecting custom taxes for the 1000-head mobs of cattle from the Channel Country in south-west Queensland that were making their way to the southern markets. When the railway was extended from Port Augusta to Marree in 1884, the Track became one of the most important stock routes in Australia as Queensland 'fats' were walked to the rail head at Marree for carriage to Adelaide.

When he was selected for the task at the beginning of 1936, Tom had never laid eyes on the infamous Birdsville Track. He had driven up to Lyndhurst plenty of times, but no further. Harry had only marginally more knowledge of the country Tom would be travelling through. His experience was limited to a couple of reconnaissance trips he'd made up to Birdsville since landing the mail contract—to introduce the new Ding service to the families of the Track and to sew up deals for freight loading for the northern cattle stations. He generously decided to send along one of his travelling companions from one of these trips to act as a guide for Tom's first run.

'He was like a sore rear to a boundary rider,' Tom recalls. 'Couldn't stand the weather, couldn't stand the water and he didn't know the way.'

In addition to the questionable 'guide', Harry sent Tom up north with a glittering new tandem-drive-axle Leyland Cub, a raise in wages to 35 shillings per week, strict instructions to be certain to sign the postal paperwork and leave Marree at 11 o'clock Friday morning, and a word of advice: 'Remember, Tom, when dealing with men, an ounce of loyalty is worth a ton of cleverness.' And Tom would need all the goodwill he could muster: Some of the folk of Marree were none too pleased with the arrival of Tom Kruse nor the era of motorised transport on the Track in general.

'Old Mr Scobie, that's Jimmy Scobie . . . he had the store at Marree,' says Tom. 'There were two stores in Marree those days—Scobie's store and the Carter store. Mr Carter was delighted, totally delighted. He said it was the greatest thing that could happen to the country. But Mr Scobie, in the beginning, he was very anti the Dings. Hell, he was treating us like a black snake. I said, "Look, I'm only a driver here and I'm pleased to have the job."'

At the time, Jimmy Scobie was the biggest freight supplier along the Track and he feared that Tom and his truck would see the end of his camel operation. 'I tell you, he was really roaring about it,' Tom says. 'I can understand it from his side: If you want to hurt a man, hurt him in his pockets.'

Jimmy Scobie and others like him, who preferred the old ways, knew that the large carting trucks spelled the end for the camel strings that had padded the Birdsville Track for more than half a century. The Afghan camel drivers and their beasts had been gradually disappearing from their homes at 'Ghan Town' on the north side of the railway tracks in Marree ever since lightweight buckboards, then V8 utilities, began replacing the mail horse, and station owners started buying vehicles and ferrying their own supplies. Harry Ding's high-capacity haulage truck was the final straw.

Whereas the mail was always carried by horse in the early days—either by horse and buggy or packhorse—camels were the traditional means for carting stores and supplies to and from the stations of outback Australia. Horses were faster, making the trip from Marree to Birdsville in about ten days, but they were more susceptible to the heat and lack of water typical of the terrain. Camels, on the other hand, could shoulder 300 kilograms or even up to 450 kilograms—at least three times the weight that a horse could carry—and could endure the harsh desert conditions much more readily. They were slow, but steady and reliable, making the same trip in 24 days.

Harry had seen the camels being loaded for a trip to Birdsville when he had visited Marree a few months before taking over the mail service. Wooden cases containing five dozen large bottles of beer were propped up either side of the pack, or 70-kilogram sacks of flour and sugar—always double-bagged to protect the contents from animal urine, sweat and saliva—were laid in pairs on each side. Then the line of animals, each one connected via a light rope in his wooden nose-peg to the tail of the one in front, was ushered to its feet amid much camel griping, spitting and verbal complaining. When all was ready the cameleer walked off into the desert, his string of 70 beasts plodding along behind him.

George Farwell, in his 1950 account of the inland, *Land of Mirage*, reported that animosity towards the pioneers of new forms of transport was not new: 'When motor trucks first began to push outback, undercutting the rates of Afghan carriers, sometimes without profit, the drivers complained that broken glass was spread to cut their tyres. On occasions there were fisticuffs beside the track, and knives flashed. But the Afghans remembered similar scenes a generation before, the advent of their camel teams having angered the bullock drivers and teamsters they displaced.'

It was New Year's Day, 1936, and 115 degrees F (45 degrees C) the day that 21-year-old Tom Kruse inaugurated the HE Ding service on the Birdsville mail run.

Mr Fred Hey, clerk of the Diamantina Shire Council, his wife, and Mrs Gloria Willis, wife of the brawny Birdsville policeman, Bob Willis, were Tom's first passengers. Tom's teenage offsider, Jimmy Simmons, and his 'guide', Kevin, were also onboard. There was only room for two in the cab, so the women rode inside with Tom, while Mr Hey, Kevin and Jimmy clung on top. The Heys had come south with Harry Williams, the previous mail driver, in his 1934 Ford utility, one of the first V8s to carry the mail. Now they were travelling back with Tom Kruse in his six-wheeled Leyland Cub. Along the way, Tom met up with Harry, who was completing his last trip, and whose friendly advice and helpful directions proved more useful than any assistance from his personal guide.

Harry Williams had been the Birdsville mailman on and off since 1926. When Harry Ding came along and undercut Williams's tender to the Postmaster-General's Department by 30 per cent he was forced out of the mail business.

'Dad lost his livelihood,' says Williams's son, George, an 83-year-old retired motor garage owner from Broken Hill, now living in Adelaide. 'He wasn't all that happy, but that's life. My dad was getting 35 pound per month and had to do two trips a month—the postal service'd have you doing it for a pound a month if they could. And we got tuppence per pound on any freight we carried. We only had four-cylinder Dodges, Dad and I, so we couldn't carry much.'

The biologist Francis Ratcliffe discovered the joy of passing for freight on one of the Williams Dodges when he rode the Birdsville Track with Harry and George on one of their final runs. Unfortunately for Ratcliffe, Harry's lauded Ford V8 was temporarily out of commission. When Williams pulled up in one of his old Dodges the well-bred English scientist was astounded by the proposed means of transport.

'I have seen some warriors in my time, but that antiquated Dodge had them all licked hollow,' he wrote in his account of his Australian adventures, *Flying Fox and Drifting Sand*. 'I can best describe her by saying that there was not a single part of her . . . which had not been bashed and broken and rather obviously repaired. The sides of the bonnet had been discarded as unnecessary; one of the lamps was smashed, and from it a length of wire dangled hopelessly; the cap of the petrol-tank was a tobacco-tin held in place by a strap; and there was no sign of a spare wheel or tyre. Later I learned with something of a shock that she had no brakes—not merely bad brakes, but no brakes at all: the shoes had been taken out of the drums. What a vehicle, I thought anxiously, with which to tackle one of the longest and loneliest, and driest mail runs in Australia.'

However, the decrepit Dodge came to earn Ratcliffe's grudging respect by struggling gamely through bog after bog and he found himself impressed by the doggedness and 'she'll be right mate' demeanour of his driver, seventeen-year-old George Williams.

Young George had begun his career as a Birdsville mailman early in life. 'I left school at fourteen—in 1932—and you got a driver's licence at fourteen them days. I'd learnt to drive since I was ten, o'course,' he says. 'But when I left school, Dad said, "C'mon lad you've got to go to work now." We had several of those old Dodges so sometimes we'd be going up together and sometimes I'd be on me own. The first night I slept out by myself, tell you what, I was a bit nervous . . . coming back empty, no lights or anything . . . and when it gets dark you just stop and camp.'

A few months after George's last run up the Track with his father in late 1935, Tom Kruse embarked on his first trip as the new Birdsville mailman. As he'd been firmly instructed, Tom and his party left Marree on the Friday promptly at 11 am. They camped the first night at the dry Cooper Creek crossing and set off the following morning to attempt the infamous Ooroowillanie sandhill 170 kilometres from Marree. Tom had been warned about the Ooroowillanie.

'Being down Lyndhurst, there was all sorts of stories that you'd hear prior. If well-wishing was anything, I would never have had any troubles,' he says.

He had on board some coconut matting that Harry had given him. The idea was to lay it down like a carpet on the sand over which the truck could glide without becoming bogged. Harry had made enquiries with the two other big outback carriers—Glasson's Motors, who serviced the area east of Broken Hill, and Bottom and Clarke, who operated north of Broken Hill up to Innamincka and Cordillo Downs—and had settled on the coconut matting as the best solution to the problem.

'Ooroowillanie—she's pretty soft sand there,' recalls Monty Scobie, Jimmy Scobie's nephew. The sandhill was only about 3 kilometres from the Scobie family homestead at Ooroowillanie station, where Monty lived with his father, Alec, mother Ellen and six siblings. He remembers a constant stream of stricken travellers stumbling into their yard for help. 'Gawd, I was a little bit of a kid going around with no boots on, then. They used to always get stuck there. They used to walk up to the homestead and Dad'd go over and help them. We used to have strips of bullock hide that Dad'd take over in the buckboard.

'Yeah, they had a lot of trouble at Ooroowillanie. And you couldn't go round it. I went round it once. Gawd, it was rough and it was slow.'

At the approach to the sandhill, Tom's passengers disembarked to lighten the load. The women stood on the hard claypan at the foot of the dune, the hems of their long skirts just high enough to avoid dragging in the dirt, their straw hats sheltering their faces from the fierce summer sun. Tom lay down the matting, reversed the truck, then charged at the dune. Fred Hey photographed the big, heavy Cub toiling to make the top without sinking into the sand. The truck climbed halfway up the face of the hill and came to a stop with its front wheels off the mat. Tom slowly backed down to the bottom and made another attempt. And another. Each time the truck climbed a little further up the soft, slithery surface. But each time the Cub's wheels spun, rents appeared in the coconut matting. By the time Tom made it over the top and skidded cautiously down the other side, the brand-new mats were torn to shreds.

'Yeah, I remember Tom coming along as the mailman. It was good,' says Monty. 'We didn't get 44-gallon drums until Tom came. Williams couldn't bring 'em with his little ute. We used to get petrol in two four-gallon tins in a wooden case.

'Dad used to cart his own loading, and then he found out he'd get it cheaper by bringing it with Krusey. Groceries and that, he used to send the order down to Adelaide and go down to Marree and pick them up. He bought a 1927 Chev utility—made to carry half a ton and he wouldn't want a tin of jam over, either . . . He couldn't drive no good—he couldn't drive a bar of soap with a mallet! Terrible driver he was. He screwed a lot of axles off. But I don't know . . . those old cars . . . they went! They was amazing, you know.

'Gawd, we had some hilarious mailmen on that trip . . . Billy Long—he was half Chinaman—he had a Chev. And Harry Williams with his running boards. They had some of these old motor cars with mudguards on 'em—the old Dodges. One of 'em he called Myra. He broke down in the [Mungerannie] Gap once; fixed the tailshaft with the wall of a tyre—you put the side of a tyre in the tailshaft, then that's the weakest point. If you break anything then, you only break the rubber, and you sit down and light a fire and burn another one.

'I'd just finished school when Tom started. Used to get the lessons up in the mail every fortnight. We'd look forward to Tom coming. He was handy: If the car broke down—wait till Tom comes and he'll fix him.

'Then Fred Teague and Ken Crombie. Kenny made a clutch up out of the bottom of a 44-gallon drum, once. A lot of people wouldn't believe that. But it was true, all right. I know how he done it. When you've got a long way to walk, you improvise.'

To the list of memorable Birdsville Track mailmen, Monty would one day be able to add his own name. Fifteen years after Tom first drove up to the house at Ooroowillanie, Monty Scobie became the newest mailman of the Track—working for Tom Kruse. But that wasn't until 1951.

In 1936, at 3 pm on Sunday 3 January, Tom and his party arrived in Birdsville, having successfully completed the first Tom Kruse/HE Ding mail run from Marree.

The arrival of the mail was the highlight of the fortnight in the inhabited little pinprick of a town that was Birdsville. Without the single radio transceiver at the Australian Inland Mission (AIM) nursing hostel and the twice-monthly visits from the mailman, the town was completely isolated from news of the outside world. At the mailman's arrival, the welfare of neighbours along the Track would be eagerly enquired after, letters and parcels from family and friends down south pounced upon, and fourteen-day-old newspapers squirrelled away for relaxed cover-to-cover reading in the quiet hours of the evening.

When Tom pulled up on that Sunday afternoon in 1936 he was received with a flurry of excitement. Most of the residents of the town gathered in the wide, dusty street between the hotel and the post office to meet the new mailman and marvel at the lumbering great truck he turned up in. Mr Harry Afford, the local postmaster, storekeeper and part-time barman, hurried over from the hotel to greet the new arrivals and take charge of the mailbags. Mrs Gaffney, the hotelkeeper, was there as were Mrs Hagen, who owned the second general store in town; old Joe B, the Betoota–Birdsville packhorse mailman and Mr Celcus C ('Celcie') Morton, from outlying station The Bluff (later called Roseberth). Police officer Bob Willis embraced his road-weary wife, introduced himself to the new mailman and welcomed him to town. Then the group wandered across the road to the hotel for a celebratory drink before the job of unloading began.

Harry had given Tom two pounds with which to buy a drink for the premiere Ding passengers upon arrival in Birdsville. The ladies settled themselves at a table near the window while Tom moved to the bar and rested his hands on its wide surface. He waited patiently to order several five-shilling bottles of beer.

Finally Mr Afford approached Tom and started laying saucers on the counter in front of him.

'Er, no, Mr Afford, it's not tea or coffee, it's beer we want,' he said politely.

'That's right, and that's what you're getting,' the barman replied. 'The saucers are to blow on the beer to cool it down,' he joked.

'The queer part was,' Tom says, 'They had no refrigeration in those days, just a bag hanging down over a bit of charcoal and water dripping on it and hoping for a bit of air. The water evaporating kept the beer cool.'

Tom's first southbound passengers were Cecilia and Eleanor Morton, from Roseberth, 34 kilometres east of Birdsville. Mrs Morton, wife of station owner Celcie Morton, was accompanying her daughter, Eleanor, to attend college in Adelaide. 'She was the first lady to come south on the mail,' Tom says. 'Mrs Morton was a good traveller. She'd have one little bag. And good food they supplied, too . . . passing pieces of cake around. I can always remember good food.'

Mrs Beryl Schaffer was another early passenger. 'Mrs Schaffer and her daughter, Daphne . . . used to always come down to Adelaide at Christmas-time. They had the station, Waverly, and owned a store at Windorah. She was a good horsewoman, Beryl, and she could swear like a trooper—she wouldn't pull her punches. She was a good traveller too.'

Many years later Tom ran into Mrs Schaffer's daughter. 'You wouldn't remember me . . . ' she began tentatively.

'Yes, yes I do. Tell you what, you were a crying little bugger,' he told her in his trademark matter-of-fact way.

Tom's return to Marree marked the successful inauguration of the HE Ding Birdsville mail service. However, it would be several weeks before Tom had another trouble-free run such as he enjoyed on that first journey. On his second trip to Birdsville, the brand-new Cub snapped a universal joint at the Mungerannie Gap, a dry sandy run-off about halfway between Marree and Birdsville. His was the only vehicle on the track so there was no use waiting for help to happen by. Fixing breakdowns yourself or walking for assistance were the only options. Tom abandoned the disabled Cub and walked back 8 or 9 kilometres to Mungerannie station, where he explained his predicament to the owner, Ted Wade, who was keen to attempt making a replacement universal joint in the station blacksmith shop. Tom dissuaded him from this idea, preferring to retrace his steps 45 kilometres back to Mulka where he thought it more likely that shopkeeper Poddy Aiston might have some useful bits and pieces at his drovers' store.

'Could I possibly borrow a horse off you, to ride back to Mulka?' Tom enquired.

'Yes, if you can catch one. But I won't lend you a saddle, you're too heavy, you'll bugger it up. And only ride him on the soft ground; you'll ruin his feet.'

'Right, no worries, Mr Wade,' Tom sang out, setting off on the trip back to the Mulka store.

By the time he reached Ooroowillanie, just over half the distance, the feeble old horse was feeling the strain of carrying him, so he jumped off, cracked the horse on the rump and continued to Mulka on foot. Poddy Aiston was surprised to see the new Birdsville mailman reappear in his yard a few hours after he'd waved him off. Poddy had an admirable supply of pipe, bolts and bits of metal but nothing that would repair a broken universal joint, so he lent Tom his own Dodge to complete the run to Birdsville and back. The Cub remained where it was for several weeks until new parts were sent up from Adelaide to repair it.

With the Cub out of commission, Tom drove Harry Ding's 1934 Ford on the next mail run. There was little freight loading scheduled for the trip and Harry thought the Ford buckboard would suffice until the Cub was roadworthy again. There were no northbound passengers on this occasion so when Tom stopped at Ooroowillanie for the customary cup of tea, he invited Alec Scobie, Monty's father, to join him on the run to Birdsville. Tom enjoyed Alec's company and having someone to yarn with helped the kilometres pass more quickly.

'Well, I coaxed him to come for a ride and we got caught in a very heavy rain at Goyder Lagoon and spent a fortnight living on potatoes!' Tom recalls. 'There was over four inches of rain, and that's a big rain. We twisted an axle trying to get through the mud . . . Couldn't drive forwards. We could drive backwards . . . in low gear, but then again, you've got to think of the amount of petrol you have. It's better to pull up where you are while you've still got petrol in the tank, wait until the roads are dry, and then drive out.

'The Birdsville Hotel used to always get crates of potatoes so we had them done in every different way. Look, it's amazing how you can cook potatoes . . . you can have 'em grilled, baked, chips, raw . . .'

Their predicament occurred in the days before Harry's drivers were equipped with radio communication. Tom had no way of alerting anyone to their plight so he and Alec Scobie settled down to wait for the country to dry out. Eventually Harry Ding received word from Birdsville that the mailman had failed to arrive and set out on a rescue mission from Yunta, two weeks after Tom had left Marree. When Harry and his companion found the stranded travellers at Goyder Lagoon, he elected to stay with the broken-down Ford while Tom drove Harry's car on to Birdsville with the mail and, from there, back to Marree. When the Cub was fixed, one of Harry's drivers drove it up to Goyder Lagoon to retrieve the broken-down Ford and cart it back to Yunta.

This incident inspired Harry to install a radio base station at his Yunta garage and equip all his long-distance trucks with radio transceivers. He teamed up with Alf Traeger, who had worked with John Flynn to establish the AIM/flying doctor radio network and its 'mantle of safety' over the outback, and together they designed and engineered portable radio sets that used the trucks' batteries for power. Over time, Harry's Yunta base station, VHU9, became the hub of a radio network that extended over a sparsely inhabited region of more than 120 000 square kilometres of northern South Australia and south-western Queensland. The Kidman company bought transceivers for their cattle stations and Harry lent sets to the managers of Lake Harry, Dulkaninna and Mirra Mitta stations so that they could keep tabs on the passage of the Birdsville mail truck, which was assigned the call sign VHU6.

By 1937, the driver on the Marree-to-Birdsville route could call Yunta at specified times if he chose to report progress. Furthermore, if the mail fell too far behind schedule Yunta would commence a 24-hour listening watch and everyone on the network would listen on the hour or half hour for news of the mailman's troubles. In this way, Harry's radio network created its own mantle of safety over the HE Ding drivers of the inland.

Several years later, Con Burt, a handyman working for Harry Ding, became another unsuspecting victim who innocently accepted Tom's offer to take a ride with him up the Track. Con had come to Marree at Harry's behest to make improvements to the new Kruse home. The expected five- to seven-day journey that Tom offered him during a lull in the building job turned into a six-week slog through rain and mud that left Con cursing his luck and vowing never to set foot on the infernal mail truck again.

By this time, Tom had been driving the Track for a while and could usually predict when conditions would be bad. In the wet season he would monitor the Diamantina River on every trip and when red floodwaters from the big monsoonal Queensland rains were on their way down south he'd switch from the shorter, smoother inside road that ran across Goyder Lagoon to the longer, gibber-strewn outside road that traversed Sturt Stony Desert. It would normally take two to three weeks for the water to make its way down the dry, thirsty channels of outback Queensland before reaching the flat, grey surface of the lagoon. But sometimes, as on this occasion, conditions caught him unawares.

'We were on the inside road on Clifton Hills station, at the southern end of Goyder Lagoon, and it started to rain. Clifton Hills wasn't where it is now. It was up in the

Diamantina country, only 60 or 70 miles down from Birdsville on the eastern side of the river. We struggled on for a bit, poking along the edge of the sandhills and digging through the mud. I was relieved when we finally crossed the Diamantina and got to Burts Hole. But we couldn't go any further. I think there was about six or eight of us all together. Bill Plush and Mrs Plush, from Palpararra, Con Burt was there and Mrs Wilson with little Billy still in arms. And raining! I tell you what . . . Bloody water coming through the cabin all night. Amazing. You couldn't roll the swags out or anything. Just continual rain.

'We had a truckload of stuff there but no meat to eat. I remember the Clifton Hills musterers came along and Bill Plush and I borrowed a couple of horses off them to see if we could go and get a bullock somewhere. For a couple of days we went out on these horses through the claypans. Poor old Bill was that sore . . . I was used to riding bareback. Hell, to ride in a bloody saddle was a novelty. Anyhow, the second day we finally came across a few mob of cattle that'd got cut off in the water. It was some of Jack Gaffney's steers and we packed one back on these packhorses.

'After a week or ten days Bob Gaffney and Ron Michell decided to poke down and see if they could reach us. They knew we'd left Clifton Hills. They only had a Ford V8. I think they had three or four attempts. Each time the country was drying up a little bit more and they finally got down on the outside road to rescue the women and children.

'We were stuck a long time at Burts Hole. It was a big rain that year. I think there was four inches while we were there. It was awfully boggy.'

When the country dried up enough to free the heavy mail

truck Tom plated and dug his way to Birdsville and waited there for a further week or so until the Diamantina had receded enough to attempt the return journey safely on the outside road. It was almost six weeks before he was back home again in Marree. Con Burt completed the renovations on Tom's house but never ventured north on the mail again.

Following an adventurous introduction to the tribulations of running a mail service on one of the toughest and most isolated routes in Australia, Tom quickly settled into his new job and life in Lyndhurst began to take on a regular routine. In alternating weeks, when there was no mail run, he would cart goods and supplies from the railway siding out to the surrounding sheep stations—up the Strzelecki Track to Avondale (14 kilometres); Mt Lyndhurst (37 kilometres) and the big, 10 000-square-kilometre Murnpeowie run (126 kilometres); northwest to Witchelina (52 kilometres); and southwest to Myrtle Springs (47 kilometres)—and backload with bales of wool. Every couple of months or so, Harry Ding would come up to check on operations, but Tom was largely left to manage for himself.

Lyndhurst itself was 'a gibber-strewn waste cut in two by the railway', according to local resident Hans Mincham. The railway siding and the local store/post office, were in the western half of the town. Tom lived near the store in a crude galvanised iron shack that Harry had had erected for him—one of his employees, Don McRae, built it with Tom's help. From there it was a short walk across the railway line to the hotel, where Tom would sometimes have meals and often enjoy a beer and socialising on Saturday nights.

Like all the thirty or so townsfolk, Tom adopted the habit of meeting the train, the Marree Mixed freight and passenger train, when it pulled in on Wednesday and Saturday evenings on its journey from Quorn to Marree. This was invariably followed by a short walk to the sliding panel of the large galvanised iron store where Tom Yates, storekeeper, postmaster, siding caretaker, butcher and chairman of the school committee, lost no time in sorting and distributing the mail.

In January 1936, shortly after Tom had completed his second run up the Birdsville Track, one of the passengers to alight from the Mixed on Saturday night was Hans Mincham, a freshly minted school teacher arriving at his first appointment. The following day, he accompanied Tom, whom he remembers as 'full-faced; healthy-looking, in fact rather good-looking', on a run to Murnpeowie station, and planned then to accompany him up the Birdsville Track during the September school vacation. '[Tom] was strong and burly,' Hans recalls, 'but a jovial person with a very, very easy-going personality. The hardest thing in the world would be to have a row with him.'

Hans ended up making the trip with another Ding driver when Tom dashed south to Yunta following news of his brother's accident. Once there, Harry bluntly informed him that he wouldn't be returning up north but instead would fill Curly's tragically vacated spot in the Ding transport operation. Following Curly's death it was a lot to take in, but Tom accepted his employer's orders without question and resumed work-life at the Yunta depot as instructed.

It was August 1936. The Birdsville mail run had been established for eight months and was operating smoothly thanks to Tom. It was time to try another young buck in the driver's seat. Harry needed Tom's skills and experience for another trailblazing venture—long-distance livestock haulage.

3

SHEEP, TRUCKS AND DRIVERS

B ack at Yunta, Harry kept Tom busy alongside the other Ding drivers carting wheat and wool and increasingly doing long-haul stock transport from the railyard at Cockburn on the South Australia–New South Wales border to various parts of Queensland and New South Wales. Transporting livestock long distances by road was a new undertaking in the 1930s. The big sheep stations in Harry's area were clustered along the Broken Hill to Port Pirie railway line and inside the dingo fence on the Central Australia railway line from Adelaide to Alice Springs via Marree. Sheep from these runs only needed to be walked or transported by road over distances of up to 160 kilometres to be loaded onto the rail trucks. Cattle were still being walked hundreds of kilometres to the railheads in large, lowing mobs, the crack of the drovers' stockwhips keeping them on the move.

Harry's long-distance loads were usually stud sheep

purchased in South Australia by the large station owners for their properties in Queensland and NSW. These big, sturdy sheep were brought in to improve the standards of the stations' flocks or, in some cases, to restock the station after a long drought. The sheep were a valuable and finicky cargo that required constant care and attention on the part of the driver. They had to be inspected at regular intervals and those who had lost their footing on the slick floor of the wooden decking had to be manhandled back onto their feet before they were smothered or trampled by their nervous travelling companions.

Harry had secured a contract to transport sheep by road from Mount Bryan station, out from Burra in South Australia, directly to Dirranbandie, just over the Queensland border—a one-way journey of about 1300 kilometres. Previously they had been sent by rail to Port Adelaide where they would be shipped around the New South Wales coast, then taken overland again by rail to Dirranbandie. When Ding learned that 2000 to 3000 merino sheep were being shipped this way each year, he bought a new truck and outfitted it for long-distance livestock haulage.

'I remember being a Diamond T driver. I know we did six weeks once and never ever got out of the cab,' says Tom. 'Harry had bought this new Diamond T with a Hercules motor to cart stock, and we towed a trailer behind it. Used to be 54, 55 hours straight. That bloody Hercules engine used to smoke like a train, and those poor damn stud sheep all covered black. Some of those poor ewes . . . their eyes all red. Ahhh, terrible.'

Besides the usual hazards of the stony bush tracks, the driver also had to keep a sharp lookout for overhanging tree limbs or other obstacles that could make short work of a load of sheep, or any other passengers riding on the top deck, as Alex Grove-Jones, former bookkeeper for the Mutooroo Pastoral Company, discovered when travelling with Tom on one of these journeys. 'I nearly had my head cut off by the power lines when I bobbed up at the wrong moment on the top deck as we slowed down at Argent Street, Broken Hill,' he recounts in his memoir, *One Man to a Thousand*. 'We had a few phone-lines to squeeze under or take off their insulators, as we had the highest vehicle that had ever been that way.'

Alex Grove-Jones recalls one of the two trips he made with Tom in October 1936, transporting a load of Bungaree rams from Mutooroo to the despatch depot at Lake Dismal, 8 kilometres from the railyard at Cockburn, to Milo station, a Barr Smith property in south-west Queensland. Harry Ding's outfit had won the contract. It was the first time that rams were transported overland from South Australia to Milo.

Harry and Tom scouted the route before the first of the four trips necessary to move the entire 389-ram load. It was a 1000-kilometre journey over rough roads, bush tracks and stock routes from Lake Dismal, to Broken Hill, north to Tibooburra, through the dog fence via the Warri Warri Gate on the Queensland border to Naryilco, Quilpie, Adavale and then on to Milo station. Harry reckoned on four days for the outward leg, taking into account that the sheep would have to be unloaded for feed and water at Paddy Paddy waterhole at Nocundra, halfway through the journey.

Tom and his co-driver, Mick Reid, transported the rams in 90- to 100-sheep instalments in a Leyland Cub equipped with a double-decker pen. Alex Grove-Jones went along on the third and fourth runs to help tend the sheep. He soon learned that the rams were not the only ones he had to keep an eye on—the seven pounds of sausages he had brought with him to contribute to the meat supply for the four-day journey disappeared in the first meal when Tom got stuck into them!

On the second trip, Tom stayed in camp while Grove-Jones, Mick Reid and another co-driver, Fred Teague, went bush to chase down a ram that had strayed overnight from the makeshift yard they had built. Grove-Jones reported that they eventually returned to camp with the sheep, only to find Tom asleep and all their tucker gone. Begging off from the ram round-up because the burrs were hard on his bootless feet—he often went barefoot—Tom had made himself comfortable and cleaned up the lot. 'I called him a bastard, and he chased me with a burning stick out of the fire,' Grove-Jones writes. 'But luckily, as I had boots on and he didn't, I made better time.'

Not a single sheep was lost in this month-long exercise and it signalled the start of many long-haul stock-carting operations by Ding drivers to and from the outback. The total of 8000 kilometres covered in the four trips to Milo took a toll on the Cub, though. A broken rear spring leaf was the first casualty, working its way out of the spring and slicing the tyre in the process. Grove-Jones lost count of how many punctures they had but he does remember that they replaced four tyres over the course of the two journeys. 'Each time we had a flat, Tom would call out, "The kinkless moulded Dunlop tyre, the fit without a kink."' Soon after Tom had repaired the spring with bits of wood twitched together with strands of fencing wire, the hydraulic brakes failed, leaving them with no brakes at all for the remainder of the trip. 'Next the fuel pump packed up, so we visited the rubbish dump at Naryilco where Tom found a petrol tank from an old Model T Ford, which he fixed on the cab roof alongside the bunk, and we had gravity-fed fuel after that.'

On the final trip, Harry Ding sent Fred Teague along to learn the ropes from Tom. Fred had only recently become a Ding driver and Harry wanted him to get a good feel for the desert country before sending him up to Marree to relieve another of his drivers, Tommy Robertson, on the Birdsville mail run.

Fred learned some of Tom's driving tricks and also experienced a good dose of Tom's playful nature. 'When running empty, Tom Kruse loved to do wheelies on any claypan that was big and slippery enough after a drop of rain, and Freddy would get a rough ride shut in the bottom deck on the back. But he took it all in good part,' writes Alex Grove-Jones.

The track near Tibooburra—or 'Tiboogibber' as Tom apparently liked to call it—was crisscrossed by narrow, sandy creeks through which it would descend and ascend so sharply that the front wheels would sometimes leave the ground as the laden truck pulled up and out of the creek bed.

'It was rough on us and the rams,' Alex Grove-Jones continues. 'When travelling empty over the same stretch on the return, Tom would throw the truck out of gear on the downhill run, hit the bottom with a crash, and then look behind with a big grin to see how Freddy was faring in the back.'

Near Tibooburra, the track also traversed a slope at such a precarious angle that Tom instructed Mick to drive along slowly while all hands draped themselves over the uphill side of the truck to help balance the load. Grove-Jones was sceptical that their combined weight made much difference but joined in with gusto nevertheless. It was safer than being on the downhill side if the truck actually tipped over, as it threatened to do.

The trips to Milo became a regular occurrence for Tom during 1936–37. Eventually, Harry bought an AEC Mammoth Major, which he assigned to long-distance livestock transport, while the Diamond T was sent up to Marree for Ken Crombie, his then mail driver, to use on the Birdsville mail run. None of the trucks Harry had yet tried on the demanding Birdsville Track had proved entirely satisfactory. Tom's initial experience with the Leyland Cub—a broken universal joint on its second trip out—soon proved typical.

The Cub that Harry had in service carting wheat at Peterborough and other places had performed well and he had thought that a new Cub with tandem drive axles—an improvement over his older Cub with a single rear drive axle—would endure the rigours of the Birdsville run. When it failed to meet the challenge of the Track, Harry recalled the Cub to Yunta and replaced it with a Ford V8, figuring that an engine more powerful than the Leyland's six-cylinder would solve the problem. But the Ford, too, was found lacking. It had a nice, roomy cabin but the drivers on the Track declared that the lighter Ford truck was prone to spring breakages, rear axle failures, ignition troubles and clutch failures. Furthermore, the engine would continually overheat in the furnace-hot desert conditions. 'People used to say why don't you make tea out of your radiator—always seems to be boiling,' Tom comments drily.

Harry hoped that the American-made 1937 model Diamond T, which had served him well for some time and which generally enjoyed a high reputation for durability and reliability, would rise to the challenge. It was a five-and-a-half-ton truck with a single driving axle and dual rear wheels in contrast to the Leylands' twin-drive axles and single-tyred wheels. Its six-cylinder diesel Hercules engine was less powerful than that of the Ford V8 but more so than the Leylands'.

Unfortunately, though, the Hercules engine succumbed to the strain of sandhills, heat and overloading: 'Going down a hill 18 to 20 miles out of Birdsville, near Pandie, the con rod came off and went straight through the side,' George Williams remembers. 'Ken [Crombie] and I carried our swags back to Birdsville, and she was laid up in Birdsville for a while. Then a bloke came up from Adelaide and put a four-cylinder Gardner engine in it.'

The Gardner engine was regarded as the gold standard diesel engine of the time—it was steady and reliable. Once its engine was replaced—in the yard of the Birdsville Hotel—the Diamond T was able to complete its tour of duty on the Birdsville Track.

The Leyland Badger was yet to be assigned a permanent role on the Track but her mettle had already been tested in 1937 when the HE Ding outfit was engaged to transport all the materials for the new Australian Inland Mission hospital being built in Birdsville. While Ken Crombie continued the regular fortnightly service, Ding employees Wally Blucher, Fred Teague and Peter Bendissi took turns driving the Badger laden with building materials back and forth from Marree non-stop. While one drove, the other tried to sleep on the back of the truck.

Monty Scobie, who carted building materials in 1952 for

the second AIM hospital after the original one was destroyed by fire, remembers hearing of the ordeals of the first team of hospital carriers.

'Teaguey, Wally Blucher and Peter Bendissi carted the first hospital,' he recalls. 'They had the old Leyland then. Oooh she was a money-spinner, that old truck. I drove it once or twice—the Badger—yeah, she was a good old truck. Peter'd sleep on the back all the way down to Marree. Then he'd get in the cabin and have a sleep while they loaded it up and away they'd go to Birdsville again. Kept on going day and night. I think it was 22 hours up and 18 back. The only time they stopped was if the goods shed wasn't open when they got to Marree to get the stuff out.

'Anyhow that got burnt down and I carted the second one in my Blitz. Eight foot by 12 foot 6 the deck is, and they've got all this timber 27 foot long. I had it running along both sides, sticking out both ends. Then when I wanted to get out I couldn't open the doors. Had to lift the windscreen up and go out under the windscreen. Get to a gate and pull up, lift the windscreen up and prop it up there, crawl through and open the gate, then back through the windscreen, take her through and go back and shut her again!'

When Harry bought the British AEC Mammoth Major in 1938 it became the flagship of the Ding fleet. It was big and powerful, with a top speed of 60 kilometres per hour. Harry had its strong, deep frame specially lengthened to take a 10 × 3.5-metre tray-top, enabling it to carry 100 bales of wool or 250 sheep at a time. At a total length comparable to that of both a truck and semi-trailer, it dwarfed the other trucks in Harry's fleet. He didn't believe that semi-trailers could handle the rough terrain his trucks were required to traverse, but with his new AEC he could carry equivalent loads. According to Harry, it was the largest single-unit truck registered in South Australia at that time. The maximum allowable vehicle width in those days was 2.6 metres—40 centimetres less than the width of the Mammoth tray, but by special order from the then premier, Thomas Playford, Harry was granted permission to operate it on South Australian roads as long as he kept to the back country and didn't drive the monstrosity into built-up areas.

Responsibility for the Mammoth Major was handed to Harry's younger brother, George, another Ding driver. It was reserved for carting stud sheep, export lambs, wool clips and any other big, heavy jobs. Tom regularly accompanied George on the 72-hour run out to Milo station and on many other trips throughout the Corner Country of South Australia, New South Wales and Queensland.

George's frequent offsider was another young lad called Bill Holliday. He was a good gate-opener and general helper but aspired to something more. In particular, he was keen to try his hand at driving the huge AEC.

Returning to Yunta from a stock run to Milo station, Tom, George and Bill ran into strife with the new AEC. The main problem was with the steering—it was incredibly heavy. Tom remembers that, once again, Bill was pestering him and George for a turn at the wheel of the empty truck. Finally Tom relented.

'C'mon Tom, giv' us a go.'

'All right then. Just be sure to hang on to the wheel,' Tom warned him. 'Don't be sitting there thinking about what you're going to have for tea. And none of this one-handed business!'

'Yep, no worries. Gee, thanks, Tom,' said Bill.

'Next thing you know,' Tom recounts, 'we've hit a dried-up track and Bill's screaming out, "I've broke me arm! Me arm's broken!"'

The AEC had lurched into a dry creek crossing. The wheels had hit deep ruts—formed from a previous truck ploughing through the mud when the crossing was wet—and the steering wheel had been wrenched violently from Bill's hands. The AEC came to a sudden, shuddering halt with the front wheels at full lock and the front axle collapsed under them.

The three men surveyed their predicament. The axle of the incapacitated truck was bent between the kingpin and the spring seat on the passenger side. Stranded as they were, halfway between Broken Hill and Tibooburra with their radio on the blink, it would be a long wait before someone happened to find them, let alone before a rescue crew was dispatched from Yunta, more than 300 kilometres away. The truck was not driveable in its present condition. However, the trio discovered that it would travel in reverse, which is what they did, crawling along in reverse gear, dragging the misshapen front axle along behind them like a demented plough. Slowly they retraced their tracks 6 kilometres back to Steven's Creek, where they knew there was a stand of sturdy gum trees necessary for their planned bush repair. They needed a strong branch to which they could secure their block and pulley, which was always carried on the truck, and they needed wood for a fire.

'All we've got to do is winch it almost straight up and pull the bloody axle out,' Tom declared to the others. 'We'll burn a couple of big logs, surround the whole thing with coals and we'll be able to gradually get it hot enough to take the bend out of it. We've got plenty of bloody strength here to get it perfectly straight.'

'And that's what we did,' Tom recounts now. 'George Ding, Bill Holliday and me. I think we were there for a couple of days, all told. Didn't even have to fix it when we got back. Nothing wrong with it. Ah, look, it might've worn a tyre on one edge. No worries, just swap 'em over and put it on the other side for a while.'

In a dried-up creek bed in the middle of nowhere the three men used their nous and their combined muscle power to repair the irreparable within 24 hours. Slinging the block and pulley over a branch of a stout old gum they winched the front of the truck off the ground. They then removed the front axle, softened it up a little over a roaring fire and straightened it by eye using a crowbar and a short piece of pipe twisted in a length of chain to gain extra leverage. Next morning they reinstalled the axle and were on their way back to Yunta.

While Tom was kept busy with long-distance stock carting, the mail run was under the charge of Ken Crombie. Ken had spent his childhood at Mungerannie station and he knew the Birdsville country like the back of his hand. In fact, he had driven the mail in Dodge buckboards for his brother-in-law, Harry Williams, and, long before, his father had run the mail with a team of horses—eleven changes between Marree and Birdsville.

Tommy Robertson had originally taken over when Tom Kruse was summoned south, then Fred Teague filled in for a while, but it was Ken Crombie, who was married and had his home in Marree, who ran the mail for several years in the period between 1937 and 1941. During that time Tom would make the trip north occasionally to fill in when Ken needed a break or the Diamond T required repairs.

'The only time anyone went back to Yunta was when whoever was working at Marree had to bring the vehicle back to Yunta to give it a facelift,' Tom explains.

Since Wally Blucher had joined the Army and gone to the War—reluctantly relinquishing his grip on the Badger—Tom would take the Leyland up the Track with him on these relieving runs. Taking it through its paces on the 500-kilometre route he immediately christened it 'the best of the bunch'. It had a more powerful engine than the Cub and it could carry a larger load than the Ford. By that time the Badger had also received a major upgrade, in the form of a replacement Thornycroft rear bogey and transmission.

Harry had bought the 1924 XB model Thornycroft from Mr Crawford, the owner of Erudina station, to cart wool around Yunta and Lyndhurst. Tom had frequently driven the Thornycroft to and from the railway siding soon after he began working for Harry Ding. It was a thrill for him the first time he climbed into the Thornycroft's cab, remembering when, as a child, he had first seen the very same truck being delivered brand new to Erudina station. Big trucks like the Thornycroft were a rarity on the roads in the 1920s and Tom's father had taken him out to the main road through Waterloo to see the impressive new vehicle en route from Adelaide. Tom's uncle, Arthur Stremple, had heard about the impending delivery and had written to alert the family of the event.

'I remember him writing down very clearly,' Tom says. 'I

remember Stremp saying they've arranged to get this truck and gone down to get it. He was still carting wool with donkeys those days—I think it could've been 1924, something like that. I was only a kid.'

'He used to write quite frequently to our mother and if he was ever down here he used to enjoy buying a tin of Minties and giving it to the kids. Hell, I can remember every Christmas, regular as clockwork, there'd always be a 7-pound tin of Minties and half a case of cherries from Arthur Stremple.

'Anyhow, we saw this truck going through—Waterloo was on the main highway from Adelaide to Broken Hill in those days. It was extremely unusual to see a big truck like that going through. There used to be a Brockway going up and down from Burra to Adelaide, and a chap with a GMC that us kids used to bludge a ride with … give him a bit of a hand. But that was about it.'

When Tom finally got to drive the Thornycroft himself about ten years later, he was less impressed with the truck's performance.

'Curly was with us the very first time we went up to Lyndhurst, in the old Thornycroft. Weak as damn water. There's a couple of little hills there inside the Common out at Lyndhurst—not sandhills, hard ground. I don't remember what kind of load we had but I remember dropping down and dropping down and finally we had to hit the joey box. She was revving at peak but there wasn't enough power, and finally it just petered out … we couldn't get up. We had blocks and all that sort of thing. Had a hell of a job getting out of that.'

In 1939, only four or five years after Harry had purchased

the Thornycroft, it came to a sad and sudden demise at Carrieton in a spectacular crash in which, remarkably, no one but the truck was mortally wounded. Harry's trucks occasionally came to grief—going skew-whiff in a bog and losing some of their load—but serious accidents were rare. This time the cabin and front end of the Thornycroft were completely destroyed when the truck crashed head-first down an embankment, spilling its entire load of wool bales. The truck was beyond repair but enterprising Harry, reluctant to write-off his investment completely, realised that some of its rugged and well-designed driveline components could have a second life in the Badger. The Leyland had the more powerful diesel engine but was saddled with a single rear drive axle, whereas the Thornycroft's superior transmission, dual rear axles and more robust tail shaft were under-utilised behind its less reliable petrol-driven motor. Harry's mechanic, Archie McRae, did the swap at Harry's workshop at Yunta.

'It was a lot of a job . . . adapting those parts to the smaller truck, but once in, we had no further trouble,' Harry wrote in his memoir *Thirty Years with Men*.

The transfer of the Thornycroft main and auxiliary (joey) gearbox and rear axles to the Leyland chassis improved the Badger's performance no end. The only disadvantage with the new-edition Badger was the brakes—or lack of them. But all agreed that brakes were more decorative accessory than necessity in the Marree-to-Birdsville desert country and thus the Leyland's feeble front brakes were declared 'good enough'. Harry was so pleased with the result that he searched for other Thornycrofts from which he could construct similar hybrid trucks. He did end up purchasing several more but no further transplants were done and they were simply used for spare parts. Thus the Badger became completely unique.

'It made a hell of a difference to the Badger,' says Tom. 'With the Thornycroft jazz in behind it, it was twice as strong as what the Leyland was. There was no such thing as brakes. But in heavy sand she'd just keep going. No she was; she was great.'

The same year that the Badger was granted a new lease on life, Tom was assigned a job that was a slight diversion from the usual daily grind. Harry had selected him to assist with Dr Cecil T Madigan's expedition to traverse the Simpson Desert from west to east across its approximately 400-kilometre centre. Ted Colson, a pastoralist from Blood Creek station, had set out from Mount Etingambra and crossed the southern edge of the Desert with an Aboriginal tracker three years earlier, but this would be the first documented geographical survey of the 'dead heart'.

In addition to supplying a truck and driver to the party, Harry would also be relaying all radio communications for the explorers through his base station at Yunta, including three nationwide radio broadcasts for the Australian Broadcasting Corporation.

In the early 1920s he had supplied transport to Sir Douglas Mawson and his fellow scientists and students for two- to three-week expeditions to the mineralised and ancient glacial areas about 30 kilometres north of Olary, so it seemed only natural that Dr Madigan, an Adelaide University geologist, like Mawson, should also call upon Harry to provide transport for his party.

In a letter to Harry, Mr R Grenfell Thomas, a member of

one of the early geological expeditions, recalled the spring dray and horse that Harry had supplied for an expedition in 1921. 'It looked a bit frail and spindly but it got us there and back. I seem to remember that the horse you provided was a sort of dapple grey and Douglas Mawson used to encourage her to greater efforts by calling out "Come on Polly, let's hear from you." Whereupon Polly would respond with a slight acceleration and much farting.'

Eighteen years later, Polly and the dray had been superseded by Tom Kruse and a Ford BB three-ton tray-top with dual rear wheels.

'Tom, you're wanted in the office,' one of Harry's men called out as he strode across the yard of the Yunta workshop.

Hell, what have I done wrong now, Tom thought.

'You wanted to see me?'

'Yes, you've got to take a few hours off to get yourself looking a bit reasonable—do some washing and suchlike. I've got an easy job for you,' said Harry.

An easy job? Hell, this is strange, Tom remembers thinking.

'You'll be going up to Andado station—driving a group of explorers from Adelaide University. They've hired one of our trucks to get them to the start and they'll be needing a driver. I want you to go.'

On 25 May 1939, Tom drove 222 kilometres from Yunta northwest to Hawker in the Flinders Rangers, where, in the middle of the night, he and the truck boarded the train carrying the members of the scientific team north from Adelaide. 'The train, the usual mixed one, was fully booked up and there was no sleeping accommodation for Tom,'

Madigan noted in his popular account of the expedition, published in 1946, *Crossing the Dead Heart*, 'not that that was much worry to him. He slept as usual on the seat of his vehicle, which was on a railway wagon. He had no ticket, but the railways later prised a fare for him out of the expedition, raising a rather nice point over which we differed, my argument being that you pay for a seat on a train, theirs that you can't travel on a train without a ticket.'

When the train stopped at Marree, Tom was pleased to see a familiar face on the platform. Ken Crombie was driving the Birdsville mail at the time, and he and Tom enjoyed a chat while the train took on water and the mail was sorted for points further north. When three or four whistles sounded people reappeared from the hotel and other locations to which they'd scattered, and the train was soon on its way again.

At four o'clock the following morning they pulled into Abminga railway siding, 16 kilometres from the Northern Territory border and the closest stop to the party's launching point into the desert. It was a struggle to offload the truck sideways in the dark only aided by the light of hurricane lamps. From the siding, Tom would ferry the party to Andado station, on the western edge of the Simpson Desert, which Madigan's team would be using as a staging base before setting out on their desert trek.

Harry chose Tom for this assignment because he was the most experienced bush driver among his men, and as soon as Madigan saw Tom in action, he happily endorsed Harry's choice. 'In Jack Bejah and Tom Kruse it was felt that we had the best camel man and the best outback motor driver the country could provide, and time proved that our confidence in them was justified,' Madigan wrote.

For Tom, his minor involvement in the expedition was a delightful diversion from daily life. 'It was extraordinary,' he says. 'We were all eating at the station, getting three feeds a day . . . plenty of meat. It was something different from having to drive eighteen or twenty hours a day. Madigan was really great. From my side, it was quite a thrill to be associated with the whole thing.'

It was 130 kilometres from Abminga to Andado. Before setting out for the Andado homestead the scientific team stopped at Charlotte Waters in the beautiful Finke River region to rendezvous with their camel string, which had been making slow progress from Marree.

'Our first meal was in the Finke,' Tom recalls. 'Right in the heart of the Finke. It was an experience. They were all sleeping on the ground and going without hats and things . . . toughen themselves up a bit. I remember the cook was short of blankets so I gave him a couple of mine . . . Don't think I ever got them back.'

At Charlotte Waters Tom was delighted to catch up with Jack Bejah, the camel man, and his assistant, Andy, both of whom he knew from Marree. Jack was the son of long-term Marree resident and famed cameleer Bejah Dervish, who had accompanied the explorer Larry Wells on his expedition across the Great Sandy Desert in Western Australia in 1896. Bejah demonstrated great feats of stamina and endurance during the near-deadly journey, prompting Wells to name Bejah Hill in the centre of the Great Sandy Desert for him in recognition of his efforts.

Now Bejah's son was following his father's example by joining the Madigan expedition to the Simpson. Jack had selected Andy, in addition to Nurie, a young Afghan lad, to help tend the camels.

'Jack Bejah, I knew him very well from Marree. He was the roadmaster's clerk on the railways,' says Tom. 'He wasn't doing much with the camels then 'cause Harry Ding was there. And Squeakin' Andrew, the Aboriginal, I knew him well, too. He had a high, squeaky voice. He was the bottlo at the hotel—the pub yardy. He used to drain all the beer bottles and the wine bottles. Used to get as drunk as a monkey at times. Hell, he used to get himself drunk. Proper drunk. He was very clean, though. He was a proper cleanskin.

'But Squeakin' Andrew was most unreliable. I used to say, "Hell, Jack, I think I'd've chosen someone a bit different to Squeakin' Andrew." He's good . . . but then again, he's likely to walk off . . . see a mate. He's most unreliable. You might find the camels haven't come back and he's walked off. He'd think nothing of walking home bloody miles; those fellows can live on air.'

After spending the night at Charlotte Waters, the scientific team piled in and on Tom's truck and they set off for Andado. The railway line around Abminga ran through endless, flat, gibber-strewn terrain, but as they headed further northeast the country became smoother and more sandy. Two sand ridges, each about 18 metres high and capped with a layer of loose, shifting, red sand, had to be crossed before reaching the homestead, and these gave the men a chance to see a bit of Tom Kruse, the off-road driver, in action.

According to Madigan, the first sand ridge was the more difficult of the two. 'One wondered if our truck would ever manage it . . . Kruse charged it at full speed from several hundred yards away, wildly and recklessly, but just failed to reach the top. He decided to back down and charge again . . . At the second charge our truck reached the summit, and on starting again on the pipes it succeeded in running down the far side.'

The pipes Madigan referred to were two pieces of 6-metre lengths of 7-centimetre water piping that were always carried on dual-rear-wheel trucks like the Ford, to provide traction for the tyres. The Birdsville mail drivers had discovered that these were easily the best aid for extracting trucks from sand or mud bogs when simply ploughing through the morass failed. The end of the pipe would be inserted from the front between each pair of wheels. When the clutch was engaged the tyres gripped the piping, drawing it under, and the vehicle ran along the pipes. They could be re-fed under the truck until it reached hard ground.

In the week Tom spent with Madigan's party he made multiple trips between Andado and Abminga. The Andado Bore No. 1 was the limit to which motor vehicles could be used and Tom would leave the expedition there. It would be the last reliable source of water for the explorers before reaching the township of Birdsville on the eastern side of the desert, so Madigan wanted to ensure that the camels drank their fill before they set off the following morning. However, they found that winding the water up through the bore by the hand pump was so slow that most of the water had leaked out of the tube by the time it reached the surface.

'But the enterprising Tom Kruse soon altered this,' Madigan wrote. 'He detached the end of the wire rope from the windlass and fixed it to the rear of his truck, leaving a few turns on the windlass, and then went ahead with the truck, thus making a sort of miner's "whip" with the truck instead of a horse. The windlass looked as if it would fly to pieces at any moment as it whirled round, but the tube shot up practically full and the camels were soon watered at the trough.'

Next morning, Monday 5 June 1939, Madigan and his party mounted their riding camels and turned towards the desert, waving farewell to Tom as he turned back for Andado and the railway. It took them one month to cross the 'dead heart'.

'At exactly four o'clock on July 6th, the camels went down in front of the pub,' Madigan recorded. 'There to meet us were gathered the leading citizens of Birdsville, including Norman Carralan, the policeman; Harry Afford, the hotel manager; Dorothy and Bob Gaffney, daughter and son of the proprietress; Ben Barton, the schoolmaster; and stockmen and townsmen I did not know. We took the camels to a wire yard nearby, threw off the loads, put our personal gear into Bob Gaffney's car and dumped it at the hotel again, and then, in accordance with the custom of the country, both expedition and town crowded into the little bar. We were rather late into the bar even then I think, to satisfy the best traditions.'

Madigan's official Simpson Desert expedition concluded in Birdsville, but after a few days' respite in the town most of the party decided to extend their adventure and proceed on camel down the Birdsville Track to Marree rather than take the mail truck back. They set off down the inside track, keeping to the west of the Diamantina River, the same side as Birdsville, until the river floods out into Goyder Lagoon.

Madigan opted for the shorter inside track, even though

he was apprehensive about crossing the lagoon at its southern end. Recent rains meant that the countryside was prettily lush and green but accordingly boggy and treacherous in parts. Evidence of the difficulties caused by the muddy terrain was presented when the party saw ahead of them 'a large circular disc like a notice board, stuck up on the end of a sand ridge. When we arrived at it we found it was the end of a forty-gallon [sic] petrol drum of a familiar yellow colour, that had been cut out of the drum. There were other ends lying about, with holes in them where smaller discs had been cut out, and the tracks of a truck were still clear.'

Madigan had discovered the remains of the most famous bush repair ever. It happened to the Badger.

Ken Crombie was driving the mail then, with his offsider, his nephew young George Williams, when the Diamond T they were riding in broke its front stub axle. Wally Blucher was on the Track, too, at the time, carting 100 tons of wire in the Leyland Badger for the dog fence in Queensland. Knowing that Wal would soon be by, George and Ken waited by the disabled Diamond T for a lift back to Marree. Soon enough, Wally came along and the three of them piled into the Leyland. One hundred or so kilometres down from Birdsville they struck trouble again.

'There was a thunderstorm and we got a bit bogged and did the clutch plate—at about Sheedy's Hole on the Diamantina, two to three mile off the road,' George recounts. 'Everything else was okay so we slept on the problem. Next morning, Ken said to me, "I wonder could we make one? You're pretty handy, what'd'ya reckon?"

'"Good thinking," I said. That set the bells ringing in my noodle. We cut the bottom and the top from a 44-gallon drum—we weren't too sure how strong we had to make the centre, so we put double thickness—the bottom and the top. The drum was from the truck—we always carried drums on the truck. We used a chisel and hammer to cut it out—that's all we had . . . used the railing around the back of the truck as an anvil. And we had a very old dog file.

'We were there about three days fixing it. Oh, it was pretty rough—our clutch plate was about one and a quarter inch thick, and it's normally about three-eighths of an inch thick. And there was no clutch release . . . But it drove. You had to idle it right down and plonk it into low gear, then keep going. It was pretty rugged but it done the job and got us out of the problem.

'The story's been blown up over the years. Different people reckon what a marvellous thing it was. As far as we were concerned we didn't think it was anything. That was what the bush was about in those days—there was no support, you had to sort things out yourself.'

The story of the fuel-drum clutch plate and how Ken Crombie scavenged bolts from the truck tray and other non-essential parts to fasten the makeshift plate to the intact hub and facings, has become a part of Birdsville Track mythology, with Fred Teague and even Tom, himself, credited with the famous repair. However, Tom readily confirms that he wasn't even there when it happened.

'There again, you see how stories go, they get it all upside down,' he says. 'Kenny, George and Wally, all in the poor old wagon to come back . . . Er, the motor's running, there's no movement. Wally always had a 32-volt drill on the Badger—it'd run off the 24-volt battery quite easy; between that and a hammer and chisel . . . that's how the clutch plate ended up. And, well, once they got the thing bolted up . . . "Don't touch the clutch, don't touch the clutch! Start her in gear and don't cut the motor."'

With George—the only surviving member of the original trio—able to recount the true story of the clutch plate repair, the only remaining mystery is what happened to the makeshift part afterwards. Tom says it was under the seat of the Badger for a long time before it disappeared. Harry Ding wrote in his memoirs that the clutch plate finished up at the 'Adelaide Technical College' as an example to show students what could be done with basic materials and a good dose of bush inventiveness. George, however, always believed that it ended up in England—of all places.

'We got back to Marree,' George continues with the story, 'and then I took the truck to Quorn and put seven ton of fuel on it and went on to Yunta. We unloaded it and put it in the garage and then they pulled out the gearbox and replaced what needed fixing.

'I heard that this remittance man down there, who used to come to our garage and watch us work, asked Harry what he was going to do with the clutch plate and Harry said it had done its job; he didn't want it. He said this bloke could have it, and when he asked him what he was going to do with it, he said that he was going to send it to England to have it put in the Leyland museum.'

When Madigan stumbled upon the circular remains of the drum ends several miles south of the Andrewilla Waterhole on Goyder Lagoon in July 1939, he was forced to admit that the fantastic report he had heard about Ken Crombie's repair was true. Five months earlier he had read a brief account of the repair—'Mailman at Marree: Oil Drum Clutch Holds Out', in the 23 February edition of *The News*—with some scepticism. But now, here before him, were the discarded remains. 'So this was where the Birdsville mailman on his last trip on this route had cut clutch plates out of petrol drums to repair his ruined clutch!' he wrote in his journal incredulously. 'We had read about it in the newspapers, but though I have the greatest respect for the ingenuity of the bush mechanic, I had thought this was going a bit too far in good stories. However, here was proof of it. Hammer, cold chisel and file were probably his only tools.'

4

LIFE IN MARREE

By 1942 Tom and the Badger were back on the Track together—cementing what was to become a famous union. Harry Ding's transport operation now numbered twenty trucks and nine mail runs. He had depots in Marree, Lyndhurst, Hawker and Olary, in addition to the home base at Yunta. Since Ken Crombie had given up truck driving and had gone to work for the railways, Harry needed someone competent and reliable to run the Marree-to-Birdsville operation. He offered Tom the position of resident Marree manager.

When Tom returned to life up in the north of South Australia he was 27 years old with a new bride in tow. She took one look at her new home and said, 'Oh my God, what a place. If I die don't bury me here!'

In fact Marree was quite a lively little country town in the '40s and '50s. It even had its own billiards saloon for a while, which was one of several new buildings erected in the 1920s with the prospect of the extension of the Port Augusta to Oodnadatta railway line north to Alice Springs. Mr Carter's general store, office and billiards saloon was described as a handsome building and a fine addition to the main street. Monty Scobie remembers the pool hall being a great attraction for the local folk.

The young Mrs Kruse had never been to Marree before. 'It was the 2nd or 3rd of February and it was a very hot day,' she recalls. 'There was a little bit of a rise coming into the town and as we came to the top, Tom said, "That's Marree." All you could see was a glimmering heat. I was shocked . . . absolutely shocked!'

'Yeah, it was a fairly warm day,' Tom says. 'We came through the Common gate and I said, "You'll see Marree in the distance there, through the mirage . . . " Well . . . she didn't burst into tears but she wasn't very happy.'

Tom and Valma Fuller had been married only a week previously, on 24 January, at the Methodist church in Pirie Street in Adelaide. Their wedding photograph shows Tom, sombre and serious in a dark suit; Valma girlish and happy. Having had their wedding ceremony during the war years Valma had eschewed the froth and extravagance of a traditional bridal gown, opting instead for a simple knee-length frock with a lace collar, a matching hat and a posy of flowers. They had spent their honeymoon in the city, shopping for homewares and furnishings for their new home in Marree, then Tom's brother, Reg, had taken the couple back to Yunta, where they loaded up the Badger and set off for their new life together. When they arrived in town the local residents welcomed the young couple with a 'Welcome to Marree' party.

Tom had been courting 22-year-old Valma for five years before their marriage. Her parents owned a sheep property, Wabricoola, a few kilometres out of Yunta, and she and Tom had got to know each other soon after Tom moved back to the town at the end of 1936.

'It's rather strange. I can always remember how we first met,' says Tom.

'Oh yes?' says Valma with an amused, sceptical look in her eye, waiting to hear his version of events.

'Yeah, Snow said, "You'd better come up here, I've got a nice girl up here for you." I was never interested in women anyhow. Then when I got there he pointed you out, "There's girlie Fuller walking over there now." "Hell," I said . . . '

'Oh, go on with you,' she laughs fondly at him. 'We met at a dance at Waukaringa.'

Phyllis Bruce, Harry Ding's younger sister, who followed her brother from Olary to Yunta and bought the Yunta store and post office with her husband, remembers Tom and Valma from the early days. 'Tom was big; and the greasiest man you could find. But when he was going to a dance . . . *oh*,' she sighs, 'he'd clean himself up and there'd be big Tom standing in the doorway, with a big, beaming smile . . . the *cleanest* man you could imagine.'

'I'll never forget when I first saw him dressed up,' says Noreen O'Donohue, who knew the young couple in Marree. 'When he got dressed up he was so handsome . . . Now we can understand how Valma fell for him. We used to say he was the handsomest man of the north. But we only saw him dressed up a few times. Mostly he'd have on an old shirt, old shorts, big boots with no laces, or no shoes at all, no socks, no belt—just a piece of rope around his waist. But he was a worker. By gosh he could work.

'It would've been a shock to Valma, coming to Marree to live. I think she wondered what struck her, being just married and Tom having to go away every fortnight. But she coped. Valma's like Tom—she'd cope anywhere. And she was such a happy lady . . . such a jolly person. I never saw her any other way.'

Valma says that she knew when they went to Marree that Tom would be away for five days most fortnights. 'I used to go with Tom quite a bit before we had children—if there were no passengers. When I got back from a trip I'd think I wouldn't go next time, but then a week or so later he'd be preparing to go again and I'd think, hmmm, stopping here on my own . . . or . . . And I'd go with him again.

'I used to enjoy sleeping out in the open, looking at the stars. At Birdsville we'd sleep in swags in the back room at the hotel. I always travelled in the cabin, except going up to the Birdsville races . . . we had quite a few passengers then and I travelled on the back.'

Valma regularly accompanied Tom on the mail run until after their first child, Pauline, arrived at the end of 1943. Tom was away when it came time for Valma to give birth so Harry Ding drove up to Marree to take her to the hospital in Peterborough, where she had family nearby.

When Valma and Pauline were ready to travel they took the Mixed train back to Marree, where Tom was introduced to his new daughter. Thereafter, when Valma accompanied Tom on the mail run she would bundle baby Pauline into a tin bath that served as her bed and her bath. But as Pauline grew older and more restless and the three other children came along the family increasingly stayed behind.

While Tom refamiliarised himself with the rigours of the Birdsville mail run, Valma set about creating a home in the small desert community, where summertime temperatures reached well beyond the old century mark and the average rainfall was described as '10 inch or nothing'. Their house was across the road from the school and the police station, on the southern side of the railway line where the white community lived, a couple of streets back from the hotel, post office and general store. On the northern side of the line was Ghan Town where the Afghan families of Marree lived.

Most of these 'Afghan' camel drivers had grown up in Baluchistan—at the time, a small Indian state on the Pakistan–Afghanistan border but now a province of Pakistan. 'Ghan' or 'Afghan' was a derogatory nickname assigned to the camel drivers by whites who didn't care to know better. The first of these camel boys had come to Australia in January 1866. They were brought to South Australia along with 122 camels from Karachi by pastoralists Samuel Stuckey and Thomas Elder to facilitate transport to and from their outlying pastoral runs after the Great Drought of 1864. The Baluchi camel boys came in search of a better life and many of these cameleers settled permanently in Australia, planting date groves and building mosques to bring some familiarity into their strange new homeland.

Marree's original mosque was demolished in 1956. The town's most famous Afghan resident, Bejah Dervish, was believed to be between 95 and 105 years old then and maintaining the mosque was a job for a younger man. But the second generation of Afghans were less enthusiastic about the devout Muslim ways, so another of the town's Afghan elders, 86-year-old Syed Goolamdeen, made the decision to pull the mosque down and dispose of its imported woven prayer mat and silk-swathed Koran rather than have the mosque fall into ruin due to neglect and what he perceived to be a lack of Mohammedan respect.

In 1942, when Tom and Valma were getting settled in Marree, the 100 or so Aborigines and Afghans living in the northern half of the town were equalled in number by the European Australians living in the southern half. Victor Coe was head teacher of the Marree school, in charge of 21 white students, and Mounted Constable Alec Collins, a rotund Englishman who despised the ferocious Australian summers, maintained the law.

Other residents of the town that Tom remembers fondly include, Herb Tilmouth; Archie Price the camel man; Robin and Flo Russel; the Bejah family; the Khan girls; Max Payne on the railways; Ron McGuiness on the Ghan; George Bell; Allan Crombie; and Billy James, a former Birdsville mailman. James ran the mail with a horse-drawn buggy in the early 1900s and was quick to dismiss the travails of the current mailmen, such as Tom Kruse, in their modern, new-fangled motor cars and trucks.

'It's 49 years since I held the contract,' he told *Land of Mirage* author George Farwell outside his Marree shack one afternoon in 1948. 'We went from waterhole to waterhole . . . We weren't too slow either. Motor mailman reckons he's doing fine if he hits Birdsville in three days. That's if he's not held up, which he is mostly. When there's floods, even an inch of rain—or heavy drift, the joker might take a week. Ghost, my horses did it in eight days. Regular. Look here,' he said, tapping Farwell's knee with the stem of his pipe. 'Look here, in my day we ran to a time-table. We made every station on the run to the exact half-hour. If we were sixty minutes late in Birdsville the postal cove wanted to know why.'

For Tom and Valma, despite her initial misgivings, Marree in the 1940s was a companionable community. Tom's essential role as the Birdsville mailman shielded him from the prospect of military service and, from their isolated spot in the centre of Australia the fighting of the Second World War was mercifully far away. Valma took care of her growing family and modified the small house that Harry Ding had purchased for them to suit her needs.

'I got a lawn going and planted a few trees around,' she recalls. 'There was plenty of water but it was bore water ... good for washing and bathing because it was soft—it had soda in it—but no good for drinking. All the years we were there, we never ran out of rainwater, ever. I remember once it got low, but we never ran out.

'The house was all iron. And very, very low rooms. Tom could put his hand up and touch the ceiling in the kitchen and the dining room and the lounge. And in the summer it was hot. Oh, it was terribly hot. It was better to get outside than try and stop inside in the summer.'

Beyond the cramped living quarters and summertime heat, the biggest problem in the early days in Marree was the frequent dust storms—an ordeal that everyone in the town learnt to cope with. They had no choice.

'It'd start at about nine o'clock in the morning,' says Valma. 'I'd get up and do the washing at about four o'clock and get the washing dry before it'd start—you knew it was going to start by nine. It'd blow from the north all day till about five o'clock, then it'd go down, and you'd start to clean up. I mean, you couldn't go to bed with it like that. The sand and dust'd go right through the house. You'd have to take your bedding out and your curtains down. You'd use a wheelbarrow to take the sand out.

'Not every time, but half the time it would turn around then and blow from the south. It used to start again at about seven o'clock, eight o'clock at night. It wasn't as bad at night. It used to blow, but it never used to blow as much dust as it did in the daytime.

'It was pretty awful,' she says in a matter-of-fact way. Such rigmarole was just part of daily life for the women of the outback. 'Three or four days out of the week it would be blowing like that. You had a job to even have a meal . . . trying to hold something over the table while the dust was flying. We had it on and off for a few years . . .

'It was the summers that were bad. You didn't get it in the wintertime. In the winter the winds didn't pick the dust up like they did in the summertime . . . you'd look outside and it would be red, and it'd be rolling in.'

Throughout the 1940s and even through the 1950s the dust storms raged.

'Our chooks blew away,' laughs Tom and Valma's youngest daughter, Helen. 'Well, they weren't there the next morning, anyway. And the petrol drums used to blow away. Phillip and I would have to go and roll the drums back. It seemed like miles when you'd have to run and push this one, and run and push that one, trying to get them all back home again.

'The wheelbarrow had to be brought inside to take the sand out. Our place wasn't dustproof—one wall used to just fill up with sand. And the beds would all be covered with a layer of dust. You'd just hop in . . . didn't take any notice . . . you'd get up in the morning and you're another colour from lying in the dusty bed.'

'Dusty! Was it ever!' exclaims Celia Teague, who came to Marree when her husband was appointed the local policeman in June 1949. 'We lost everything in those dust storms. If it wasn't nailed down the dust and wind just took it . . . then when we did have rain we'd have buckets of it. We were flooded in for six weeks, twice.'

Despite the vagaries of the weather, Celia holds happy memories of her five years in Marree. 'Tom and Val were friendly with everybody. They lived almost next door to us and two of their children were almost the same age as our two children . . . on Sunday mornings, the kids'd all gather at Coverdale's shop and Jack'd dole out the ice-cream so he'd have room to get the beers cold. Supplies came up on the Marree Mixed on Saturday night—fruit and veg., and bread. And Coverdale's got the ice-cream up. Meat we got from local drovers. They'd kill just outside of Marree and bring meat in it.

'Valma was involved with the Country Women's Association and the Red Cross . . . she played tennis and was always involved with all the social activities. Tom'd play tennis and go up the pub for a drink, but he was away most of the time. I remember him coming home once and we were out playing tennis and he jumped out—bare feet—picked up a racket and began playing tennis with us.'

'Yes, that's right. Tom wasn't around much at all,' says Valma. 'All the time we lived in Marree, he was away more than he was home. Normally I didn't know when he'd be back, either, till the truck drove in. There was no radio at Marree. Etadunna station was the closest place with a radio.

'When he was in town he'd be doing things on his truck, or someone else would bring something around and want it welded or something . . . He's always liked his visitors.

'Every week in Marree there'd be a dance. And race weekend was always a big event. I recall partying all night Friday night and then at seven or eight in the morning, with no sleep, having to start cutting all these sandwiches. And there'd be another party Saturday night, after the race.'

'I remember the dances,' says Helen. 'Mum and Dad were very social. There'd be parties at our place and we'd hear people laughing and we'd be all excited, then about eleven o'clock at night they'd all go off to the dance.

'I'd always get a new outfit made. We'd go to the races, but not the dance . . . all the other kids were allowed to go, but Phillip and I weren't old enough.'

'Everyone had to get new dresses,' agrees Valma. 'John Martins sent up dresses in boxes for the women—there was no cost to have them sent up—then you'd choose one and send the rest back.'

'The Marree race weekend was the Queen's birthday weekend,' explains Celia Teague. 'People came from 500 to 600 miles away. We'd have parties all over the place—parties at the police station, at the store. By Monday or Tuesday it would all be over and everyone'd leave for home. They'd always call Bill over saying that someone was refusing to leave—being drunk and disorderly—and Bill'd have to come over and arrest him. But he'd get there and they'd want him to have a drink with them . . . want him to have one for the road.

'Yes, we had some great times in Marree. We were all in the same boat up there.'

Out on the Track, Tom was happy to find that the road had improved somewhat in the six years since he'd first driven it. 'It was all different, entirely different. It wasn't like it was on the first initial stage,' he says. 'They were working on it by then, all with pick and shovel o'course. The road was a piece of cake. No comparison whatsoever. Naterannie had all been clayed, bulldozed into a straight track. Even Ooroowillanie had been all chopped down. You used to have to go into Mulka; cross sandhills to get out to Ooroowillanie.

'I remember running over a snake there once, and the damn thing came up in the cabin. It hadn't gone out the side—we couldn't see its track. I don't know if it got curled up in the bloody wheel, or what, but anyhow, it got up in the cabin—got in behind the battery box there in the old Badger and curled itself up. I reckon we could've been an hour there finding the bloody snake. Didn't know whether it was up in the load, or where the hell it was, but we didn't get back in the truck till we found it.'

Although the Birdsville Track in 1942 was less taxing than it was the first time Tom drove its length back in 1936, it was still a route that would challenge modern four-wheel-drive enthusiasts. The road that Tom spent seven days of every fortnight traversing in his overladen two-wheel-drive Leyland Badger little resembled the Birdsville Track of the new millennium. Back then the Track consisted of two faint tyre trails that often required seat-of-the-pants intuition to decipher. As it wound over windswept sandhills and spooled out across hard claypans the famous Birdsville Track would disappear altogether for kilometres at a time, the thin evidence of the previous journey having disappeared under deposits of drift sand or a powdery layer of bulldust. Motor traffic passed through too seldom to confirm the route.

Today it is a wide, graded roadway—straight and flat. Like any remote gravel road there are the occasional corrugations and sand-filled depressions to contend with; stones litter the hard surface and rocks and potholes make for a bumpy ride, but it is a far cry from the Birdsville Track of Tom's day. Now roadworkers from South Australia's transport authority regularly maintain the Track and travellers can journey from Marree to Birdsville in a two-wheel-drive sedan in eight hours. The number of motorists who travel the Track has swelled from the handful who drove it in the 1940s, mostly out of necessity, to a figure of 25 000 people who now follow it each year seeking adventure, achievement and a sense of the Australian outback.

Tom's delight with the improvements that had been made to the Track when he resumed the mail run in 1942 may account for a little overenthusiasm in his recollection of the state of the road. Although there had indeed been some attempts to improve the Track, Naterannie and Ooroowillanie were still a headache for Monty Scobie when he was driving the mail in the 1950s.

'Ah, Ooroowillanie, she was bad. It was a terrible sandhill, that. A lot of people used to get bogged there . . . it's loose, that sand. You had to put the plates down even to get over it with the Blitz—and she's four-wheel-drive. We had a stack of steel plates there. You'd leave some there—the wide ones. Then Tom got some cut down narrow and they were better, but you had to take 'em with you—slide 'em in under the tray. If you left some behind people'd take 'em. They were seen as far away as Quilpie, those little narrow ones.

'The wide ones, you'd have to leave 'em all stacked up. If you didn't, there'd be a dust storm and they'd be all buried. You'd just see one or two sticking up out of the sand.

'Now, Naterannie wasn't too steep, but it's a fairly long pull over there. Naterannie's a fair bit of flat sand; seven or eight mile, I s'pose. You'd do a bit of plating. It'd take a couple of hours to get over Naterannie.'

The sand ridges of Naterannie and Ooroowillanie were the points at which the sandy fingertips of the Simpson and Tirari deserts probed the Birdsville Track. In the Cooper Creek country, where Tom and Monty would face up to them, the 15-metre-high sandhills were a creamy colour, but away from the watercourse and further north, near Birdsville, they became a brilliant red. These drifting hills were usually about 500 metres apart. In between each rise there would be a hard claypan, which could rapidly transform into a treacherous swamp under heavy local rain. The sandhills ran in a north-west to south-easterly direction and could extend from 80 kilometres up to 300 kilometres, so driving around them wasn't an option. Over the top was the only way.

'The driver had to know his stuff when crossing from the west side, loaded,' wrote Harry Ding in his memoir. 'If he cleared the top he was faced with a near-vertical drop. So he just had to take the truck over at the right speed so it would slide down the eastern side.'

The plates that Monty Scobie refers to were 2-metre by 60-centimetre iron sheets—bits of old water main cut open and rolled flat, which the South Australian government had donated to Harry. They each weighed 51 kilograms and in summer they were too hot to handle without using insulating sacking. The lengths of iron would be laid on the upward slope of the sandhill like two metal carpets, spaced so the truck's wheels would run over them and take the vehicle over the crest. When the iron track did not extend far enough the plates would have to be repositioned after the truck passed over them until the vehicle had cleared the top. Dragging the plates around and re-positioning them in the sand was an exhausting experience for the drivers, especially in the summer.

'Oooh they were hot!' Tom exclaims. 'And you could tell when the dust storms were coming . . . the electricity! . . . Especially in the sandhills. The sparks'd fly off your fingers. But [the plates] were really the answer when it came to heavy sand. Even then you'd still go back and have a bit of a fast run at it if you could—charge at it like a bull at a gate. You might go five, six times, going an extra foot each time, and then finally get to the stage where, righto, we've got to plate now. If the sand was really heavy . . . come to the last plate, put down another line of plates. If there's a gap there . . . Right . . . Stop . . . put down more plates to fill the gap. Then you get the shovels out . . . knock a few bumps off and lower the sandhill.'

Life as the Birdsville mailman settled into a fortnightly rhythm. On alternating Thursdays, Tom would spend the day loading the truck with freight and goods to be delivered to the northern stations. These supplies would arrive on the Marree Mixed—the twice-weekly train that ran between Quorn, in the Flinders Ranges (with a connection to Adelaide), and Marree; arriving at its northern terminus on

Wednesday and Saturday evenings. The mail would travel from Adelaide on the Ghan, which stopped at Marree in the wee hours of Friday morning, on its way to Alice Springs. At the Marree Post Office the postmaster would sort the mail and have all deliveries for the Birdsville Track ready to go with Tom at 11 am.

'There was a separate contract for local carting,' Monty explains. 'Old Alec Brooks had a horse and cart and he was the carrier round the town. He'd cart the mailbags from the railway over to the post office; he'd cart the beer over the pub and stuff over to the store.

'Stuff for Birdsville they'd leave in the goods shed at the railway station. They had a big goods shed there and a platform about as high as your truck . . . you could come on the outside and load up. The first layer was pretty easy. Loading the second layer wasn't too good.'

The Badger's load ranged from drums of petrol, post-hole diggers and lighting plants to cases of five dozen bottles of beer for the Birdsville pub, which each weighed about 100 kilograms; vegetables and dry goods for station folk; sacks of flour requested by the cooks on the Kidman company cattle stations (who believed that South Australian grain produced superior bread); and even items of furniture.

'Thursday was always a day of loading,' explains Tom. 'Weight'd go to the front, on the floor . . . windmill heads, cases of beer—six, eight, ten or whatever may be—that'd all go to the front. Crates of potatoes—you'd always put them somewhere where they wouldn't crunch when the rope pulled tight.

'There wasn't a lot of petrol in those days. I think Clifton Hills only used to get two drums every month; same thing for Pandie and same at Durrie. Three times a year I'd take [the supplies for] Kidman's up to Glengyle or Durrie stations.

'Bags of flour and sugar—always double-sacked. They had to be double-sacked with camels and it was just something they continued doing. You'd want to put them somewhere where someone wasn't going to poke a hole through them. Sometimes there'd be more people on the damn back than anywhere else. You'd usually know how many . . . there might be six or ten going for kickoff and you'd have to load so as not crush anything. Say a saddle was going up . . . in those days a good saddle was worth a couple of hundred pounds, so you wouldn't want to have it sat on— not on the back of a damn truck; it's made to sit on a horse.

'Furniture used to be the worst. Someone'd say, I'm getting a little suite or a cupboard or some damn thing. We'd carry it on the hood—up on the roof—where people aren't going to sit on it or stand on it.

'Spare tyres used to hang along the side. We used to carry two or three of them. You might throw a rope over the side and hook it through and just let them hang there to help keep the load on.

'The tuckerbox was always on the side, and the swag'd be up top for someone to sit on. Actually the tuckerbox was very convenient. It wasn't all tucker either. Someone'd ask, where can I carry this camera, or some little thing . . . "Put it in the tuckerbox," I'd say.

'I used to always carry a waterbag in the front of the cabin under my feet and we used to carry one of those 24-gallon drums of water on the back of the old Leyland. That'd be the minimum. And only use it when necessary because you'd make a point of pulling up at a bore or somewhere so you wouldn't have to touch the water [in the drum].

'Actually water was no worries. But you'd have to watch people, they can think they're going to wash themselves in that drum of rainwater. Hell, there's bore water for that.'

While Tom was preparing the load, Valma would be busy gathering provisions for his tuckerbox. It was a generous tuckerbox—a wooden case, 1.5 metres long and 30 centimetres wide, with sturdy handles at each end—that a smaller man than Tom would have had difficulty lifting—and Valma made sure it was well stocked.

'I'd always have jam, a bit of treacle, tomato sauce, and all sorts of extra goodies to eat. Matter of fact, Valma used to go to a lot of trouble with the damn tucker at different times. We used to have a standing order down at the bakery in Hawker for a dozen loaves of hi-top bread. I always think if you've got a slice of bread to eat, you can dip it in a bit of water or a bit of syrup and you've got a meal.

'It's amazing how that hi-top bread could carry, too. But then we never used to just leave it out in the sun. I'd have it on the side in a little cavity where the wind couldn't get to it and you could get it out easy without unloading.

'Not always, just sometimes, I'd get a wheatbag of ice and sawdust from one of the train guards. Unbeknown to most people I used to know a few of those train guards on the Ghan. I'd say, "Look Marty, we want a bag of ice," and he'd put one aside. He was very generous . . . and he had a lovely head of hair, old Marty.

'You'd put the ice down deep in the load and things'd stay cold for days—a couple of bottles of beer, or butter. There used to be quite a few people who'd get butter in billy cans—

you'd wrap a [wheat] bag around them and put them down in the load. It'd still be good, even when you got to Birdsville. To get fresh butter was a bit of a change. Otherwise, from November on, it was all tinned butter.

'Summertime was always a bit of a worry with tucker, but wintertime was a piece of cake. You'd come back with a load of fresh beef. There used to be that many drovers on the road, and they were always anxious to kill a beast. When they killed they could only carry half . . . either leave the other half lying there, or you take it. And you wouldn't take more than you need, either. You don't take meat just to carry it—it goes rotten. Look, in those days if you had a lump of meat in your pocket, you had a full meal.'

One reason that Tom's tuckerbox may have been so large was that it was often called upon, like the Magic Pudding, to expand when necessary to provide meals for his passengers, too. 'Often people would say, "Look, can I get a ride",' explains Tom. 'No worries. But then again, in plain words, how can you sit down and have a feed when someone's sitting there hungry. It was common to share the tucker with anyone travelling with us . . . you'd say to 'em, "Look we've got our own tuckerbox, don't you worry." That hi-top bread was a bit of a godsend that way.'

But Monty was a little more cagey than Tom. He'd had his fill of disorganised freeloaders. 'Ah, you'd always be sharing your tuckerbox with passengers,' he gripes.

'One fella, he come once and he's got no tucker. I got to Mulka and they was away—he was gonna be the caretaker there over Christmas. He had no tucker and I had to give him mine—a lot of tinned stuff I had.

'Next time he goes, I said to him, "Now, you got your

bloody tucker? Where's your tuckerbox? I'm not taking you up without your tuckerbox."

'"Oh yes," he said . . . he had 25 pounds of self-raising flour and a bunch of celery!'

Fully laden, the Badger assumed its characteristic humped shape. The radio with which Harry equipped all his long-distance trucks was always on the back, along with tools, spare motor parts and extra quantities of fuel and oil. The mail drivers routinely carried spare axles, tyres and spring leaves, among other things, to repair their vehicles trackside. The Badger was less prone to these types of breakages than any of the previous vehicles employed on the Track, but even the Badger had suffered the indignity of having both axles removed at the side of the road when a failure in the differential incapacited the front axle. Cannibalising pieces from the rear axle sufficed to get man and truck home. It had to be a completely disabling mechanical failure such as a broken con rod, snapped crankshaft, damaged crown wheel and pinion, or some equally serious trouble, for a driver to call Yunta for the assistance of a mechanic or to obtain a replacement vehicle.

Once the steel plates and a long-handled shovel for getting through the 'soft stuff' were stowed on board in an easily accessible spot, the load would be secured with a few ropes. Sometimes a tarpaulin was tied over the lot, sometimes not. Then, with a last stop to be made at the post office on Friday morning, Tom and the Badger were ready to embark on the Track.

5

DRIVING THE BIRDSVILLE MAIL

Friday morning, with the load stowed and securely fastened, Tom would drive around the corner to the post office, where the mail and any northbound travellers would be waiting. Places would be found on the truck for the passengers and their belongings. There was room in the cab for two or three people, and any extras were relegated to a spot on top of the load. Women and children were given priority inside. Those outside had to endure the sun and dust, coping as best they could.

Margot Baker travelled with her parents on the mail as an eight-year-old, back in 1950. She and her mother were given a space in the cabin, but Mr Baker had to make do on the back. 'As a result of my father riding on top of the truck he got sunstroke and had to go to the hospital when we got to Birdsville,' Margot recalls. 'He had fair skin and red hair—the worst possible combination. He was in bed for two days while my mother and I stayed at the Birdsville Hotel.'

Margot and her family had emigrated to Australia from England only six months previously. This was their first experience of the harsh Australian outback.

'We were told that the mail coach would take us to Birdsville en route to Windorah, where my parents were to work. I'm sure they didn't realise how far away and isolated it was. I know they were somewhat surprised to see the mode of transport.

'While Dad was in hospital, Mum got on the pedal radio and spoke to the owner of the property at Windorah. After a heated conversation she decided it was not for us and we returned to Adelaide. However, the total experience was one we wouldn't have missed. It gave us an insight into the vastness of this country and we realised we had a lot to learn about our new homeland.'

Florence Wade, a prim, well-dressed, 40-year-old spinster from Adelaide, was able to ride inside the Badger's cabin when she travelled the mail alone with Tom, although there were many other aspects of her first outback experience that she found unusual. She described them in great detail in a long letter to her sister, including the fears that crept into her mind at night.

'About 9.30 pm the mailman said he thought we would camp for the night and he made up my bed in front of the headlights on the road—said I might have the headlights on all night if I wished—and went off to his own swag at the back of the truck ... The night was not cold, fortunately, as nights go, but I soon grew cold, being used to hot water bags and whatnots, and the road was so jolly hard that I tossed and turned all night, and of course began to wonder what I would do if a dingo came along and bit me and such-like thoughts. Then I properly got into my stride and began to wonder what I would do if the mailman suddenly died in the night and I was left there all alone—it seemed so entirely a world apart. We had not seen a soul from midday and did not see anyone at all until we arrived at Birdsville next day.

'The mailman is a young married man,' Florence continued, 'huge in size—wears the dirtiest old battered felt hat, khaki shirt with no coat and the biggest pair of greenhide boots I have ever seen. But as a driver—a perfect wizard, which indeed he needs to be—no roads in the bush, just track, and very often not even that—and the things that that overladen truck was asked to do amazed me; and do it she always did with the persuasion and perseverance of the mailman. He is a model of patience and nothing daunts him— when things break he just gets out and mends them somehow or other, and when we came to what you would think was an impassable sandhill he just got her over an inch at a time by putting iron plates under the wheels.'

In addition to the occasional holiday traveller, Tom's northbound passengers often included drovers and stockmen returning to stations up the Track and further on. After delivering a mob of cattle to Marree it was common practice to send the team, or 'plant', of horses back with a couple of men while the majority remained behind, enjoying the hospitality of the Marree Hotel. They would then hop on the mail truck to catch up with their mounts.

Shirley Deans, one of Tom's passengers in 1949, recalls drover Bill Gwydir travelling hundreds of kilometres in unorthodox style. Shirley was on her way to Pandie Pandie station. Her only female travelling companion was a nursing sister on her way to the AIM hospital at Birdsville. 'Tom made a comfortable seat for us both on bags of sugar at the top of the load,' Shirley remembers. 'Also on board was Max Homes, policeman from Marree, a couple of stockmen, and Bill Gwydir, who travelled the whole way perched on the running board.'

On average, there would be passengers on the mail about every second trip, but the arrangement was not as profitable for Tom as it should have been. 'Well, you can't have both. You can't have workers and payers. Look, the only people who ever used to pay'd be someone going up to Kidman's,' says Tom. 'If they were sending up a cowboy or something like that, you'd charge it to their account. Oh, there'd be the odd person that might pay. But look, most times you wouldn't have the heart to take the money.

'Going over the sandhills, they'd all have to get off . . . People'd work! . . . Digging out the tyres. Look, I tell you, some of those ringers could really work. At the first smile on the sun they'd be saying, "What do you want done now?"

'"Well, look, we've got a few flat tyres here, just pump them up," I'd say. They'd be happy to oblige. Look, I know in 1944, when it was really sandy . . . hell, you wouldn't've ever dared to take a cent off a person.

'There again, some of them were a bit bloody lazy too . . . Look here, if you want a free ride, you pull your weight.

'Then when Monty took over, an old blackfella said, "The mail's buggered now. It's like getting on a train. You gotta pay before you get on."'

'Yeah, well, they were supposed to, but if they didn't have any money . . . well, they didn't,' says Monty. 'Ah, if a drover wanted a man and I could get one in Marree, I'd take him up for 'im . . . wouldn't worry about him. But Tom and I were supposed to get half, see. If I carted all these passengers and Tom knew there were three passengers on the mail and he didn't get a half of those three fares, well, he might've thought I was pinching it, see. That was the point.'

'Monty, really, I tell you what, he did an excellent job,' says Tom. 'And very honest. The day the term finished, Monty came over with a bag of money. He said, "This is what I owe you, and I've kept half." Look, you couldn't get anyone more honest.'

Along with northbound passengers, the Marree mail would be ready to go by 11 o'clock, Friday morning. Letters and parcels for each station and the town of Birdsville were contained in separate canvas sacks. Some were fastened with a lock or crimped with lead; others were sealed with string and beeswax. The bags were not supposed to be opened by anyone but the official postmaster, although exceptions were sometimes made in the isolated country of the Birdsville Track, far from the bureaucratic eyes of the Postmaster-General. Occasionally the Marree postmaster would also hand over a large, sealed wicker basket that the mailmen despised. The light, unwieldy basket was always in danger of being crushed or catching the wind and flying off the back of the truck. It was an annoying inconvenience for something as frivolous as a lady's straw hat—frequently the contents of the basket—and Tom and the other mailmen would invariably 'go crook' at the object of their frustration.

Tom would also be given a couple of small bags for road mail. Inside would be deliveries for doggers, drovers, stockmen and other itinerants who lived along the Track.

'I might say, sometimes there used to be more road mail for some of those drovers than what there was for people living along the Track. If it wasn't collected, you'd just [take it back to Marree] again and it would go the next time. There could be letters from their girlfriends or wives. And for the drovers it was very important to get their trucking dates— when the train'd come up to Marree to load their mob of cattle. They had to know if they'd have to put a bit of a spurt on, or have to kill a bit of time.

'Scobies—Monty's mother and father—always got their mail by road mail and they used to get more letters than certain other people. It would just be addressed to "Mr Scobie, Road Mail".'

The mail, in fact, was a minor part of the Badger's load, but it represented the means by which everything and everyone else was ferried up and down the Track. The mail contract provided a kind of financial retainer that allowed the passenger and freight service to operate. Tom would fling the postal bags up onto the load—stuffing them into crevices behind wooden crates and hessian sacks to prevent them from coming adrift during the journey and blowing about in the dust, kilometres from anywhere. It was the Royal Mail, after all, and had to be afforded the appropriate protection.

Once the mail was onboard, official protocol dictated an immediate departure from the post office. 'When you load up the mail you're not supposed to stop again. You're supposed to go straight out of the town,' explains Monty. 'All the drunks, they used to have to come down to the post office. I always had arguments with 'em. They'd want me to go up the hotel [to pick them up] and I'd say, "No, you bloody walk down here."'

'Yeah, leaving Marree was always a bit of a damn nuisance,' Tom says. 'Some of those drovers coming down from Queensland . . . they might be three months on the road. They wouldn't be paid until the end of the trip, and of course then some of them would really think they're Lord Nuffield. They'd be—in plain words—stupid bloody drunk. It used to be a horror sometimes. I remember one chappy walked off the top of the load—over the back. He's up about 16 feet high. If he hadn't've been full he'd've killed himself, I'm sure.'

Cargo complete, Tom would climb up into the Badger's driving seat, turn over the engine, and pull out onto the unsealed street. He'd give a wave and tip his hat to passers-by as the truck trundled past the Marree Hotel, then he crossed the railway line and headed north. About a kilometre out he passed through the Common gate, whose fence encircled the township and delineated the town land. The truck ran along smoothly as it approached its top speed of 40 kilometres per hour; the road was flat and smooth and hard-packed at the southern tip of the Track. In an hour they'd be passing through the dog fence (42 kilometres from Marree); they'd be at the first stop, 968-square-kilometre Dulkaninna station (83 kilometres out) by lunchtime; at Etadunna station—a big run at over 2600 square kilometres— by late afternoon.

'At Dulkaninna you used to go right through the yard— through the sheds,' says Tom. 'Monty always used to say, "I don't know whether they're putting it up or pulling it down." Only half the wall finished, and petrol drums all over the place.'

The ramshackle nature of Dulkaninna station impressed all who saw it: 'Despite the melody of its name, it was nothing but a tiny tin shack, no more beautiful, and hardly more commodious, than a hen-house,' an early mail passenger, the biologist Francis Ratcliffe, observed.

Dulkaninna was home to the Bell family, and Tom enjoyed catching up with the youngest son, George, five years his junior, as he passed through. Other than a couple of years spent droving in the late 1930s and a short stint living in Marree, George Bell had lived on Dulkaninna all of his adult life. Dave Bell, George's father, had brought his family of six up from Adelaide in 1932, travelling for five weeks in a convoy of dray, trolley and sulky to take up the pastoral lease that had once belonged to his grandfather. They arrived three days after George's thirteenth birthday and set up home in a cane-grass and tin shed built in the 1890s by George's great-grandfather. Over the following months the family set about rebuilding the original homestead and restocking the run with cattle. Dulkaninna station, now more than doubled in size to 1964 square kilometres and still owned by the Bell family, has been George's home virtually ever since.

It was 500 kilometres from Marree to Birdsville and for most of Tom's era there were only five stations on his run. Lake Harry, Cannuwaukaninna, Ooroowillanie, Mirra Mitta and the Mulka Store all closed down while Tom was on the Track. Others, such as Mount Gason, Goyder Lagoon and Kalamurina, and the missions at Kopperamanna and Killalpaninna were abandoned and desolate before Tom ever set foot there.

Originally there were fifteen stations along the way but drought had dispensed with ten of them, leaving only the most resilient. Those, too, had been restocked on several occasions when the cattle had died from want of feed and water or had been sold off down south to salvage some return in the face of prolonged dry spells. Each station encompassed at least one of the government bores that had been sunk along the Track in the late 1800s and early 1900s to tap into the underground reservoir of the Great Artesian Basin. The bores were some compensation for the lack of permanent surface water between the waterholes of the Diamantina and the dwindling Hergott mound springs that had given rise to the nearby township of Marree. They were spaced at 40-kilometre intervals, estimated to be the distance that a mob of cattle could walk before requiring water.

During the droving season, which stretched from April to September, thousands of 'fats'—prime beef on the hoof—would make the long walk down the Track in dusty herds of 500 to 1000 beasts. As the country dried out thinner, less profitable 'stores' would amble toward Marree. If the drovers were lucky enough to find feed along the way and their animals fattened up, they might be classified 'forward stores' or even fats by the time they made the railhead.

It was one of the epic sights of the inland: great herds of cattle advancing across the plains, while behind them in clouds of dust rode the drovers.

By Friday evening, all going well, the mail truck would have reached the Cooper Creek, a 5-kilometre-wide sandy furrow in the sunbaked plains, 145 kilometres into the journey. Tom and his passengers would usually make camp there, among the clumps of dry desert grass and coolibah trees. After a simple meal, Tom would lay out his swag on the ground and turn in for the night. 'To sleep in the Cooper Creek and find kangaroo tracks around us in the morning was really unbelievable to an eight-year-old,' says Margot Baker, reflecting on her journey on the mail truck in 1950.

But some of Tom's passengers were less taken with the joys of casual bush camping. Kay Tucker was an infant when her mother, Dorothy Garnaut, carried her on Tom's truck. 'I have no memories of this trip but my mother often spoke of the hardships they experienced, and how they took a week to travel from Marree to Birdsville . . . Mum sat up all night nursing me on her lap as she was afraid to sleep on the ground.'

Tom and the other mail drivers liked to make the Cooper by nightfall because it was a plentiful source of wood for a campfire. It also made crossing the sandhills on the north side of the Cooper a marginally easier task.

'What I used to try and do is get to the Cooper Friday night and hit the sandhills first thing in the morning, because they're harder then,' Monty explains. 'On a hot day they're really loose . . . but early in the morning you're pretty right. You've got about seven or eight miles of the Naterannie sandhills once you cross the Cooper, then you get a bit of stone, then the next one you hit's Ooroowillanie, then you're right till you get to Mungerannie . . . use the plates in the Gap and then away you go.'

The timetable called for the second night at Goyder Lagoon, calling on Mulka, Mungerannie and the Clifton Hills letterbox on the way. With Naterannie at his back, it was usually smooth driving for the mailman to the Mulka drovers' store, located on the site of the Scobie ancestral home—New Well—a few kilometres south of Mulka station. Many of the place-names in the region are derived from Aboriginal words and New Well was alternatively—magnificently—labelled

'Mulkanundracooracooratarraninna' in a newspaper clipping of the time.

At the Mulka store Tom would unload mail and supplies for the lonely consumer outpost and the neighbouring Mulka station. The famous store might only average one customer per week, but he would usually spend up to 60 pounds—a considerable sum in the 1940s and 50s—on non-perishable foodstuffs such as tea, sugar and bags of flour, and stockmen's supplies such as bridles, bush blankets, waterbags, camp-ovens and shiny new quartpots.

'For years old Poddy used to have a standing order for condensed milk and tinned nectarines,' says Tom. 'Might be a few, might be half a ton. It was also the only place you could buy those little round blocks of cheese . . . ideal for the drovers.'

When Tom was just starting on the Birdsville run—before Harry Ding's trucks were equipped with their own radios—he regularly had to avail himself of Poddy Aiston's old pedal wireless when a problem arose on the Track. And he had often made his way to the shop for odd bits and pieces with which to repair a mail truck that had reached a sudden demise. 'He'd always say, if you can see something lying around, use it. He had old poles and God knows what, kicking around.'

Former police trooper 'Poddy' (George) Aiston was stationed at Mungerannie, 40 kilometres beyond Mulka, before he retired and set up a store with his wife, Mabel, to serve the drovers plying the Track. After Poddy's death in 1944, Mabel remained at the store on her own, serving her customers for a further eight years. Tom was a welcome fortnightly interruption in a lonely life for Mabel and the pair became close friends. When she eventually sold the store she stayed with the Kruses in Marree for a while before finally settling in Adelaide.

After Mulka and Ooroowillanie, the next mail stop was Mungerannie station, where Tom would leave consignments for the Oldfield family and the folks from outlying Cowarie station, who would rendezvous there to send and receive their mail. Cowarie was on the original Birdsville Track when its route followed the course of the Diamantina River and Warburton Creek, but the string of artesian bores put down by the South Australian government followed a more direct route between Marree and Birdsville, and Cowarie was bypassed.

Passing between the low, flat-topped hills and escarpments of Mungerannie Gap, Tom was about halfway through his run. This also marked a change in terrain from the sandhill country fringing Lake Eyre to the pebbly gibber plains of the Sturt Stony Desert. The ground was strewn with the reddish-bronze nuggets for which Sturt named the area.

'Our gibbers are smoother and rounder than the stones of most deserts,' Dr Cecil Madigan noted in *Crossing the Dead Heart*, describing the flat, roundish pebbles found scattered for kilometres in all sizes from a centimetre or two in width up to 15 centimetres or more. The stones—the remnants of ancient sandstone outcrops—are dark red to yellow in colour and polished smooth by thousands of years of scouring by sandy winds. Over time, they in turn erode to sand, which is swept up into the distinctive red sand ridges of the Simpson Desert.

For Tom, driving over the gibbers was like driving over a never-ending paddock of marbles. The steering wheel jiggled and jolted constantly, sending shuddering vibrations reverberating up his arms. Stones pinged and popped as they flung up against the truck's sides and undercarriage. Most of them were worn as smooth as glass, but there were plenty of sharp-edged scoundrels lying in wait for a rubber truck tyre—the threat of punctures was a constant worry for Tom and the other drivers.

'Punctures! . . . During the war years it was shocking,' he remembers. 'Hell, the old Badger was completely overloaded. Look when you've got to use a hand-pump to pump tyres up, it's far better to get out and move a few stones. I think it used to be 1000 strokes to get it to pressure. If you had an offsider you'd take it in turns . . . 300 each . . . no talking.'

The last stop for the day was the huge, 23 000-square-kilometre Clifton Hills station; 324 kilometres from Marree and about 170 kilometres from Birdsville. Tom was two-thirds of the way through his route. If struggling through the sand ridges had meant that he was behind schedule he would continue driving through the night, only stopping to rest when he neared the station homestead. During the summer, when temperatures reached 45–50 degrees Celsius and beyond—and stayed there for weeks at a time—it was not uncommon to travel in the relative cool of the night and find a patch of shade to rest in during the day—even if it was only a matter of crawling under the truck to avoid the sun's glare. It could be deadly to attempt the sandhills and all the associated digging and exertion in the midday heat.

At dawn on the third day Tom was just 150 kilometres from his final destination—if he took the shortest route up the 'inside' track. Fourteen kilometres beyond Clifton Hills station the Birdsville Track split in two. In dry times, it would be a smooth ride to Birdsville over the hard, flat surface of Goyder Lagoon, and truck and cargo would be in town by lunchtime. When the lagoon was inundated with floodwater it would transform into an endless quagmire that could trap the truck for days; weeks. Then, Tom would divert to the alternative 'outside' track running around the eastern edge of the floodplain—adding an extra 37 kilometres to the journey—until the country dried out.

The outside road was all gibbers, so Tom was particularly glad to avoid it whenever possible. 'On the inside track you don't see a stone,' he says. 'Once you're on the inside road, if someone said, look, I'll give you a thousand dollars to find one stone, you'd have to be carrying it in your pocket.'

About 30 kilometres from the end of his run, Tom would offload mail and supplies at the letterbox for Pandie Pandie station, then it was on to Birdsville, which Madigan described as 'a bare and wretched little town', while at the same time acknowledging that it was a welcome sight nevertheless when he approached it from crossing the Simpson in 1939.

The town—originally named Diamantina Crossing, then Burtsville, after 'Baldy' Burt who set up a drover's store on the spot—was the northern terminus of the Birdsville Track and the end of Tom's run. Apparently Baldy was too modest to feel comfortable with a growing township on the Queensland–South Australia border bearing his name and in 1885 it was officially changed to Birdsville. However, Baldy didn't contest a waterhole on the edge of Goyder Lagoon being named for him and Burt's Hole thus became a familiar landmark for Tom and other Track travellers.

Today, Birdsville is one of the trio of tiny Queensland towns—along with Bedourie and Betoota—that comprise the 'urban' component of the Diamantina Shire. At 95 000 square kilometres it's still only the second largest shire in the State. The official population count of 120 each in Birdsville and Bedourie and one person in Betoota, leaves a remainder of just 149 nomads and station workers to make up the shire's total population of 390 residents in an area of Australia twice the size of Denmark.

In the 1940s when Tom was the town's local postman, Birdsville was a lethargic little settlement slumbering in the sun. The Birdsville that was a thriving turn-of-the-century customs outpost equipped with three hotels, three general stores, a customs house, bank, school, printing press, cordial factory, police station and town hall, and which was serviced by a doctor, a saddler, a butcher and two blacksmiths, had not only suffered deeply from the drought of 1900, it had also been made largely redundant by Federation in 1901. Outback tourism, which has revitalised Birdsville and now ranks alongside the cattle industry as the most important in the shire, had yet to draw visitors to the area.

A small smudge of dust in the distance would signal the approaching mail truck, sending a frisson of excitement through the community. The hotel, the AIM nursing home, a school and police station, and a clutch of low, lonely stone dwellings shimmering in the heat were all that stood for the Queensland border township at that time. Mail, supplies and news of the world beyond the desert plains were eagerly anticipated by the town's twenty or so stalwart residents, and any who were about would immediately gather at the post office—a small galvanised-iron shack—to greet Tom and the Badger. Ropes would be untied and the mail sack and any loose mail collected along the way would be handed over to the charge of the postmaster, Mr Afford.

'Look, even if you arrived at midnight old Mr Afford used to enjoy opening the mail,' Tom says. 'The policeman's wife, Mrs Carralan, her mother used to write two letters a week to her daughter. From her side, it was always a total delight to get the mail. There was no telephone to Birdsville in those days. You could speak on the radio, through Port Augusta or somewhere. But old Mr Afford would always say, "it's great to get the mail. No, really great to get the mail."'

Once the truck had come to a halt at the post office, the passengers would climb down from their perches, stiff and dusty and aching for a drink, and make their way across the street to the Birdsville Hotel with Tom close on their heels. As soon as the fortnightly consignment of bottled beer and spirits was unloaded he would take a place at the bar and savour a cold—or coldish—one. On some occasions there was no beer to be had, cold or otherwise, so Tom and the Badger's appearance over the horizon was welcomed with extra fervour. The way Tom tells it, running out of beer was a serious matter—not to be trivialised by anyone.

'I think Maxy Bowden was the driver when the song, 'The Pub with No Beer', came out, and of course the Birdsville pub was always out of beer, and Maxy played it and Jack Gaffney threw him out.'

At Birdsville, Tom would stay at the hotel, where he could be assured of a bed, a shower and a hearty meal for two shillings and sixpence. The menu usually consisted of corned beef in a number of guises, unless a drover had recently killed or a stationhand had brought in some fresh beef.

The following day was spent refuelling the truck from the

drum of diesel carried on the back, patching punctured tyres and making any other minor repairs. During the war years spare parts were hard to come by and broken or worn-out components were often cobbled together with a lick and a promise. While Tom attended to the truck the townsfolk would have a day or so to read their mail and prepare any return correspondence for Tom's departure the next morning.

Sometimes Tom would have to make a 30-kilometre trip out to Roseberth station to deliver petrol or other freight. If he had to go further afield, to Glengyle or Durrie stations, his return to Marree would be delayed by a day.

If Tom was on schedule, it would be Tuesday around midday when he and the Badger would be off down the Track once again, return mail and southbound passengers on board. He aimed to reach the southern end of Goyder Lagoon the first night and Clayton Bore on the second, ostensibly putting him back in Marree by 10 am Thursday morning, where he would drop off any mail at the post office that he had collected on the return trip and drive home for a wash, a feed and a well-earned rest.

Travelling south, the sandhills presented a different set of problems to those of the northbound journey. The truck was usually without a load so, being much lighter, didn't bog as often in the deep, soft sand. Due to the prevailing winds blowing from the west, however, the slope of the hills was much steeper on the eastern side. The top of the dune would have a sharp lip—like the crest of a wave about to break over the truck. If a spot could not be found nearby where the lay of the sand was more helpful, it was a case of lowering the sandhill—shovelling a channel wide enough for the truck to pass through and over the summit.

Tom would call in at the same stations on the way back to collect the mail bags again, which invariably contained a few items of mail. Usually there would be people around the homesteads who would invite him in for a cup of tea. Stations off the Track had a mailbox—an open-ended oil drum, a tea chest or a kerosene case—standing in their stead. Sometimes a stationhand would be there to receive the mailman and sometimes there'd be a passenger waiting for a ride down south. Occasionally stockmen or drovers would appear, seemingly materialising from nowhere, to deliver their letters to Tom.

It was one such occasion that gave Tom a terrible start and led to his mounting extra illumination on the truck. It happened at night, near Mount Gason Bore. A drover, seeing the mail truck's lights from his camp, had jumped on his horse and raced to catch up.

'O' course they'd have some idea of when you were coming along,' says Tom. 'They'd see the lights—might be 10 miles away—and ride over. They'd say, "Do you mind if I have a quick glance in the light?" "Okay, you read your mail if you want to," I'd tell 'em. "There's no seats to sit on though."'

This particular drover galloped alongside the truck, waving his letter and shouting out, trying to capture the attention of someone inside, seemingly to no avail. Tom was oblivious. There was a wooden board in the driver's door instead of window glass and Tom was looking dead ahead.

'We never had glass. I had three-ply for wind-up windows . . . tea chests—there were plenty of them around.'

In desperation the drover wheeled his horse to the left and cut straight in front of the truck. *Bloody hell!* Tom thought he'd hit the horse, he was that close. He stopped as quickly as he could—'Well, the brakes, they weren't instant,' he admits—and jumped from the truck. He found both horse and rider in one piece, but the incident gave Tom such a fright that, soon after, he mounted a large headlamp high on the front of the Badger. It shone brightly, casting a wide circle of light on the driver's side.

'That one eye was far better than two weak ones. It was a beautiful light,' he recalls. Because there was only one lamp he named it the Lord Nelson lamp to honour the hero of Trafalgar who was blind in one eye.

6

The Cooper

And so it went on the Birdsville Track, week after week, month after month.

From 1942 to 1947 Tom ran the Birdsville mail for Harry Ding, largely at his own recognisance. In 1944, Harry moved from Yunta to Wilcannia in far western New South Wales, leaving Tom in charge of the Marree operation. Harry continued to oversee the business from afar for the following three years but the two men were not to meet again for another sixteen years.

Although Harry's original schedule called for a seven-day round trip from Marree to Birdsville, within a couple of years Tom was doing the turnaround in five days, conditions permitting. He'd leave on Friday and be in Birdsville by Saturday night or Sunday morning, then depart Birdsville on Monday morning and be back in Marree in time for southbound passengers to board the Ghan on Tuesday night for its return trip to Adelaide.

'We used to do it in five days, everything going all right,' says Tom. 'I might say, coming down [from Birdsville], especially round Christmas-time, there'd be so many people going to Adelaide . . . I'd say, look, if we can get away by two o'clock this afternoon, we only have to poke along all night . . . get down [to Marree] by four-ish . . . the mail can be resorted etc, give you fellows a chance to have a bit of a clean-up and pay your bills and have a few grogs, and then catch the train.'

In the mid-1940s an Aboriginal stockman and camp cook, William Henry Butler, joined Tom on the Birdsville run as an offsider and occasional co-driver. He was still working for Tom, off and on, when Monty took over the run in the 1950s.

'Oh, he was a funny bugger,' Monty says. 'William Henry Butler. I said to him one day, I thought your name was Henry. Yeah, he said, but they call me William, it's short for Henry.'

To Tom, Henry was always simply 'But'.

'I knew But from the stations,' he says. 'Sometimes I'd see him down in Marree and I'd take a bit of a bend out of him. I'd say, "Come on, But, give us a bloody hand loading the truck." He used to enjoy that. Most people'd be over the pub, see, half damn drunk. He wasn't a drinker at all, old But. Look, I don't think I've ever seen Henry have a drink.

'Anyhow, one time he came down as a drover's cook with a mob of cattle from Boulia and he didn't ever go back. That's when he started working for me.

'He was like a Pomeranian dog—used to love riding around in the truck . . . something different to riding damn horses. He wasn't a motor man, poor old But, but he wasn't a bad driver. Look, if the wire jumped off the plug he'd have no idea but he was amazing in many ways.

'I tell you, it wouldn't matter if you'd only pulled up five minutes, he'd get a fire going and soon be making damper. Put the wireless down, he'd say . . . Let's listen to a person's voice.

'Cooking was really his joy . . . grilled meat, damper . . . Out in the bush, it didn't matter if five people turned up extra. You'd say, "I don't know if there's enough damper there for you fellas." But'd say, "No worries, we'll cut it thin. I've got a knife here that will cut a slice that's twice as nice, you'll find."

'Oh, and he used to like his tinned steak and onions . . .' Tom adds. 'One year there was a really big flood. We were camped on the side of a sandhill about 18 miles down from Birdsville. "Okay," But says, "What are you going to eat today?" I said, "I think I'll have steak and onions out of the tin." So we're eating out of the tin. Suddenly he starts pulling on this piece of gristle or something—rather a strange thing, his front teeth were spaced like a picket fence, and he had this thing really wedged tight. He's pulling away, pulling, and next thing—What the hell!—a little rat tail came out between his teeth!

'No, that's quite a fact . . . Put him off steak and onions for a while,' Tom guffaws.

Henry was happy to swap the stockman's life for the chance to ride up and down the Birdsville Track in the cab of a truck rather than on the back of a horse.

In addition to the Badger, Tom now had charge of two ex-Army Canadian Military Pattern Ford Blitz buggies—four-wheel-drive trucks with a powerful, extra-low gear. Harry Ding had dispatched him to Alice Springs late in 1945 with

1000 pounds in his pocket to see what he could buy at the first army disposals sale following the end of the war.

'After the war, you could save millions of dollars worth of stuff—at Alice Springs and Larrimah,' says Monty. 'At Larrimah they had a lot of stuff—rolls of barbed wire stacked up just like hay in a hay shed. You could buy a ton of wire and go and take five ton. There was no one there to see what was going on.

'And the motor cars—all them Blitzes. Tom was up there and he come back with a mob.'

In Alice Springs, Tom purchased the two Blitzes for Harry, plus various items of garage equipment and spares for the two vehicles. Rather than putting them on the train, he elected to drive both trucks back to Marree, securing the front wheels of the second vehicle on the back of the leading vehicle. He set off on a more direct bush track running alongside the railway line in preference to the South Road from Alice Springs. In this piggy-back fashion he pushed through the desert country until the sand became too deep and he had to abandon his scheme at the railway siding at Abminga. Banking on a train coming by with an empty flat-top wagon, he single-handedly piled up a mound of railway sleepers to form a ramp. When the train came he flagged it down, drove his vehicles up the makeshift ramp onto the wagon and rode the train back to Marree.

Being four-wheel-drive, the Blitz had a decided advantage over the Badger, although it was notoriously susceptible to overheating and the cramped, narrow cab of these so-called 'Monkey-face' Blitzes made an uncomfortable ride for both driver and passenger. It was a challenge for Tom to squeeze both legs into the shallow, tapered driving well and position his feet on the narrow pedals. He also lamented the Blitzes' petrol-driven engines as fuel consumption and loss to evaporation were both high in these engines, making petrol-driven vehicles more expensive to run than diesel-driven vehicles. However, he liked their durability and especially their four-wheel-drive capability. Life was thus made a little easier for Tom, as the Blitz rarely bogged in the sandhill country and there were fewer occasions when it was necessary to free the wheels with the long-handled shovel to move the truck forward.

The Blitz was also a blessing in the mud that mostly plagued the upper reaches of the Track. Heavy local rain anywhere along its length would soon turn claypans into muddy pits and dry waterholes or creek crossings into sodden swamps, but the more serious problems were caused by monsoonal rains further north that would bring red Queensland floodwaters rushing down the Diamantina and onto the floodplains of Goyder Lagoon, forcing Tom to take the longer, stony outside track.

Tom usually knew when the wet season floods were on their way, so he could prepare in advance for the aquatic interludes. It would normally take two to three weeks for the water to fill all the cracked, parched channels south of Birdsville before finally inundating the lagoon floodplain. He would monitor the water's progress on each trip north and choose which track to take when he reached the fork, 14 kilometres north of the Clifton Hills homestead.

Sometimes extended rainstorms up north, or local downpours arriving on top of the Queensland rains, meant that the Diamantina spilled its banks with wild abandon and knocked out the top section of the outside track as well. Then mail and driver would have to divert northeast towards Roseberth station where it was easier to cross the river and then circle back to Birdsville, or float across at the town crossing using boats owned by the residents.

In those situations all hands pitched in. The locals would be on standby, alerted to Tom's predicament and the likely time of his arrival by the radio grapevine following his progress up the track. Anxious passengers would be ferried across—women and children first—then Tom and his offsider would offload the mail and freight and transport it across the water. As Birdsville was usually the end of the line, Tom would often have minimal cargo by then and only essential stores would be taken into town.

'They used to have about four or five boats there,' says Tom. 'What they called the big boat, you could put about two and a half ton in it and still be quite safe. That's quite a weight. You'd only take the necessities, o'course. Apart from the mail, might be potatoes and onions, and someone might say, well, we're awfully short of sugar.

'The thing is, the Diamantina could be in a roaring flood, and you know that six weeks after, the water'll be back in the channel. Then there'll be green everywhere . . . taking up the water . . . it's not very long before it's back to normal.

'It might only be a fortnight, three weeks, you might've had a little bit of trouble getting up to the town—the mud and all that sort of thing. Once the water went down to, say, two feet, you could reverse over it. Most people drive through it, but reversing's the shot. If you go forward, the bonnet's down under the bloody water. If you go backwards, the water opens up . . . like Moses . . . Fair dinkum, you go backwards and the water rushes away and the front of the motor car hasn't got a drop on it . . . if you're going fast enough. Well, I mean you don't charge into it, but you say, okay, give her some curry.'

Tom remembers a hair-raising time when he and one of his later workers, 'Seamus' (Allan) O'Brien, crossed the Diamantina in Tom's AEC Matador. '[Seamus] was anxious to get to the hotel. I reckon it was over four feet of water. And the Diamantina runs fast—about four miles an hour at the crossing. Going over the stones you could feel [the truck] shifting—hell, you could feel [it] wriggle from under you. Four feet's a lot of water. It was a high truck, too. Old Celcie Morton used to say, you've got to be a possum to get up in the bloody thing and a goat to get out of it.'

The Diamantina channel near Birdsville is only 20 metres wide at the crossing but the river would regularly flood out to 10 or even 30 kilometres of water. For Tom, the river in flood represented an exhausting addendum to an already tiresome journey. In both the dry and wet seasons, the Track was a menace. The scheduled five-day journey up and back was often impossible; instances of punctuality few and far between.

In 1947, Tom bought the Marree-based business, including the Badger, the Blitzes, the Marree house and the mail contract, from Harry Ding, who had been gradually disposing of his depots to the men he had left in charge when he moved to Wilcannia three years before. And so, on 1 January 1948, exactly twelve years since first driving the Marree-to-Birdsville mail run, Tom Kruse became the official contractor for the service to the Postmaster-General's Department, for annual compensation of 396 pounds.

With a four-wheel-drive truck, the trusty Badger and more than a decade of Track experience under his belt, Tom felt comfortable with his new business venture. He knew his vehicles inside and out, his customers had become his friends, he had a reliable offsider in Henry Butler and he had endured and overcome the best and worst the Birdsville Track had to offer. But there was one more challenge in store for him, something that no Ding driver had had to deal with— something that had not happened in more than 30 years: the Cooper Creek flooded.

It was 1949. The end of the previous year had seen the most intense dust storms that residents of the Track could remember. Another major drought, like those of '29, '35 and '44, was feared imminent. But in March, rain fell with a vengeance and the whole back country was soon inundated. The Cooper was roiling with floodwater. It filled Lake Hope, 50 kilometres upstream of the Birdsville Track crossing, and slowly, inexorably, inched toward the roadway. Tom sent word for a boat, and steeled himself for the unappealing prospect of ferrying freight at both the north and south ends of the Track.

Shirley Deans, travelling with Tom to Pandie Pandie station that year, remembers racing against the water. 'It was the year of the great floods,' she says. 'We crossed the Cooper just before it came down and reached Lake Eyre for the first time [in memory]. When we drove into Clifton Hills at dusk on the fourth night Mrs Rowlands had kerosene tins of hot water, soap and clean towels lined up for us all—the first proper wash I'd had for days. Then she gave us a good feed of steak and onions. When we left the next morning she gave me two fresh loaves of bread. I have never forgotten her kindness.'

The rain kept coming and, sure enough, the Cooper cut the Track about 20 kilometres north of Etadunna station, with the Kopperamanna and Naterannie sandhills now rising up like beach dunes either side of the waterway. On it went, filling up lakes Kopperamanna and Killalpaninna, that once had sustained the early Lutheran missionaries and upon which they had floated boats and pleasure craft before the mission had been abandoned and the lakes dried up. Still further it flowed, until the relentless wet tongue of the Cooper began lapping at the gaping, parched mouth of Lake Eyre.

As parts of the South Australian inland gradually sank under a sheet of muddy water, it became clear to all that the volume of water was so huge that once the Cooper poured over the Birdsville Track it would wallow there—fat and happy—for many months. Before his northern customers became completely stranded, Tom arranged to station one of his trucks in the sand dunes on the northern side and resigned himself to boating his load across the Creek.

'The Badger was always on the north side when the Cooper was down proper. It was the most reliable and, also, the old Leyland's a better weight carrier. We had a Blitz over there, too. In really wet weather, you'd say, look, we'll use the Blitz. But the Blitzes were really only fill-ins. And we had all sorts of rubbish trucks coming out from Marree . . . Some old junk wagon running up and back.'

The unprecedented flood stirred excitement up and down the Track. Even folks in the city were aware of the drama unfolding in the north of their State; the newspapers reporting the progress of the water with growing interest. Tom was regularly asked to comment on the floodwaters, and readers were kept informed of his travails to ensure that the mail got through.

'Mail Man's Race Against Floods', a newspaper headline of the time read. 'After a race against floodwaters sweeping down Coopers [*sic*] Creek the Marree mailman yesterday got his truck across the path of the floodwaters at "Dead Man's Crossing" about 30 miles south-east of Kopperamanna. Communications can now be maintained with a truck on the northern side of the floodwaters. MC [Mounted Constable] W Teague of Marree said that the floodwaters were travelling at about four to five miles a day.'

Once he had motor transport stowed on the northern bank, Tom's priority became securing a seaworthy boat to ferry his load across the creek. Fortunately, he was not alone in his needs. Disgruntled drovers contemplating swimming their mobs across were wondering how to do so without submerging tucker, swags and gear. Some were making rafts by placing their swags at each end of a bowed stick and pack bags along the sides, then using their tin plates to paddle across the creek. Getting the cattle from shore to shore was also a 'hazardous business', with some drowning when they began to swirl in the current. Realising that there was a chance that the stockmen might walk their cattle eastward to the Queensland markets instead of droving them to the railhead at Marree if dealing with the Cooper became too tiresome, the Adelaide stock agency Dalgety attempted to ease their passage south by providing a boat and boatman at the Kopperamanna crossing.

Stock agents such as Elders, Dalgety and Bennett and

Fisher managed the sales and purchasing arrangements for South Australian sheep runs and many of the big northern cattle stations. Station managers and owners ordered their farming supplies from their stock agent and the agent sold the stock and produce on their behalf at the Adelaide markets. The agents were effectively account managers and banks for their pastoral clients and their business depended on the success of the graziers.

'It all happened fairly quickly—that we got the *Tom Brennan*, because Dalgetys didn't want to lose the market for South Australian cattle,' says Tom.

'In the meantime . . . boats were quite common around Birdsville and so on. [People from Birdsville] used to have one down on the bottom of the Diamantina there, to get their gear across. They brought this boat down—the *Queen Mary*, an old galvanised-iron thing—but you couldn't even carry a swag in it. And if there were any waves, hell, it used to be hair-raising. I remember spending half a day, once, trying to get over.'

The Adelaide newspapers picked up on the story of the donated boat and it generated some favourable publicity for Dalgety. The flat-bottomed, 3.7-metre steel barge, which had been built by the Harbours Board at Port Adelaide and fitted with an outboard motor, was officially named the MV *Tom Brennan* to honour Mr TR Brennan, the manager of the stock department at Dalgety and Co Ltd.

The company arranged to deliver the boat to Marree, where, on 21 May 1949, Tom loaded it onto one of his Blitzes and set off, convoy fashion, for the Cooper. Tom drove the Badger, loaded with stores and the mail, while Gooli Khan, preparing to take up his new appointment as official ferryman, drove the Blitz.

The launching of MV *Tom Brennan* was inauspicious: ' . . . a mighty push by four whites, an Aboriginal and an Afghan and it slid off the back of the truck into the creek', one journalist reported.

The small boat struggled to do all that was asked of it, observed another reporter accompanying Tom on a later trip: 'The MV *Tom Brennan* was built to carry three tons; but it fell short of expectations. The little outboard motor took us out into mid-channel and there we found the swell almost too strong for the boat. In the centre of the lake it was at least three miles across and in places at least 30 feet deep. All around us coolibah trees could be seen with just their tops showing above the water . . . '

For Tom, even with the brand-new boat, the Cooper was a nightmare. The floods of '49 were followed by the floods of '50 and '51—the Cooper languished on the Track for the best part of three years. Tom became expert at floating mail, freight and passengers across the inland sea.

The mail run would begin as usual from Marree, in the Blitz. At the Cooper crossing he and Henry Butler would unload the truck and ferry the load across in 765-kilogram instalments. When all the cargo had been relocated, they would load up the Blitz or the Badger on the other side of the creek and continue on to Birdsville. All this rigmarole added at least another day to the outbound journey, and, of course, it had to be repeated on the return trip, but one or two crossings in the boat was usually sufficient then, as there was a minimal load on the homeward leg.

'From my side, sandhills were nothing compared to the bloody Cooper,' says Tom passionately. 'Three miles in the boat to take your stuff across . . . backwards and forwards all day. The first year it was down for six months, almost to the day, before you'd ever drive across again, and that's a long time.'

In that first year, Tom followed the drovers' tradition and crossed the creek near the ruins of the old Kopperamanna mission. The creek split into two wide channels there, forming an island in the middle, giving the cattle somewhere to have a spell from swimming. But for Tom, the island was a nuisance and he searched the banks of the Cooper for a more hospitable crossing point.

In 1950, the second year of the floods, Tom moved his operations upstream to the so-called top crossing—where a permanent pontoon barge was later installed by the South Australian Engineering and Water Supply Department to replace the sturdy little MV *Tom Brennan*.

'They made this 'ere barge thing,' Monty remembers. 'Must've been 18 foot long . . . We had a cable stretched right across the waterhole and you picked up the cable and pulled yourself across.'

In times of flood, the Track takes a 50-kilometre detour near Etadunna station to reach the top crossing, where the waterway is narrowest—about 16 kilometres upstream from where the roadway usually crosses the dry bed of the Cooper. A car or four-wheel-drive could mount the new pontoon by way of two wooden planks that were pulled up on board after it. The vessel was then dragged across to the other bank by someone standing on the deck and hauling on a length of fencing wire that was stretched between tree stumps on either side of the creek. A small rowboat tethered to the bank enabled one to row across and fetch the pontoon if it was at the wrong end. Sandhills on either side of the watercourse at that point allow vehicles access to the pontoon without risk of bogging in the muddy creek flats.

But that wasn't installed until 1956. In 1950 Tom was still making do with the *Tom Brennan*.

'We were more experienced on the second round,' says Tom. 'We finally went 12 mile up. Jim Oldfield [from Etadunna station] told us to go up to what they call Field's crossing; there's only one channel there—you're not worrying about a bloody island in the middle. It's the only place between Innamincka and Lake Eyre that's one channel. A sandhill comes in from the Cooper and there's one coming down from the north and they form a little channel there for about half a mile.

'O' course when the flood's up, it's okay. But when the flood's going down—receding—you can't get close to the water anywhere. The Cooper may only remain at high flood for six weeks, then it gradually starts going back, back, back . . . there isn't enough water at the edge to float the punt, and you can't drive in there either—too boggy. You have to walk in.

'You might be walking through mud up to your knees . . . carrying everything on your shoulder—50 metres through a bog to put it onto the bloody boat . . . dragging your feet out of the mud . . . Hell, I think I left me leg behind! . . . Well, it's a long way to carry the loading, anyhow.

'On the north side of the Cooper, we dug a little trench, like a little pit, where we used to load the Leyland. We used to back in, and the sandhill became a loading ramp so you could walk off the truck without going up and down all the time. It was quite convenient.

'We just scooped it out bit by bit—didn't do it all in one day. Ah, while you're there waiting for someone to come over in the boat, you'd say, look, there's plenty of picks and shovels here, let's try them out.'

During the floods of 1950, Tom was caught up in one of the tragedies that pockmark the history of the Birdsville Track like gibbers strewn along the roadside.

The Cooper was down and there was a large backlog of freight to take over. Tom decided that he would take mail and stores up as far as Mungerannie while Henry and the boatman spent the day ferrying the rest of the load across the creek. Tom Burnley, obstreperous and contrary, with a quick temper, had replaced Gooli Khan by this time, and was giving Henry a hand.

Tom Kruse made the delivery and was on his way back early in the afternoon when he saw young Billy Wilson and his mother stumbling along the Track. It was only a couple of years since the Wilsons had moved from Clifton Hills to the old Scobie place at Ooroowillanie.

'About two kilometres down from Mulka I saw this little kiddie, Billy Wilson, and his mother, Pearl. She was in tears.

'"Hell, what's happened?" I asked them.

'"Billy just came in. He couldn't wake his dad. Something's happened. Could you possibly . . . ?"

'Well, it was pretty damn sandy out there,' Tom continues. 'I chained up the back end of the old Badger—so you only have one drive axle—takes the weight off the front—and finally got out there, about 12 kilometres out.

'Hell, the crows had picked old Wilson's eyes out. He'd

had a log on his shoulder and must've had a heart attack and dropped dead.

'Billy and his dad had gone out to get a load of wood in their Blitz. It was early in the morning, still dark. Little Billy was only four years of age, I reckon—only a toddler. Ah, he might've been a bit older. But he walked back on his own—about 8 or 10 kilometres he walked back—and said to his mother, "I can't wake Dad." She had no idea that he'd died.

'Well, we covered him with bush and went to notify the police and so forth. And I had to go back to the Cooper that night. It was about two or three o'clock in the morning when I got back there and, of course, where's the bloody boat? They'd been backwards and forwards bringing gear over and now there was no boat on this side.

'Then . . . hell, I can hear voices—I might say, on a clear night, it's amazing how voices carry on the water—someone's calling out. So I took the old *Queen Mary* . . . and finally get out in the middle. Queerer and queerer . . . What actually happened was: the *Tom Brennan* was fairly heavily loaded and they'd run into a branch and the boat had gone to the bottom. Old Mr Keith and his grandson were on the boat—Mr Keith's daughter was a sister in the Birdsville hospital and he'd make a point every year to come up and see Heather—now, his grandson was up a tree and he's still in the water—hanging on to this tree.

'"Where's Burnley?" I asked.

'"All I know is that Tom was walking that way—splash, splash, splash—and taking the Lord's name in vain," Mr Keith replied.

'Anyhow, the three of us all piled out into the water—hanging on to the side of [the *Queen Mary*]. We got old Mr

Keith in, and me and the young fella pushed it along. The water was chest-high and damn cold. The bottom's up and down . . . sometimes it'd go over your head for a couple of seconds and then you'd be back. Probably only 500 yards of water, 'til we got to the nearest point.

'We finally got back to Kopperamanna, and then we had a hell of a job, finding Tom Burnley. We got the old Blitz and drove it around, lighting fires up and down, all round the sandhills.

'He finally came in . . . no clothes . . . in the nude—he'd ripped them off. He'd been swimming, swimming, in the nighttime—no idea if the land was 500 yards away or half a mile away. Then stumbling around in all those burrs. That night we had to tie him down on the cyclone bed because of the prickles in his feet.

'Anyhow, poor old Mr Wilson. Finally the coroner came out from Marree. Janet Dunn and I—she was a sister in Marree, later—we made a coffin out of galvanised iron and wrapped him in a new campsheet, and Mr Keith read the funeral service. Poor Mrs Wilson, how awful for a person. It was sad in many ways.'

7

END OF AN ERA

It was the Cooper Creek that sapped Tom's spirit and drove him away from the mail run. After three years of wrestling with the floodwaters he could no longer bear the financial, physical and emotional strain and was searching for a way out.

'The Cooper was . . . excuse me for saying it . . . bloody awful,' he says in a low voice. 'When the Cooper was down it was no good. You couldn't make any money. All we did was build up a debt.

'For six months you've got three miles of water in between. Everything's got to be handled and everyone's got to be paid. Instead of one vehicle and one man or two men doing the job, you might say it's a three-man job with at least two vehicles. Mrs Aiston always used to say, that the Cooper only crossed the road twice in 75 years. And we had it three years in a row . . . three winters straight.

'It was just after we started from Harry Ding, and I know from Harry Ding's side, the Cooper used to worry the life out of him—"Whatever's going to happen if that Cooper comes down?" he'd say. It used to be the worry of Harry Ding's life.

'Look, I don't know how to describe the Cooper. Say, from Oldfield's side, it couldn't've got any sweeter . . . gold, proper gold: fat cattle. From my side . . . couldn't ever think of anything worse. The thing is, with the Diamantina, it's not very long before it's back to normal. The Cooper was a different piece of cake altogether . . . entirely different. It'd be six months to the day before you could drive across again.

'I don't know how to put it into words,' he says searchingly. 'Look, it's like saying to a person, it's a chilly night tonight, you've got to sleep in the nude tonight whether you like it or whether you don't. You can dig a hole to put yourself in the ground but that's it . . . I don't know how to describe it . . . your hands are tied . . . totally tied.'

By the middle of 1951, the third year of the floods, Tom was nearing the end of his tether. People everywhere were advising him to give up the mail run and find a more rewarding line of work.

'Different ones were saying to me, hell if you can get away from this job, you'll do all right . . . I really feel you should bail out etc, etc.'

Tom's family was also feeling the strain. It could easily take him the entire fortnight to complete the run when the Cooper was down, and Valma and the children were on their own more often than not. Valma's parents were also eager for the family to move nearer to them and for Tom to seek regular work in Adelaide.

Knowing that Tom was considering his future, Celcie Morton, owner of Pandie Pandie and Roseberth stations, dropped a business proposition in his lap. Celcie needed the mail run. Like the township of Birdsville, he was at the end of the line and needed a regular, reliable freight service to keep supplies for his stations rolling in. He was anxious to make his business opportunity attractive enough to tempt Tom into staying on.

'Look here, we're at the end of the road,' Celcie said to Tom. 'We still want supplies, we still want mail. Please, stay.'

'If you can stop the creek from flowing ... yes,' Tom replied. 'But otherwise ... there's no way we can keep going, Mr Morton ... if you keep a man's head under water long enough, he'll drown.'

'Right. Here's what we'll do,' Celcie stated, looking Tom straight in the eye. 'We'll pay all your bills and bring everything up to date for you. I've just bought all Bert Griffiths's gear. The day the Cooper dries up and you can get somebody else to take the mail run on we'll sell it to you cheap and give you enough work to pay for it. If you get other work offered on the side, no worries, go ahead and take it and come back and do ours later. I'll have a firm letter drawn up and give you a formal agreement if you accept my offer,' he concluded decisively. 'We want you to stay around, Tom.'

'So that's how we first cracked along,' Tom says. 'See, Bert Griffiths had all this earthmoving gear. Just after the war, he got the contract to put in all these new dams in Queensland to stop all the cattle going out of Queensland to South Australia. Big tanks, they were, too. Well, he wanted to retire so he sold some of his gear to Celcie—an old 5R series tractor and a scoop and some other things—and then we ended up with it. Oh, look, it was all worn-out gear—nothing new.

'Then Brooks, at Clifton Hills—they were strong

supporters of ours because they were selling 5000 head of cattle per year and needed supplies for all their men. They said, look we'd love for you to have something new. We'll buy you a tractor and give you plenty of work to pay it off. And that's how we came to buy the D6. Brand, spanking new.'

Before the new arrangements could take effect, Tom would have to find someone willing to take over the day-to-day business of running the mail. He would retain the contract but he needed a capable and reliable man to take responsibility for delivering the mail, passengers and the panoply of freight demanded by his northern customers. Until the Cooper dried up, though, he knew it would be difficult to attract anyone to the job.

While Tom was mulling all of this over, Monty Scobie lobbed into town for the annual Marree race meeting in June, on a break from ringing in the Northern Territory. Tom ran into him at Allan Crombie's house, where he was griping about his latest station job and lamenting the impact of the dreaded Birdsville disease on the stock up north. Horses stricken with the mostly fatal disease, the result of grazing on a certain small plant, would suddenly lose all strength in their hind limbs, stagger and keel over. On some runs entire paddocks were infested with the weed and the affected stations suffered a chronic shortage of horses.

Years ago, back in the '30s, when Monty was a slip of a boy just entering his teens, Tom had been instrumental in getting him his first job at Cannuwaukaninna. Even then he was recognised as an excellent stockman, having inherited the Scobie gift for droving and stock work. Tom knew the family as a clan of honest hard workers and now here was Monty, ripe for the picking.

'Monty, ah, how about a bit of a change?' Tom ventured, placing his tea cup in its saucer and laying his hand on Crombie's kitchen table.

'What'd'ya got in mind?' Monty replied, interested.

'How'd you like to be a mailman?'

'Gawd, I don't know nothing about trucks,' Monty scoffed.

'Look, not a problem, we'll get you fixed up with a good chariot. At least she won't crumple in the legs like the damn horses. What do you think?' Tom prompted.

'Well, I'd be happy to give it a try. Not too sure about that bloody Cooper, though.'

'Monty, no worries. We'll wait 'til the Cooper goes down and then hand over the reins. Smooth sailing from there on.'

The two men agreed that Monty would take charge of one of Tom's Chev Blitzes, which they would fix up together. Tom arranged for Lawtons to put on a new tray and Monty paid to exchange the Chev's petrol engine for a new Perkins P6 diesel engine for more economical running. While they waited for the improvements to be completed in Adelaide, Monty began to get a feel for his new job by helping Tom out on some other carting assignments.

'The only boatin' I done was before I started . . . giving Krusey a hand,' Monty says in his bushman's sing-song manner of speech. 'Boat-loading over the Cooper—that was a lovely job, that was. A right job and a half.

'At first they only had the *Tom Brennan*. It was only about 12 foot long but you could put a ton or more on it— you couldn't sink it. The ends was filled up with air—two tanks, one each end. If you loaded her up and pushed her down outta sight and took the load off, she'd come right up again!'

Despite Monty's assurances that the *Tom Brennan* was unsinkable, Tom Burnley had previously achieved this feat with a sewing machine and passengers onboard and Tom Kruse had also managed to send the boat to the bottom more than once.

'Well, to be quite truthful, I think we sank the boat several times,' Tom says with a conspiratorial chuckle. 'Some of it floats . . . bags of flour, they float, they'd drift. No worries. Mailbags'll float. They're bound up tight . . . never lost any mail. O'course horseshoes wouldn't float. I know the time Tom Burnley went down . . . bloody horseshoes kept the boat down in the puddle there for quite a while.'

Capsizes in the *Tom Brennan* were really no laughing matter for Tom, who, despite spending up to half the year on the water, had never learnt to swim.

'I'm a very poor swimmer. I used to really hate going across,' he confesses. 'One time I was extremely lucky when the boat went down. I grabbed a 150-pound sack of flour and floated right to the shore.'

'Tom? He swims like a stone,' Monty drawls. 'Nah, he can't swim. And Henry Butler, I don't think he'd ever been wet. I'm a bit of a dogpaddler m'self. We had an old horse at Ooroowillanie and on a hot day when the dam was full we used to swim this old horse across—about 100 yards. We'd get in there . . . If I had the reins, I'd slide off his back, hold onto his mane and kick me feet and the other fella'd grab his tail and go across that way. When we got to the other side we'd turn around and come back again. [The horse] reckoned it was good. He liked it.

'That's what we used to do swimming the droving plant across, too. The horses'd all swim . . . just hold his mane and kick your feet. And the cattle: they swim. They'd touch the bottom now and again, I s'pose.

'Old Bill Gwydir was taking a mob across the Cooper once. He said to Tommy Kempster, "You start the horses and when the horses get swimmin' you come back and get in the boat with us." So, away they went, the horses start swimmin', but Tom's horse wouldn't come back; he followed his mates. Old Billy's on the bank yelling, "Tom come back, ya silly bugger, you can't swim. You'd drown in a dish of water!" Tommy swum right across like that, about two mile,' Monty laughs, giving the table a thump and shaking his head in disbelief. 'Geez, it was funny.'

While Monty waited for his new mail truck, he and Tom helped Henry take a few loads over the Cooper, then Henry continued on to Birdsville while Tom and Monty did a couple of fill-in trips carting talc. The talc mine was 126 kilometres from the railway siding at Lyndhurst, out from the Strzelecki Track, and plenty of blokes were making a living tripping backwards and forwards with their trucks loaded high with the slippery white powder.

'We went across in the old Leyland,' says Monty. 'The joey box was worn out by that time—the cogs used to gradually sorta pull out. If you're going uphill you'd flick the accelerator and you could get the cogs back into full depth again, but going downhill you couldn't do anything about it.

'We're going down this *steep* hill at the talc mine. Tom's got one foot on the brakes, and the other one on the gear lever, holding that down. Then he says, "You want to be ready to jump out because if she slips out of this joey box she's a goner." I says, "How d'ya open this door, Tom?"

'"Oh," he says, casual as can be, "that door don't open."

'If she'd slipped out the joey box I'd've had to wait till Tom went, and followed him out!' Monty exclaims.

'We did two or three loads in the old Badger. Ah, she's a good old truck that.

'We used to get three pound ten per ton for second-grade and five pound for first-grade talc. That's 99 per cent Johnson's baby powder—all you had to do was put the scent with it.'

When the Blitz was finally ready in November 1951, Monty did his first Marree-to-Birdsville mail run as the Centre was beginning to warm. The Cooper crossing had just opened— Monty being the second person to cross, following in young Claude Oldfield's deep, rutted tracks. Some of Tom's regular customers were sceptical at first, upon hearing that Tom had appointed Monty the new mailman.

'What d'ya want to employ him for? All he's ever done is sit on a horse,' one scoffed, scornfully.

But Tom's early confidence was borne out and Monty proved to be a very capable driver. 'Monty was pleased to get away from stock work and be back in his own country and, from my side . . . well, how wonderful . . . what a relief to get away from the Cooper . . . driving those trucks up and down for free.'

Tom couldn't have been happier with his new partner and Monty was glad of the career change. It was a different line of work from the well-trodden road followed by his brothers, and their father, and his father before him. Monty

Loading the Birdsville mail at the Marree post office, July 1939.
State Library of South Australia: B47089/5

The Birdsville Track inundated by local rain, July 1939. Passengers on the mail truck found seats wherever they could and were expected to work the truck out of bogs when necessary. *SLSA: B47089/43*

Sandhill crossings. Tom scrapes sand away with his hands to free the Badger's wheels, April 1947. *Kruse family collection*

Assisted by mail passenger Max Shepley, Birdsville mailman Ken Crombie (centre) and his offsider, George Williams (right), make wayside repairs to the Diamond T's gearbox, generator and clutch, July 1939. *SLSA: B47089/95*

Tom (right) with a typical truckload of supplies for the Birdsville Track. *Kruse family collection*

Dr Cecil T Madigan (left) with his exploration party and Harry Ding's Ford at Abminga railway siding, prior to their successful crossing of the Simpson Desert in 1939. *Kruse family collection*

Ooroowillanie station homestead, home of the Scobie family. Birdsville Track, July 1939. *SLSA: B47089/77*

Tom (right) and Bill Holliday in the shade of their mud-caked truck while on a stock-carting assignment for HE Ding. *Kruse family collection*

Harry Ding's 1924 XB model Thornycroft lost its load of wool bales in this 1939 crash at Carrieton, from which the drivers, Jim Wade and Dick Hooper, escaped unhurt. Its gearboxes and rear axles helped transform the Badger into a superior Leyland–Thornycroft hybrid truck.
Kruse family collection

Max Bowden (left) and Monty Scobie take a break at Mungerannie station, April 1952. *John Heyer*

Monty Scobie watches Max Bowden cross the Ooroowillanie sandhill in his Ford Blitz, April 1952. Steel plates were laid on the sand to prevent the vehicles from bogging. *John Heyer*

Tennis partners. Tom Kruse and
Valma Fuller in Yunta before they
were married. *Kruse family collection*

Tom's Ford Blitz mail truck and Bob Bilton's 1950 model Land Rover
outside the Birdsville Hotel, January 1956.
Bob and Stan Bilton

was a third-generation Birdsville Track man. Stock work, horses and droving ran through his veins. He was easy in the saddle and with the barest flick of his wrist his handmade stockwhip unfurled like an extension of his arm, concluding each time with a resounding crack. But times were changing: horsepower of the mechanical type was the new way of the world and Monty was eager to climb aboard.

'I reckon I was lucky to get a start in the trucking game,' Monty says. 'No one else but Tom would've given me a start, I don't think. A bloke up in Alice Springs said to me once, what you want to do is get all the money you've got and all the money you can borrow and put it into road trains, because it's coming in and it's coming in to stay. And he was spot on, too. But I never had no money. I had 1000 pounds but that wouldn't go far. It cost me 750 pounds just to put the Perkins 6 in Tom's Blitz.

'When I took on the mail, they said to Tom, he'll be no bloody good. All he's done is bloody horses and cattle all his life. Tom said to me, "You want to remember that—that you don't know anything about trucks, because when I started on the mail I done a bloody lot of work for nothing you know." He was good like that, ol' Tom. He'd be a couple of hours here fixing this up, a couple of hours there fixing that up. Well, it makes you late. And how're you going to make it up? You can't make up the time . . . you gotta take it outta your sleeping time.

'Yeah. I done all right. I was lucky I s'pose.

'She did slip the timing once, up at Clifton Hills. Lucky thing for me that Tom was there. He'd come in to pick up his mail and he fixed it up. I broke an axle a couple of times and put another one in—I could do that all right . . . always carried a spare axle—a long and a short. But apart from that ... The only time I walked away from it was the battery. It was the only thing that let me down. It was hard to start in the winter time, that Perkins.

'O'course none of the trucks had any brakes,' Monty muses. 'Tom didn't believe in that—too expensive. But the thing is, she wouldn't stop often enough. There'd be so many ruts after the rain ... You can't stop ... then you'd break a spring and when you get home you gotta put another main leaf in. The only way you can stop is change down with the gears. Well, that's all right, but it's slow ... can't miss a rut that way. And someone waiting by the road ... look, you've got to start putting your brake on half a mile away to pull up, otherwise you'd drive straight past 'em.'

After the war, in Monty's era as the Birdsville mailman, spare parts were more readily available and of a higher quality than they had been in the 1940s. The condition of the Track was improving all the time and driving a four-wheel-drive Blitz, Monty had command of a vehicle more suited to the desert terrain than the cumbersome six-wheeled, two-wheel-drive trucks that Tom used to shepherd up and down. Monty had a few delays due to mechanical breakdown but nothing of the sort that Tom and the other drivers had had to contend with in the Harry Ding days.

Unlike Tom, Monty didn't have an offsider while he was on the mail run. The Cooper had receded from the Track so there was no need for a regular helper, and even in Tom's time Henry Butler was never permanent—a 'loose man on the country', as Tom used to say. He'd help out for a while, when Tom needed him and when it suited him, but he also pursued other interests.

'Sometimes Henry'd go on his own and Tom'd be somewhere else. Oh yeah, he'd drive the mail all right, but the trouble with Henry,' Monty explains, 'is that he'd see a dingo bitch and he'd be half a day or a day late. Dogs were a pound each and he'd see this bitch and he knew she had some pups, and he'd be half a day finding them. That was the trouble with him.

'He'd scalp 'em. Put 'em in the police station and get a pound a head for 'em. He'd just put ashes on 'em and rub it in and they wouldn't . . . oh they might smell a bit—you wouldn't put 'em in the tuckerbox. But he'd put 'em somewhere on the truck.

'He was still working for Tom when I started. Then Tom give him the Blitz and he went dogging.'

In 1952, with Monty running the mail and Henry off dogging or resuming work as a stock-camp cook and handyman, the era of Tom and the Badger on the Track was drawing to a close. He was still in the vicinity—people in Birdsville and Marree would hear of his whereabouts or run into him roaming the bush—but it was no longer big, burly Tom that stepped from the Badger with a gentle smile to hand over the fortnightly mail bags.

In the transition period of 1951, before relinquishing the regular driving of the mail, Tom remembers making one or two trips with a passenger he transported at the request of Bob Jolley, the South Australian publicity manager and former outback representative for the Shell company.

'I knew Bob Jolley from Harry Ding's days, when he used to come up to Yunta. Bob said, "There's a man coming up . . . do give him VIP treatment." So this fellow, John Heyer, arrived from Sydney in a Chev motor car. I didn't know why he was there . . . just thought he was one of these bloody tourists asking, "Does the sun rise up here?"

'Other people'd make themselves known . . . I'm Ernestine Hill . . . I'm George Farwell . . . Wally Watkins and so on . . . Old Wally was as poor as a church mouse. Hell, he was proper poor. We took a bend out of him all the same— get off your arse and do a bit of work . . . 'scuse me swearing.

'Anyhow, little did I know . . . when John Heyer first came up. I reckon it wasn't until even the third time that he was speaking about doing a film.'

John Heyer, an eminent documentary producer and director, acclaimed for such films as *The Overlanders* (1943), *Native Earth* (1945), *Journey of a Nation* (1946) and *Men and Mobs* (1947), was planning to make a film that would romanticise the hardworking outback way of life and thus capture the essence of Australia. He'd been taken with *Land of Mirage*, George Farwell's recently published account of the Birdsville Track, and was toying with the idea of bringing the spirit of Farwell's images to life on screen. Bob Jolley assured him that the Birdsville Track would be the perfect setting for a story celebrating the quintessential Australia.

Heyer was producer for the Australian branch of the Shell Film Unit, which made documentaries subtly supporting the company mission such as *The Petroleum Industry* (1927) and *Cars and Motor Cycles* (1935). At the time, Shell produced up to 25 new films per year, and screened and distributed films around the world through its educational film library and its privately owned theatrettes and mobile picture theatres. Most of Shell's own films were made at the company's London headquarters, but a quarter of the annual output was produced in Australia, with the remainder made in Europe, America, Egypt and India.

By the time Heyer joined the company in 1949, Shell had made its 30th film and had sponsored Australia's first demonstration of television. Heyer's brief for this project was simply 'to produce a film that reflects the spirit of Australia'. From a range of subject possibilities he had narrowed the field to a transport operation in Western Australia and the Marree-to-Birdsville mail run.

Heyer travelled the mail route with Tom and Henry two or three times before making his decision. He saw how residents of the Track relied on the mail for contact with the outside world; he gained an impression of the outback emptiness and loneliness that Farwell so vividly described in his book; and he experienced the Cooper in flood and learned first-hand how the mailman triumphed over 5 kilometres of water.

By the end of the year he'd chosen his topic: the Birdsville Track offered the opportunity to showcase the sun-worn desert plains of the harsh Australian inland, and the mail driver's fortnightly assault on the Track would provide a natural chronology for his story.

Back in his Sydney office, Heyer started formulating his plans for the film and sketching out the storyline. He began assembling a creative team that included his wife, Janet, and his friend Douglas Stewart, the noted Australian poet, who would help write the dialogue and narration. Heyer had been assigned only a small budget to produce the film, which left little margin for storyline changes, re-shooting or other modifications once shooting was underway. It was essential that he meticulously script and choreograph the entire film before any shooting began. He and Stewart drew heavily from Farwell's book for supporting characters, vignettes and ideas.

Heyer specialised in the British docu-drama style of filmmaking, producing films that were neither cinema dramas nor documentaries in the conventional sense. Rather, he believed that reality could be mixed with scripted scenes to allow the story to emerge. He designed a dramatised documentary in which the story of the Birdsville Track would be told through a number of representative voices: an Aboriginal man would tell the story of Father Vogelsang's Lutheran Bethesda Mission at Killalpaninna; station wives chatting on the two-way radio would illustrate the importance of radio communication to the people of the interior; and the fateful legend of a stricken young mother and her two lost children would symbolise isolation and the significance of the Royal Flying Doctor Service to the families of the outback. The mailman represented all of the hardworking pioneers who had opened up inland Australia; the drovers, camel drivers, stockmen, storekeepers and farmers. The mailman provided a cohesion to the overall story, and his journey up the Track was a tether line upon which each of the mini stories and scenes could be strung.

Heyer knew that further trips to the Birdsville Track would be needed in the coming months to gather additional material for a final shooting script and, most importantly, to cast local people in the roles he had created. He realised that his central character was pivotal. The mailman must be someone the audience could bond with: someone who represented the pioneering qualities of fortitude, loyalty and mateship; someone with guts, who would uncomplainingly soldier on in the worst of circumstances . . . a real Aussie battler . . . an Australian of whom all Australians could feel proud.

It was Monty Scobie who made the connection. 'You know, the sort of man you're looking for . . . Tom Kruse might be right. He used to drive the Birdsville mail.'

Heyer had met Tom on his earlier trips up the Track— when his film was merely the germ of an idea—but on recent trips he'd travelled with Monty, and Tom's absence had meant that Heyer had overlooked him as a possible actor in his film. Somehow, Heyer felt that Monty Scobie wasn't quite what he had in mind for his leading man. He tested a few actors in Sydney and, not surprisingly, they weren't right either. By this time, Tom had embarked on his dam-sinking career and was currently scraping out a dam on Celcie Morton's Roseberth station. Heyer made the long trip to Birdsville and met Tom over a beer at the Birdsville Hotel. When Tom strode into the bar and clasped his hand in a pawlike grip, Heyer knew he had found his man.

8

The Back of Beyond

Central Australia
A vast flat wilderness
As large as Europe
And a thousand miles
From anywhere.
In all the great emptiness,
A lonely track
Joining Marree in South Australia
to Birdsville in Queensland;
Three hundred and thirty miles across
Shifting sandhills,
Stoney plains
And the flat dry beds
Of ancient streams.
A land through the burning centre of Australia—
The Birdsville Track.

A bare dry rut
Disappearing into the mirage
Over the edge of the world,
The Birdsville Track . . .

They called it
The Never-Never Country,
The Back of Beyond . . .
It echoes now to a man and his truck—
A carrier called Kruse . . .

Supplies and mail
For the lonely cattle stations
—stations measured by thousands of miles—
Where the man living a hundred
miles away is your neighbour
And your only link with the outside world
Is Her Majesty's Royal Mail:
Tom Kruse . . .

A carrier called Kruse:
Every fortnight
Fighting the sand
Seven hundred miles
To Birdsville and back.
Every fortnight
The story begins . . .

So began *The Back of Beyond*, the film that immortalised the carrier called Kruse and his trusty, timeworn truck. Filmed over a period of a year from late 1951 through 1952, the editing and post-production consumed most of 1953. 'When

Delta won the Melbourne Cup,'—November, 1951—is the answer Tom gives now when asked what year the filming was done.

It was a picture that changed Tom's life. With one stroke of serendipity he was transformed from a hardworking bushie making a simple living in small-town obscurity to a celebrated romantic outback hero revered by strangers and city folk around the nation. More than 750 000 people—about 10 per cent of the country's population at the time—saw *The Back of Beyond* during its first two years of release. The film also claimed critical success, beating 96 entries from more than 20 countries to win the title of best documentary at the 1954 Venice Film Festival. This honour was the first, and the most important, of a series of prizes that the film garnered, including first prize at the 1956 Montevideo and Trento film festivals, and diplomas at the 1954 Edinburgh, 1955 Cape Town and 1956 Johannesburg film festivals. It was the first Australian film to make such an impact on the world stage.

Shooting took place in the winter months of 1952. Heyer had experienced the Birdsville track in flood the winter before. He'd driven with Tom and Henry Butler in the overloaded old Badger, sailed across the Cooper on the MV *Tom Brennan* and bumped along in one of Tom's Blitzes. He had incorporated all of these elements into his script and now he needed to reassemble the key pieces.

Henry Butler was still poking around the Marree area and agreed to revive his role as Tom's offsider. Tom was working near Birdsville on a dam for Celcie Morton when he was summoned south for filming to begin. Valma contacted him from Marree on the radio to say that Heyer had arrived with the crew and was anxious for Tom to join them. He was specifically instructed to bring the Badger with him. Heyer wanted audiences to see the truck that for so long had characterised the mailman of the Birdsville Track and he planned to include demonstrations of the ingenious methods used to get the cumbersome old Leyland over the sandhills.

While Monty was driving the mail in the revamped Chev Blitz, Tom had the Badger with him up north. It was still his trusty and reliable wagon, serving as a general roustabout vehicle carrying supplies and water to his campsites and assisting in the dam excavations. At Valma's call, Tom threw his swag on the back and took off down the track. He assumed this movie thing wouldn't take long, so told Celcie he'd be back in a few days.

It would be three months before Celcie heard from him again.

'I was at Moorayepe—the first dam we ever built, 80 miles due south of Roseberth. And, I might say, we were as poor as a church mouse,' Tom recalls. 'When we started the dam-sinking, Celcie Morton'd made a stipulation. He said, "Don't be like most of these bloody grading fellas. They take something on then go out bush and decide they don't want to go on with it." He made that very clear.

'Well, I was away for, I reckon six or eight . . . might've been twelve weeks,' he says. 'I had no idea it was going to be so long . . . so involved.

'O'course when I came back I was given a bit of a reprimand. Old Celcie was really angry. He was roaring; going wild.'

Perhaps on this occasion Tom was slightly taken aback by the extent of the timetable hiccup he had inadvertently generated, but by nature he was completely unperturbed by the concept of lateness and serenely unaware of the passing of the hours or the artificial constraints of the calendar. Tom lived to his own rhythm.

Those who ventured back of beyond soon learned that time had a different pace in the bush—regulated by the turning of the earth, the movement of stock and seasons of wet and dry, rather than city-bound appointments and schedules. Even among the people of the outback, however, Tom was unique.

'Time didn't mean a damn thing to Tom,' says Des Thompson, 'and anyone else who dealt with him just had to get used to it.' From 1957 to 1959 Des was the Shell representative for the northern region of South Australia extending from Port Augusta to the border. Tom, with his fuel depot at Marree and his carting contract for the Birdsville Track, was one of Des's more colourful clients.

Des recounts how on one occasion, Tom invited him on a run from Birdsville—where they both happened to be staying at the hotel—down to Alton Downs, 72 kilometres south, on the northern edge of Goyder Lagoon. Des was reluctant to ride with Tom, knowing that he could well be stranded when Tom's 'one-day' excursion invariably extended to a multi-day stay.

'The problem going with Tom was that his idea of time and mine were quite different,' Des elaborates. 'A day could mean anything to Tom.

'After some discussion I told him I'd like to go but, unfortunately, I didn't have the time. Tom drew himself to attention, dressed in singlet, shorts and unlaced army boots and said, "Des, if time were my only worry I wouldn't have a care in the world, because the fella that made time made plenty of it."'

This expression encompassed Tom's outlook on life and was one that he shared frequently with those who knew him.

Even a movie man such as John Heyer was not spared. 'He was a great personality but he had some curious outlooks,' Heyer commented in an interview published several years after the film's debut. 'For example his total lack of a normal time sense. Anyway, quite different from yours or mine. I remember the first time we met. We'd arranged the meeting for lunchtime on a Saturday in Birdsville. I think I waited a couple of days before he turned up. He wasn't embarrassed. He just said—and he meant it—that he wouldn't have minded if he'd been in my place and he'd had to wait.'

With Tom and Henry in place Heyer had his most important characters onboard, but most of the others were still titles in the script. He had decided not to fill these roles until he and the crew ventured farther north and found willing 'actors' for their film. The difficulty of finding extras was eased by Heyer's wife, Janet, who, in addition to her position as script co-writer, was the unofficial public relations person for the film unit. She liaised with the families of the Birdsville Track, smoothed over problem areas and ferreted out potential supporting characters. Once the crew was on site, as the field manager she continued these duties in addition to endeavouring to keep cast and crew happy and healthy, and conducting the twice-daily check-in on the portable two-way radio with the flying doctor base at Broken Hill.

When Tom arrived back in Marree, ready for action, Janet

was horrified at his appearance. Their leading man had turned up with chapped lips and fly-infected, pussy, weeping eyes.

'Janet was really worried about my appearance. I remember that very clearly. She was really worried. Little did I know about bloody cameras and close-up pictures. Anyhow, sandy blight was quite common—look, flies, they're not too proud to settle on you. I had lots of trips to the hospital to get my eyes cleared up.

'And cracked lips, well . . . lotta drovers have a hanky over their lips. Ahhh, don't bother with that,' he says, brushing his hand aside dismissively, typically nonchalant.

With some concentrated care and medication, Tom's eyes cleared and he was declared camera-ready. Heyer and his ten-person crew left Marree in a convoy of four four-wheel-drive vehicles carrying an electricity generator; radio transmitter; wind machine; three months' worth of food, water and petrol; medical supplies; camping gear; and the usual sound and camera equipment. They also transported a track and trolley system for capturing 'tracking' shots, whereby the camera glides along on rails beside a moving subject, plus materials for constructing a tower from which the photographer could shoot overhead shots.

When word spread among the Sydney filmmaking community of the elaborate equipment Heyer was lugging into the desert to get the precise shots he desired, some of them scoffed at his folly.

For most of the shoot, the film unit worked from one of three main camps that they established within a 40-kilometre radius of each other: Etadunna station, 122 kilometres from Marree; the mission ruins at Killalpaninna; and the Naterannie sandhills. Once the main sequences had been shot, a single mobile camera unit followed Tom up the Track gathering general scenery and background shots.

Although the crew members were experiencing central Australia in winter, accustomed to Sydney's moist, mild weather, they found it difficult to adjust to the Birdsville Track's dry conditions and high daytime temperatures of 35 to 45 degrees Celsius. 'Two or three cups of tea would seem to make no impression and it became usual before having tea to drink one or two glasses of water,' the film programme notes.

They tried to work around the peak sunlight hours of 11 am to 3 pm and went to great lengths to keep the film cool to prevent its deterioration. Keeping the ubiquitous flies and dust off the camera lens and out of the delicate sound and camera equipment was another frustrating problem for the filmmakers. 'It was quite common to see flies so thick on a man's back that you couldn't see his shirt, and on occasions it was almost impossible to raise a sandwich to your mouth or take a drink from a cup before the flies got at them,' the programme notes continue. 'The only good thing about the flies was that they all got up and left like one man soon after sunset.'

For the film crew it was an experience learning about the outback. For Tom it was an introduction to the movie business. Around the campfire of an evening Tom heard many a tale about the mechanics of filmmaking. But he also learned in abundant first-hand detail how the filmmakers created images to suit the mood they wanted to convey, and how they improved on Mother Nature if she was found wanting.

When the time came to shoot the dust storm scene, which was filmed at the back of the men's quarters at Etadunna station, Heyer and Ross Wood, the cinematographer, decided that sand was not photogenic enough for a cinematic sandstorm, so they got their wind generator going—an old aeroplane engine with a huge propeller attached—and covered Tom and Henry with great clouds of dry cement. The two endured several hours in a choking, suffocating fog as director and photographer strove for perfection in retake after retake.

'John Heyer gave him a tough time with that dust,' Tom remarks now, dismissing his own discomfort and recalling Heyer's barked instructions to the ex-air force man who was in charge of the engine. '"More! more! more!" he'd yell, until this bloke was afraid of what it might do . . . take off or something.'

By Tom's account, Heyer was a hard taskmaster who demanded that every scene fit the vision he had in his mind's eye and that every line was word-perfect. All Tom's lines were scripted and every movement choreographed, rehearsed and repeated until it was just so.

'John Heyer always got what he wanted. He had it all planned out beforehand, before he got up there. And he knew exactly what he wanted,' Tom says. 'It wasn't on the spur of the moment. Oh, no, it was all written out. That's dead right. And . . . well . . . when you've got a head like a sieve . . . '

'No, no, no you're not using the right word,' Heyer would scold Tom each time he detected a diversion from the script—no matter how slight.

'Right.' Tom would humbly accept the rebuke and try again.

'And don't put your words in. You're saying "and" too much.'

'Er, right, John.'

'You're saying "er" and "ah" too often. Please leave that out.'

'Right.'

'No. Now look, you looked at the camera. What the hell did you do that for?'

'Sorry, John.'

'Smile a bit more. Is that how you look when you're happy? No, you lifted the wrong hand. Now lift your hat . . .'

Tom chuckles now at his memories of Heyer as a stubborn and unyielding director. 'Yeah, no joke. But anyhow . . . won't go into that,' he says, setting aside the difficulties between actor and director of half a century ago.

'I hadn't intended to use Tom Kruse at all,' Heyer admitted. 'Working with unprofessionals exaggerates the time problem but professional actors are expensive and when I'd balanced the saving in cash against Tom's marvellous movements and his expressive face, Tom was the inevitable choice. [He] was a nice chap all right, but he made me sweat a lot. You remember that shot where Tom is lying under his truck, banging a wheel—the camera draws back to reveal the gramophone and then his wife comes out to shout that the food's ready. That took one whole day to shoot. Tom couldn't seem to get the mechanics of it right. Everything would go fine and then he'd pause or glance at the camera, and then we'd have to start again from scratch.'

Despite the minor frustrations that he sometimes caused Heyer, Tom's inclusion in the picture was fortunate. Heyer's budget for the film was a meagre 15 000 pounds which, as he pointed out, would not stretch to employing professional actors. Tom, like all the locals who appeared, was not paid for his involvement. He took part because it was a change from the ordinary daily drudgery, like his assignment to the Madigan expedition. He was happy and honoured to be offered the role. As it turned out, his 'holiday' on the film set took a lot longer than he expected. But, as always, patient and unflappable, he saw his accepted task to the end without question.

'Never give in boys, never give in ... No, look, the pay side of it never even entered a person's head,' Tom says. 'Honestly, it was never something that entered a person's head. It was just something different, a bit unusual. There's always someone ... say a whipcracker: I'd like you to stand up there, I'm as drunk as a monkey, you hold this bit of cigarette paper in your mouth and I'll cut it in three strips and I won't even touch your nose ... Or, I can ride a bucking horse back to front ... Or, Gordon Scobie saying, look, I could stand on the bar here at Birdsville, I can drink a butcher of beer, turn a somersault and it'd be empty and I wouldn't spill a drop ... All stupid things. Well, not stupid, just a bit of a lark. That's all it was. Helping out.'

After sixteen years—on and off—driving the Birdsville Track, Tom was accustomed to helping writers and journalists wishing to enliven their stories of the outback with a turn on the mail truck. Ernestine Hill, author of *The Great Australian Loneliness*, *Flying Doctor Calling* and *Water into Gold*; Wal Watkins, author of the fictional work *Race the Lazy River*, based the Birdsville mail run and dedicated to Tom Kruse, 'who showed me the Cooper'; and even George Farwell, author of *Land of Mirage*, *Vanishing Australians*, *Cape York to Kimberley* and *Australian Setting*, had all sought free passage on Tom's truck while they captured the country in cattlemen's quotes and evocative desert prose.

'Well, Ernestine Hill used to say, "I'm as poor as a church mouse" . . . and she wasn't just saying that to pull the wool over a person's eyes,' Tom says. 'Same as George Farwell saying, "Well, I don't know if I'll ever hit my straps or whatever happens, but help me if you can."'

Tom was not a publicity seeker and whether the efforts of these authors and writers ever amounted to anything was of no consequence to him. For Tom, these requests for help were, again, a pleasant diversion from the loneliness of the fortnightly run: some company in the cab and an eager ear was recompense enough for an extra body onboard. However, starring in *The Back of Beyond* was clearly different from having someone travel on the mail truck for free while he or she wrote a story or collected notes for a book. In this case Tom had broken away from his paid livelihood to collaborate with Heyer. When he agreed to do the picture he hadn't given it a second thought. Later, when filming extended to three months rather than the three days or so he was initially expecting, it was too late to change his mind or withdraw his offer, even if he'd wanted to. He'd made a commitment and it was not in the Kruse handbook to go back on a promise.

Heyer also wanted Valma to act in the film. He particularly wanted her to play the role of the stricken mother whose sudden death leads her two young daughters to embark on a futile search in the desert for help. However, out of shyness, Valma refused to take part, so Janet Heyer agreed to lie down on the ground and be filmed. But Heyer was accustomed to getting his way and he triumphed in the end, catching Valma on the spur of the moment and directing her to call out to

Tom in the backyard of their Marree home: 'Come on Tom! Your dinner'll be all cold!' This was a phrase that fell naturally from her lips—one she has uttered in vain to Tom thousands of times before and since. She now readily admits to being grateful she was forced to overcome her self-consciousness and reflects proudly on her brief cameo.

Tom and Valma's two daughters, Pauline and Helen, also took part. They were cast as the two lost children, Sally and Roberta, who set off into the desert with their puppy, a billycart and a few sips of water, never to return, Roberta whistling a haunting tune on her wooden flute as they innocently wandered into the sandhills. It was a scene that touched the hearts of many when the film eventually reached the public. Valma made special new dresses and bonnets for her girls and sent them off with Tom and the crew for the day's filming.

Unfortunately, when the reels arrived in Sydney their section of film was found to be irreparably scratched and the scene was re-shot in beach dunes somewhere near Sydney. At Heyer's request, Valma sent the clothes over for the young replacement actors to wear. She was terribly disappointed that the dresses and bonnets appeared in the final film but not the girls for whom they were made.

It is unclear whether the legend of the lost children is based in fact or merely an evocative amalgamation of stories of outback tragedies. A newspaper review of the film claimed that it was based on a true tale related to Heyer by Flynn of the Inland, the founder of the Royal Flying Doctor Service, shortly before his death.

The scene at the Killalpaninna ruins was another of Heyer's re-creations—one that he borrowed directly from

George Farwell's *Land of Mirage*. In his book, Farwell gives a poignant description of life at the Lutheran mission there through the eyes of Uley, the last full-blood Aborigine left in his traditional tribal area of the Lower Cooper. John Heyer transferred these images directly to film, casting Malcom Arkaringa as a representative of the 500 Dieri Aborigines who had once lived at the mission under the care of Father Hermann Vogelsang. Father Vogelsang and his missionary 'brothers' had sailed from Germany to Adelaide in 1866 to embark on a four-month wagon journey to Lake Killalpaninna. There, these men in their long dark coats and tall top-hats had learned the indigenous languages and endeavoured to teach the scriptures to the local Aborigines.

Malcolm, a stockman at Etadunna station, had in fact been reared at the mission and his sense of grief for the demise of the settlement was genuine. Heyer later claimed the mission scene to be his favourite sequence in the film.

When Heyer visited the Killalpaninna Lutheran mission in 1951, he determined then that it would be one of the dramatic highlights of the film. Upon his return to the site a year later he was dismayed to find that the climate had taken a heavy toll on the 80-year-old adobe buildings that had stood empty for more than 30 years. The original lectern still remained in the church but there was nothing else left besides the mud-brick walls encompassing an interior mountain of sand. With scant regard to the historical significance of the site, Heyer instructed his crew to toil for several days constructing the apparent remains of wooden pews and re-creating the interior of the church in another building.

'This kind of thing hadn't occurred to me,' he said. 'We only had five shovels—one emergency shovel for each truck.

Fortunately the people who had built the mission had also built a couple of houses that looked the same from the outside. One of them was filled with sand, like the mission, but the other one still had its dividing walls inside—for rooms—which had prevented too much sand from driving in. It was much easier to knock down the two walls than dig out tons and tons of sand. And it really was just like the original mission building.'

The building Heyer commandeered may originally have been the home of the mission manager, Pastor Bogner, as his house had been inhabited more recently than all the others. When the Lutherans withdrew from Killalpaninna in 1915, Bogner stayed on for a further three years before selling up to an optimistic English couple, Lance and Beryl Powell, who lived there and worked the property for ten years until they were finally driven away by drought. When *Land of Mirage* author George Farwell saw the dwelling in 1948, its seven large rooms and arched entrance were fairly well preserved, whereas little remained of the stores, church and schoolroom. At the mission outstation at Kopperamanna there was even less to see; the ruin of Father Vogelsang's house almost completely buried by sand and only scattered evidence of the small church and blacksmith's shop that once had stood there.

By mid-1952, when Heyer was actually filming *The Back of Beyond*, the Cooper had receded from the floods of the year before and Tom and the mail were able to drive across the creek bed as usual. However, Heyer had seen the Cooper in flood at the end of '51. He liked the drama that the floodwaters brought to the story and he was determined to include this in his picture. The *Tom Brennan* was still sitting at the creek bank at the top crossing and there was still plenty of water in large pools hundreds of metres wide that would enable Tom to act out the procedure of boating the mail across the creek. Heyer was particularly keen for Tom to re-enact an incident that had occurred when he travelled with him on a reconnaissance trip the previous year.

'Well, in plain words, that time I fell in the bloody water, that did actually happen,' Tom says. 'That wasn't a put-up show. The starter rope broke, and down I went . . . They did that about a hundred times and it was a freezing-cold day.' Naturally, Tom glosses over the potential danger this represented for him as a non-swimmer.

Many of the scenes in *The Back of Beyond*, like Tom's plunge into the creek, were embellishments of actual events. But there were others—what Tom calls 'a put-up show'— that Heyer created entirely from his own imagination. Tom's dance with the dressmaker's dummy on the banks of the Cooper, for instance, was something that he found silly. But Heyer had an artist's eye and knew what would work on screen. This simple sequence, accompanied by the honky-tonk piano music of the era, became one of the most loved moments of the film. It also revealed a hint of Tom's true character—Heyer had really come to know his actor's personality. Tom's playful nature emerges during the dance and viewers could see that he is remarkably light on his feet for a man of his size and build. He nimbly circles the mannequin with impish style and claps his hands with a grin. Doffing his hat to his plastic partner at the end of the dance is classic Kruse.

Heyer also beefed up one of Henry Butler's scenes to make it more humorous. In the film we hear Henry tell of the time he made a wooden gear wheel, carving it out of a coolibah branch with his penknife in an unsuccessful attempt to replace the damaged one in a truck he was driving. 'But o'course he didn't move. We put him in and start her up and she strips all the teeth off him, just like [she's] shaved him with a razor,' he laments onscreen.

'Him good wood, coolibah, you can make all sorts of things,' Henry steadfastly concludes, undeterred by the timber's failure to stand up to the rigours of the metal gear assembly.

'You and your wooden gear wheels,' Tom laughs.

In fact, according to an account in Maddock's *Mail for the Back of Beyond*, Henry had actually once whittled a coolibah tail shaft for the Badger when it's tail shaft snapped in the Naterannie sandhills.

'Old But was always going round, saying "Coolibah! Coolibah!"' Tom remembers. 'He kept saying, "I can make all these splines," etc. In my book that's what machines are for . . . but he was willing to try.'

While Tom walked two days to the Mulka store for some metal tubing for repairs, Henry patiently carved and shaped his wooden part. Upon his return, Tom expressed doubt about the suitability of the timber tail shaft, but fitted it to the Badger and started the engine for Henry's benefit. Despite his fine workmanship the Badger failed to move and would only budge when Tom's more sturdy but decidedly less artistic length of metal was bolted over the break.

Coolibah wood may have had myriad uses but forming a truck tail shaft obviously was not one of them.

•

Other Track locals joined the cast of *The Back of Beyond* in various roles. It was a young David Brook, now secretary of the Birdsville Race Club, mayor of the Diamantina Shire and owner of Cordillo Downs and Murnpeowie cattle stations among others, who knelt in the sand at Birdsville, studiously learning animal tracks from his Aboriginal tutor, Maudie. It was the Marree policeman's son, Peter Teague, and his mate, David Coverdale, son of the local storeowner, who implore Tom for a lift out of Marree and swing on the Common gate as Tom departs up the Track. Jim and Ida Oldfield, owners of Etadunna station, appear in the film watching for the mail and chatting on the radio—roles they had each played thousands of times in real life. Linda Dixon, who was proprietor of the Birdsville Hotel after the Gaffneys and who then took over the Mulka store when Mabel Aiston moved to Adelaide, dourly welcomes Tom to her lonely shop halfway up the Track. The Birdsville policeman's wife, Mrs Barlow, played the part of a traveller with her child waiting by the end of the Track for a lift into Birdsville. Henry Butler obligingly gives up his place in the cab for her and takes a seat in the armchair lashed onto the top of the load.

The chair, incidentally, was the subject of some argument when it was finally returned to Marree at the end of the shoot. As Tom's journey up the Track for the film was not a genuine mail run—Monty was running the regular mail as usual while filming took place—a representative load had been cobbled together. The dressmaker's dummy, swags, crates and a laundry tub that travelled upside down with its four legs poking up above the Badger's cabin were piled on, along with full petrol drums and cases of beer, to make the load more interesting and to heap it up high for full dramatic effect. Mr and Mrs Russell of Marree willingly lent one of their armchairs to the cause to add some more flavour to the load. Naturally they looked forward to returning the chair to their loungeroom when all the excitement was over, expecting it back in the same condition in which they'd provided it. But by the time it had been down on the ground at the Cooper Creek and taken across the water and had clouds of cement blown over it and had Henry sit on it in his working clothes and so on, it was looking rather travel-weary, even quite dilapidated. When it landed back in Marree Mr Russell complained rather bitterly that some of its newness had been lost.

'Well, it didn't improve it,' Tom admits with typical understatement. 'It was all scuffed up and Joe Russell screamed like a stuck pig.'

The irate Mr Russell could only be placated by the promise of a replacement armchair, which was eventually dispatched to him at Shell's expense.

Muslim cameleer Bejah Dervish of Marree also made a cameo appearance. Tall, elderly and regal, he offered viewers a rare glimpse into his Muslim lifestyle when he allowed the camera to capture one of his prayer sessions. Likewise, Mintulee, known as 'Old Joe', the last of the rainmakers in the Birdsville area, shared an ancient cultural ceremony when he performed his raindance for Heyer and his crew. There is no mention of any responding precipitation, but when Sandy, the Aboriginal rainmaker of Etadunna station, demonstrated his technique he sang and danced for the cameras with such enthusiasm that he brought down 75 millimetres of rain in six hours—bogging the film unit for three days.

Sandy's rain was a minor setback, however, compared

with the endless problems caused by the sand and grit. Severe dust storms with sudden wind gusts reaching 130 to 150 kilometres per hour, twice wrecked the film unit's camp in the Naterannie sandhills. Sand whipped about by smaller storms frequently covered their vehicle tracks, leaving them bewildered as to the location of that day's film site or their return route to camp. A haze of dust in the air often reduced visibility to a few metres. Heyer tried to protect the exposed rolls of film by making regular trips to Leigh Creek to post them back to Sydney. But the constant besiegement by sand took a heavy toll. Shortly after returning to Sydney at the completion of the shoot, Heyer discovered that all the sound tapes had been damaged beyond repair—the voices of Tom, Henry and all the others scoured off by the sand and carried away on the wind.

After all their efforts it was an enormous blow. There was no hope of rerecording the original voices so Heyer decided that he and scriptwriter Douglas Stewart would perform most of the dialogue with help from professional actors in Sydney. Dubbing was an accepted technique of the times, in fact, most of the so-called documentaries of that era featured cultured professional voices and a rather theatrical narration. Indeed, Heyer may have always intended rerecording some portions of the audio in a Sydney sound studio once filming was complete, but it seems certain that he meant to use at least some portions of the original sound—and re-recording all of the dialogue was a daunting prospect. Valma clearly remembers Heyer's keen disappointment when he learned of the loss of the audio tapes.

It was a letdown, too, for the actors, who now found their voices eerily distorted on screen.

'Your voice has changed a bit,' Valma says to Tom, tongue in cheek, when they sat together recently, watching the film for the umpteenth time.

'Well, I might say, it's a good thing I'm deaf,' is his playful reply.

'And Mrs Oldfield, old 8LX, she's never ever spoken with a plum in her mouth in her life,' he says, referring to the mistress of Etadunna station by her radio call signal while watching her chat to her neighbour at Cowarie, 133 kilometres away.

'Yes, Ida Oldfield, she was quite upset when she heard her voice,' Valma agrees. 'She was very upset. It was much too squawky.'

For the rest of Australia, though, Mrs Oldfield was the genuine thing, and the man on screen was the real Tom Kruse, the fair dinkum, true-blue original movie star version. *The Back of Beyond* premiered in Adelaide on 5 May 1954, at a charity event to aid the Crippled Children's Association. His Excellency the Governor, Sir Robert George, and Lady George, swathed in a white ermine stole, crowded into the Shell theatrette with the other invitees for the opening of *The Back of Beyond*'s three-night season. Tom and the Badger were on their way to immortality.

9

EG KRUSE ESQUIRE, MBE

When filming was finished Tom returned to dam-sinking, and life on the Birdsville Track returned to normal; the fun and high jinks of the movie world merely a blip on the flat, sun-baked horizon.

Eighteen months later, in Sydney, Melbourne and Adelaide, excitement began to mount with the release of the first previews of *The Back of Beyond*. In March 1954, Tom and Valma travelled to Shell House in Adelaide to attend a private screening of the film followed by a celebratory dinner. Everyone who took part was invited, along with Shell agents from around the State. Tom was delighted to have an impromptu reunion with one of his co-drivers from the Ding days. Harry's brother, George, who was then the Shell agent at Yunta, sat opposite the Kruses at dinner. Bob Jolley, the Shell PR man, and his wife were also there—Bob brimming with pride at his early role in securing the picture for his State.

Programme booklets were handed out to audience

members. '[*The Back of Beyond*] is designed in an impressionist style and is not the story of one man or one family or the story of the Track itself,' the introduction read. 'Rather is it an impression of life in the inland, the great open spaces beyond the sunset, in which the Birdsville Track is the stage and the people along it are the actors. To the people of the Birdsville Track, as representatives of the people back of beyond, we dedicate this film.'

Tom and Valma were both happy with the final product. Film critics attending similar private screenings in Sydney and Melbourne were likewise impressed with the film. The opportunity to review an Australian film was a relatively rare event in the early 1950s and the reporters had nothing but praise for Heyer's contribution. Brian McArdle, writing for Melbourne's *The Age*, remarked on the inherent paradox of the film: it was quintessentially Australian, yet depicted a part of the country that few Australians had seen, or were ever likely to see. He recommended that as many of the general public as possible see the film.

The *Sydney Morning Herald* film critic instantly recognised *The Back of Beyond* as an Australian masterpiece, his awe of the film's graphic desert imagery inspiring his pen to overflow with superlatives. 'The Shell company's [*The*] *Back of Beyond* brilliantly tells its story of a Central Australian journey in ruthlessly simple images, as hard and white and intimidating as a carcass picked clean by vultures,' he wrote. 'It is an environment that will not compromise with man. Even the animals face it with dismay. Dingos seek to nibble at dry bones. Snakes are always on the prowl. Oceans of sand are ready to annihilate unvigilant wanderers.'

The film had its public premiere in Sydney at the inaugural

Sydney Film Festival in June 1954. Within weeks it was being shown in country towns and outback centres all over Australia. Film distribution was an issue of great concern to Heyer—what was the point of making great films if very few people get to see them? He loathed the grip that the big American commercial studios had over the content in Australian picture theatres. In fact, one of the primary reasons that he had joined the Shell Film Unit was its vast distribution network.

The Shell Company of Australia had opened its Educational Film Library in 1935, in the middle of the Depression, and it had since become one of the most important channels for distributing educational and documentary films free for loan around Australia. In 1937 the company began incorporating theatrettes into its refurbished capital city office buildings and eleven years later the first Shell mobile film units were born. These picture theatres on wheels, complete with movie screen, projector and projectionist, travelled the countryside bringing cinema to many remote communities for the first time.

The mobile film unit now kicked into action for *The Back of Beyond*. Some film critics initially found it surprising that the film was being released only in 16 millimetre format, unsuitable for screening in commerical movie houses, but with Shell's great reach it was soon being shown in Shell theatrettes, schools and town halls all around the country.

Through word-of-mouth popularity, demand for the film grew rapidly. Even then, the Birdsville Track was part of Australia's folklore.

From the institute building in Manoora 5 kilometres from Waterloo—the tiny South Australian town in which Tom grew up—and a town hall in rural Queensland to a school gymnasium in Western Australia and Shell House in Adelaide, projectors whirred and young minds soaked up every detail. Boys and girls everywhere imagined bumping along the Track with Tom by their side, or fancied themselves at the wheel of the Badger, squinting through the dust, slapping the driver's door and urging their truck forward over the sandhills.

'How many imitation mail trucks were made out of Meccano sets and played with in the dusty spots of the backyard; re-creating the excitement, dangers and sheer ingenuity of the drivers to ensure the mail went through,' muses John McKay, who saw the film as an eight-year-old, eschewing memories of the heather-covered glens of his Scottish homeland for these thrilling new images of the great Australian outback.

Certain images drew visceral reactions from children in the audience, leaving an indelible imprint—being startled when a snake appeared, slithering along the ground; being haunted by the two children walking into the wilderness with their dog, in the heat, with no water. Others became favourite scenes: Tom circling on the claypan to gain speed; the old truck battling through the sand with images being thrown up in the vehicle's headlamps of ghostly coolibahs and low bushes growing each side of the Track.

If the picture-show man wasn't coming by, Shell fuel agents arranged to borrow the film through the company. They set up folding chairs in the town hall and invited residents in. Schools borrowed it for their students. Five- to seventeen-year-olds were herded through assembly halls in shifts. They were mesmerised.

Nearly 50 years after the film's release, first impressions of *The Back of Beyond* still linger. Such was the dramatic impact that many Australians clearly remember where they first saw the film and how deeply it affected them.

Rod Thurlow, a ten-year-old at the time attending Murrayville Consolidated School in Victoria, remembers gathering with his classmates in the school canteen with the old blinds drawn. Twelve-year-old Kim Lesouef saw the film when the Shell company sponsored a travelling science exhibition to schools throughout Western Australia. 'The star of the show was *The Back of Beyond*. It made a profound impression on me and kindled my love of deserts. How I envied Tom and his lifestyle,' he comments.

In a little, old tin bush hall, 50 kilometres from the nearest town, young Peter Thomas dreamed of the day that he could drive and go to the back of beyond himself; his head filled with images from the film as he filed out with his parents by the light of kerosene lamps. Teenaged Mal Roberts returned time after time to the large, narrow screening room upstairs in the Shell building on North Terrace in Adelaide. Coming from a family that neither owned a car nor had experienced the outback, he was completely enthralled by Heyer's depictions of Tom and his truck and the Birdsville Track.

'*The Back of Beyond* Comes Home' announced the newspaper headline. The film that had captured audiences in Australia's capital cities had its eagerly awaited premiere in Marree on Saturday 24 July 1954. All of the town's population scrubbed up and turned out for the event, which doubled as a fundraiser for the local school. The town hall overflowed with excited patrons. Families and workers who could, travelled down from Mungerannie and stations along the Track. Residents further north would attend Birdsville's premiere scheduled for the following weekend.

'Actors' who were there absorbed good-natured ribbing from their mates about their new 'movie-star' status. Most of them had not yet seen the film and shuffled their feet self-consciously, wondering how they would look on screen and how their own small part fitted into the whole.

Special guests for the evening included Shell PR man Bob Jolley, John and Janet Heyer, and the big man himself—Tom, who was dashing back from a dam site for the occasion. Tom and the Heyers, each party driving hundreds of kilometres south or west for the event, made it into town with only hours to spare.

Carrying a reel of the distinctive yellow film with them, John and Janet had once again motored from Sydney, as they had done several times in the past three years. This time, their car's differential gave out at Broken Hill. A series of urgent messages went out over the radio from the Flying Doctor base until they found a local pilot who agreed to fly them onward. Meanwhile, another copy of the film was put on board a plane in Adelaide and flown to Leigh Creek, where Bob Jolley picked it up and continued on his way to Marree.

While the Shell employees were assembling—and ensuring that at least one of them would arrive in town with the anticipated picture, Tom was steadily grinding along in the Badger. It was a 640-kilometre journey home from his work site in western Queensland. Just as in his former mail days, the radio network relayed his progress southward, a message from Etadunna station advising: 'Tom will arrive Marree about six o'clock.' The premiere was set for eight.

With just enough time for a quick haircut, bath and shave, Tom arrived at the town hall in style, Valma proudly on his arm.

The evening was a grand success. Naturally, the substituted voices came as a bit of a shock to some, but others didn't even notice. Overall, the locals were tremendously pleased with the cinematic portrayal of their lives and neighbourhood. Response to the film was so positive that the audience demanded a repeat and it was shown again on Sunday night to a similarly rousing reception.

The opening music was greeted with applause, which swelled again with the distinctive humming beat of the old Leyland, followed first by the wheel tracks and then the body of the familiar old Badger as it reared over the top of a dune and ploughed into the sand at the bottom. As each new character appeared cheers rose up in sequence from the audience. When Tom approached the dressmaker's dummy, grasping her armless shoulders, twirling her to the scratchy music from Henry's wind-up gramophone—his 'music machine'—and doffing his hat to her at the end of the dance, the audience erupted with delight, catcalls and wolf whistles ringing out from the men. Tom smiled broadly and took the teasing from friends and neighbours in his stride.

After the screening there was a short presentation in which John Heyer thanked Tom and Valma for their contribution, and then made a startling announcement: *The Back of Beyond* had been awarded the Grand Prix Assoluto, one of the highest international filmmaking awards. Heyer himself had only learned of the honour hours before, the news coming to him over the Flying Doctor radio in Broken Hill. He was still in shock. It was only the third time in film history that the prize had been awarded. The coveted golden seahorse from Venice represented the pinnacle of documentary filmmaking.

For the locals—unaware of the lofty cinematic heights to which the prize elevated Heyer and the picture—thoughts quickly turned to the rowdy celebrations and merriment to follow back at the Kruse home. Tom had specially brought a bullock back from Queensland. It was time for one hell of a barbie.

The Back of Beyond was John Heyer's seventeenth feature film; it cemented his reputation as Australia's most successful filmmaker. He was 38 years old.

After another five films and more than 40 years later Heyer still regarded *The Back of Beyond* as the best he'd ever made.

His persistence and vision had paid off. Constructing a mobile tower on the back of a truck and manoeuvring it over the sandhills, striving for close-up shots in a pre-zoom lens era—the perfectionism and dogged determination for which he had been derided by his peers in 1952 brought a power and impact to the film that affected two generations.

By 1960, more people had seen this film than any other Australian film. It was eventually translated into fifteen languages and is now reported to have been seen on movie screens, at film festivals and on television by more than 25 million people worldwide. In 1970, John Heyer was the first Australian film director to be awarded an Order of the British Empire (OBE), for achievements in cinema—in no small way on the strength of this, his most successful film. It inspired a generation of Australians to travel 'back of beyond' and most especially to make a pilgrimage up the Birdsville Track.

'Dear Mr Kruse,' a hopeful traveller describing himself as a 'New Australian with a desire to learn as much as possible about this vast country', wrote from Peterborough, on 9 August 1954:

You may receive this letter with a certain surprise, but after we (a friend of mine and I) heard and read a lot about your regular mail trips to Birdsville, we decided to ask you whether you could take us with you on such a trip during our next holidays in September . . . I should appreciate it immensely if you could give me an early reply. And in case your answer is positive, would you please let me know what the general conditions are (expenses, permitted luggage, time of departure and arrival and so on). Could you possibly give me also information about the best connection from Birdsville to the nearest main railway station in Queensland?

Thanking you in anticipation,
Yours sincerely,
Heinz Thiede

Hundreds of other naïve film fans wrote from much further afield. Letters flooded into Birdsville and Marree from all over the world. Left to Tom, responses to these cheerful little communiques would be a long time coming. He makes no secret of his aversion to writing anything down.

'I'd sooner cut a load of wood with a blunt axe and load it on a high truck, than write a letter,' he's been heard to announce on more than one occasion.

Valma began by trying to answer each letter, but was soon overwhelmed. Correspondents from England, America and

South Africa asked Tom to be their pen-friend. They were all terribly curious about Australia and its people, and had endless questions for Tom. If he didn't have time to write to them, they asked, could he perhaps find someone else who'd be willing to be their pen-pal? Even if all the residents of Birdsville and Marree and the stations in between had agreed, they could only be matched to less than one week's supply of eager writers. The letters kept coming for months.

Many of the letters revealed the ignorance of the writers for the scope of this tiny community huddled on the edge of the desert. Of the 600 letters from England that arrived in Birdsville one month, one was addressed to the 'Lord Mayor of Birdsville', another to the 'Manager of the General Post Office'. One woman wrote asking to be put in touch with 'all the headmistresses of all the girls' schools' in the town.

Television brought *The Back of Beyond* to 16.5 million viewers in one sweep when it was presented by the Ford Foundation in America. The first of two English television broadcasts on the BBC was arranged to celebrate Empire Day on 24 May 1954. As Britons emerged from a damp, cold spring, they sat down in front of their television sets to images of a dry, brown land as foreign and barren as the moon.

'It was another world to me,' said the then teenaged Bob Batty, who saw the film before he emigrated to Australia. 'I'd never seen real desert conditions before, other than the "Foreign Legion"-type feature films of the day. The enormous distances, the hostile country and climate, and the difficulties Tom encountered and overcame were a revelation. I don't think that any film I've ever seen has made such an impression on me.'

Sister Barrand, who had been in charge of the Marree

hospital in 1952, wrote from her home in Manchester to tell Valma how delighted she'd been to see Tom and so many other familiar faces on her television screen. 'It was such a thrill it made me wish I was right back there.'

In addition to enjoying the film for what it was, Sister Barrand also found *The Back of Beyond*, a welcome break from the endless newsreels on television about the Queen's royal tour with its eternal rounds of civic receptions in all the big cities. Young Queen Elizabeth was on her first tour of the Commonwealth since ascending to the throne in February 1952 and the news was full of her visits to such exotic faraway places as Jamaica, Ceylon, Uganda, Panama and Australia.

In April 1954, as the young Queen Elizabeth sailed for home at the completion of her first tour of the Commonwealth since her ascension to the throne two years previously, various films were screened aboard the royal yacht for her entertainment. One of them was *The Back of Beyond*. So impressed was Queen Elizabeth with Tom's efforts to get the Royal Mail through at all cost, that she added his name to the New Year's Honours list for 1955.

In early December, the official letter, marked 'personal and confidential', arrived at the Kruse home in Marree from Government House in Canberra.

> *Dear Sir,*
> *I have the honour to inform you that Her Majesty the Queen would be graciously pleased to appoint you a Member of the Most Excellent Order of the British Empire and I am therefore directed by His Excellency the*

Governor-General to ask you to telegraph me whether this honour would be acceptable to you.

In conformity with the necessity for secrecy at this stage, kindly confine your telegram to 'GRATEFULLY ACCEPT' or 'BEG TO DECLINE'.

Should you wish to decline, I should be glad of a confirmatory letter setting out your reasons.

Please treat this matter as strictly confidential, until advice of your proposed honour is published in the daily press.

Yours faithfully

ML Tyrrell
Offical Secretary to the Governor-General

Finding the liveried envelope from the Governor-General among the usual assortment of correspondence, Valma opened it with trepidation. She sat in stunned silence while reading the letter through, then rushed to put the kettle on for a restorative cup of tea. Tom—a Member of the British Empire! She was bursting with the news. As usual, Tom was away, this time on an errand to Adelaide, and she was too obedient to share the news with anyone else. She sent the return telegram, 'Gratefully accept', and impatiently waited for Tom to come home.

'Actually, it was rather queer,' says Tom. 'I remember thinking, hell, what's this about? That letter came over from Canberra when Seamus and I were going down to get the new tractor. Must've been '54, I reckon. Seamus and I came down in the Blitz with one of those round army trailers behind it [a bow-fronted semi-trailer] and picked up the D6 and the new scoop.

'And that was when the letter came. Well, it was. Exactly.'

Tom and Valma had to keep their secret for another couple of weeks before the news became public on Saturday 1 January 1955. The New Year's Honours announcements took up most of page three of Adelaide's *The Advertiser* newspaper. Tom was among 2000 of the Queen's subjects to be recognised, and he was not the only mailman—another bush postie, Frank Banks of Laverton, Western Australia, also received an MBE. That year's list of Australian recipients also included the famous mile-runner John Landy, mountaineer and Everest veteran Eric Shipton, and seven newly appointed knights.

When the list was published in the daily newspapers, the carrier called Kruse was immediately elevated to Mr EG Kruse Esquire, MBE. Telegrams began arriving at the tiny Marree post office on Monday 3 January; the postmistress completely bewildered by the deluge of telegraph mail.

11.15 am, 1 January, 1955, Marree, Sth Aust.
EG Kruse Esq. MBE
On behalf of my colleagues and myself I offer sincere congratulations on the well merited honour bestowed upon you by Her Majesty the Queen.

RG Menzies, Prime Minister
Canberra

Sid Crawford, founder of Commercial Motor Vehicles Ltd (formerly Crawfords) from whom Harry Ding had purchased the now-famous Badger, sent his best wishes from Adelaide; as did Bob Jolley.

More congratulatory messages rolled in over the following

few days from John Heyer; the Director General of Posts and Telegraphs for the Australian Postmaster-General's Department; the Minister for Health; the Director of Posts and Telegraphs at the Adelaide GPO; and the Director of W Chorley and Co, Tailors and Shirtmakers, Hatters and Hosiers, of Sydney, who enclosed a bar of the MBE ribbon, 'as a small token of the pleasure which we all received in witnessing *The Back of Beyond*, the film in which you figured so prominently. We feel sure that you will be very proud to wear it.'

Tom and Valma were advised that Tom's investiture was scheduled for 11.30 am on Friday 24 June, at Government House in Adelaide. But in the early winter of '55 it started raining over the inland again. Floodwaters surged down from the north and the fickle Cooper slithered across the Track for the fourth time in seven years. Tom suspended dam-sinking operations and hastened back to Marree to attend to the mail. It was impossible for him to sojourn in Adelaide for a knees-up with the Governor-General.

'Thank you very much for your letter of 19th June, advising that your husband was unable to be present at the Investiture held at Adelaide on 24th June,' wrote ML Tyrrell, responding to the letter Valma had written on Tom's behalf. 'The Governor-General quite understands your husband's difficulties.'

A creative alternative was proposed. Lady Slim, wife of the Governor-General, Sir William Slim, was about to embark on a tour of the outback, travelling by an RAAF plane to visit Australian Inland Mission hospitals in remote centres such as Derby in Western Australia, where she would open a new Royal Flying Doctor base. Her first stop would be

Birdsville, on Monday 18 July and if Tom could rendezvous with her there, on that day, his medal could be presented then. The Governor-General himself would not be in attendance but it was a novel solution for Tom's inability to travel to Adelaide to receive his badge.

So they tried again, and the stage was set. Birdsville buzzed with excitement. First a film premiere and now this! On the appointed day, Eric Salmon dusted off his policeman's dress uniform, only to find, to his dismay, that he could no longer button the jacket across his stomach. Young David Brook, all cleaned up and dressed for best, reappeared after a brief absence with an outlandish reverse-Mohawk type of hairdo, styled especially to meet Lady Slim. He said he'd wanted to be like old Inky, a bald saddler in the area, and he'd cavalierly taken the clippers to his head. Mrs Brook was horrified.

All the residents gathered at the Birdsville Hotel and waited expectantly for Lady Slim's plane to land on the airstrip out front, or for Tom to turn up in his truck. But once again the Cooper intervened.

It was a landmark occasion that was not to be. Lady Slim touched down as expected, but while she waited, medal for EG Kruse Esquire in a white-gloved hand, Tom was sloshing through chest-deep muddy water, 350 kilometres away. The Cooper was 10 kilometres wide and running at 3 kilometres per hour. Tom looked up and saw the RAAF plane fly high overhead.

'I hope we make it in time,' the previous day's newspaper had quoted him as saying. 'We will try hard.' But his efforts came to naught. His best suit, which Valma had carefully packed for him, lying flat, deep in the load, was never taken from its nylon bag. By the time he struggled into Birdsville days later, Lady Slim and his medal were, once again, hundreds of kilometres away.

It was not till the following April that Tom finally made it to Adelaide to have his MBE officially awarded. He was asked to join the 1956 New Years Honours recipients at an investiture at Government House. 'Dress will be—uniform where appropriate, morning dress, short black coat and striped trousers or lounge suit,' the Governor-General's offical secretary informed Tom by letter. Recipients were also invited to be accompanied by two close relatives, if they so wished.

Tom elected to wear a double-breasted grey suit, and brought Valma and twelve-year-old Pauline with him to Government House. It was a small group that lined up to receive their decorations from Sir William Slim. Lady Slim also attended the ceremony, and of the four or five awardees, she requested to speak in private only with Tom and his family. The Governor-General's wife had a genuine interest in the outback and a deep admiration for the people who made their homes there. She was eager to talk to the man who had dedicated much of his working life to serving them.

A photograph taken shortly after the ceremony shows Tom Kruse, MBE, in a clean suit and tie, hair neatly smoothed down with oil—almost unrecognisable as the familiar Tom Kruse of the Birdsville Track, known for getting about in filthy shorts and bare feet, hair wild and woolly. Pauline carefully unpins the medal from her father's chest while Valma stands proudly at his side. She had splurged on a new dress for the occasion, pairing it with a matching handbag, hat and gloves.

The official citation for Esmond Gerald Kruse, Esquire, appointed a Member of the Civil Division of the Most Excellent Order of the British Empire on the 1 January, 1955, reads:

In all weathers Mr Kruse makes a fortnightly journey between Marree and Birdsville, calling at all properties adjacent to the track, delivering mail, provisions and supplies for the families scattered through this remote area.

Tom Kruse is not only a romantic figure but something of an institution, having earned the love and respect of all residents of the outback. He has risked his life on many occasions in carrying out this service.

LEAVING MARREE

In early 1955, Monty Scobie relinquished his position as Birdsville Track mailman, opting to establish a trucking business of his own. He escaped in the nick of time.

'I was lucky to get in and out between floods,' he says, stepping into the kitchen from his workroom in the enclosed verandah at the rear of his home in Clare. It is there that he carries on his father's tradition: hand-plaiting stockwhips from strands of kangaroo leather—twelve strands over a core of buffalo hide plaited over again with another sixteen and finished off with a cane handle and a replaceable cotton cracker. Each one was a week's work and engraved with 'M. SCOBIE MAKER'. A fine piece of craftsmanship of which old Alec would no doubt have been proud.

Monty removes his hat and hooks it over the corner of the door. His bushy black eyebrows emerge from under the brim in surprising contrast to his smooth grey hair. 'I started in November '51 and it'd just dried up. Then I drove for three and a half years and that contract was finished. Tom got another bloke to take on the mail then, and Tom bought my share of the Blitz. Well, that bloke went up there and the bloody Cooper was down. My lucky day I s'pose. I had three and a half years to the bloody day without it.'

Luck played some part, but Tom also knew that Monty was very reluctant to take on the Cooper. They were both aware that the Queensland water was on its way and Monty's aversion to dealing with all the rigmarole the floodwaters brought with them was probably a factor in the timing of his decision to leave the mail. He'd seen what Tom had gone through back in '51 and now he knew the business from the inside, too.

'See, there's no money in it,' Monty explains, reiterating the source of Tom's misery three years before. 'You gotta have two buses—one each side; you've got to boat-load it over—get the stuff off the truck, onto the barge and push it all uphill on the other side. All that for five pound a ton. Well, that's not much for a full day's work. And you've got to have an offsider. By the time you've paid someone there wouldn't be anything left.

'Look, it was hard enough without the Cooper. I got wages—whatever the award rate was for driving a three-ton truck—and then we split the profits. Trouble was, you'd have to have five ton to make it pay. We had five ton on a three-ton Blitz: well, they was buggered. They'd bog anywhere.

'And then there's the stuff along the road . . . if you've got five ton to Birdsville, well, that's all right, it was 17 pound 10 a load. But if you've got some to Dulkaninna and a bit more here—Etadunna, Mulka, Clifton Hills—by the time you get to Birdsville you're lucky if you had a half a load. If I had a full load for Birdsville I'd get a quid out of it, otherwise . . . very little.'

Tom knew all the problems and completely understood Monty's desire to get away. K & S and Co—the Kruse and Scobie partnership—dissolved on good terms. But Tom still needed someone to run the mail. His dam-sinking business was just beginning to turn a profit and he had no interest in returning to the mail full-time.

Up stepped young Vivian Oldfield, who thought he'd try his hand at it. He went out on his first trip in July 1955, just as Tom was preparing to dash to Birdsville to meet Lady Slim. He had no idea what he'd let himself in for . . .

'Marree: Saturday', was the dateline for a newspaper story reporting Oldfield's first trip.

> *Mr Tom Kruse, the mail contractor, left Marree this afternoon with the idea of being in Birdsville on Monday to meet Lady Slim.*
>
> *Mr Kruse was to have left on the 400 mile trip yesterday. But on Tuesday, one of his trucks, driven by Mr Vivian Oldfield, broke down in the path of the flood-swollen Cooper Creek. It took Mr Kruse a day to repair it and get it back to Marree. He had been working on it until today. Mrs Kruse said today he had spent this morning welding the truck and repairing the outboard motor he will use to cross the Cooper . . .*
>
> *In Adelaide this afternoon, Territory colt-breaker Bill Travers said, 'If anyone can get there, Tom will.' Mr Travers arrived in Adelaide at noon on the train. 'Tom told me he would be doing his best to get there when I saw him in Marree last night but it looks [like] an*

Local children in front of the Great Northern Hotel, Marree, circa 1949. *Celia Teague*

Jeffrey, Valma and Helen Kruse with their dog, Harvey, outside their Marree home. Goods for the next Birdsville mail run are stacked on the verandah. *Kruse family collection*

Unloading Birdsville mail and supplies from the MV *Tom Brennan* at Tom's landing depot on the north side of the Cooper Creek, circa 1949.
Celia Teague

A mob of cattle bound for Marree swims the 5-kilometre-wide Cooper Creek crossing on the Birdsville Track during the floods of 1949.
Kruse family collection

Tom (left) and Bill Holliday repair a bent axle from the AEC Mammoth Major in an isolated creek bed, 300 kilometres from their Yunta home base. *Kruse family collection*

EG Kruse Ltd, Earthmovers and Carriers, shifting camp. Tom (left) would hitch all his vehicles together and crawl to the next worksite at 15 to 20 kilometres per hour to economise on fuel and drivers.
Kruse family collection

John Heyer (right) directs, while a cameraman films Tom in his Ford
Blitz in a scene for *The Back of Beyond*, 1952. *Film Australia*

Famed cameleer and Marree resident Bejah Dervish chats with Tom
during filming for *The Back of Beyond*, 1952. *Film Australia*

Tom's publicity photo for *The Back of Beyond*, released in May 1954.
Film Australia

Tom's daughters, Pauline (with cart) and Helen, play the parts of the two lost children in *The Back of Beyond*, 1952. *Film Australia*

Tom inspects the wreck of the Badger at Gilpininna Dam during South Australia's Jubilee 150 mail run re-enactment, May 1986. *Neil Weidenbach*

At the Northfield shed Tom works patiently on the Badger's restoration. *Neil Weidenbach*

Sitting on a plastic milk crate, Tom drives the Badger's undercarriage with delight on the vehicle's first test run in July 1998. It had been 40 years since the truck was mobile. *Neil Weidenbach*

A moment of relaxation for Tom and my father, Neil Weidenbach, during the restoration of the Badger. *Colin and Helen Hamp*

On the Birdsville Track once again: the restored Badger loaded as for a typical mail run, October 1999. *Mark Metzger*

Tom and Valma celebrate their 60th wedding anniversary, 24 January 2002. *Brett Hartwig*/The Advertiser

impossible job.' Mr Travers, in Adelaide for treatment of
a poisoned arm, was taken to the Marree DBNS [District
and Bush Nursing Society] hostel on Wednesday night by
Mr Kruse. He is a colt-breaker on Etadunna station, eight
miles on the Marree side of Cooper Creek.

Mr Travers was stranded in the bed of the Cooper
before the flooding began on Tuesday night, when he
went to pick up a broken down truck.

'Tom came out from Marree with a couple of gas
bottles and a welding outfit' Mr Travers said. 'According
to him, no truck can be broken down. He just got to work
and welded the truck together again.' . . . Mr Travers
described how Mr Kruse's other mail truck, driven by Mr
Vivian Oldfield, had become stuck on the creekbed on
Tuesday night. 'Vivian went to sleep on Monday night
and when he woke Tuesday morning the floods were all
round him,' Mr Travers said. 'He took the Birdsville mails
from the truck and hid the bags in some bushes on high
ground. Then he walked 20 miles into Mulka for help.
Doug Scobie drove out and pulled the mail truck, which
had broken down, on to high ground, where Tom found
it on Wednesday. He fixed our truck up and then his own.
My poisoned arm was hurting like blazes all the time.
I stayed on to help get the trucks out, athough Tom
wanted to take me to Marree right away. He's the most
tender-hearted coot you ever struck in your life.'

'Oh, young Oldfield? Nah, he didn't last long,' Monty
chuckles. 'He started off, see, he got to Cannuwaukaninna . . .
oh, leaky radiator or something, so he walked into Etadunna
and Jim come down and fixed him up. Then he went off to

fill the water drum—I had a 22-gallon water drum under the tray—and he pulled in too close to the bore drain and got bogged. So he walked back to Etadunna and Jim come and pulled him out again.

'Then he went up to the Cooper. The bloody flood's coming down. So he thought he'd go down to Killalpaninna and cross there in front of the water. But he couldn't get it up the bank—I don't know what happened there, perhaps he didn't have it in low range. Anyhow, he carried all the mail bags up on the bank, left the truck there and walked up to Mulka, and Doug come down and pulled him up the bank and he got in it and away he went. And that was his first trip.'

Vivian earned the nickname 'the walking mailman' and never did a mail run again.

Max Bowden was next in line to accept the challenge and he and Valma, who was taking care of the business side of the mail in Tom's absence, formed a happy team for several years. Since Max and his wife lived in Marree they knew Monty and the Kruses. In fact, when Max was transporting loads of timber and other fencing materials for jobs up north he'd travel in convoy with Monty so the two Blitzes could give each other a hand through any troublesome spots on the way. A fencer by trade, Max was a bouncy, happy-go-lucky fellow with a cheerful nature.

'Maxy and Valma got on really well,' says Tom. 'Actually, Maxy was really great. He'd say, "Well, I said to Mrs Kruse, 'I think we ought to have two new tyres on the back, and that there.'" Everything Maxy said would always finish up with "and that there".'

'That's right! "And that there"!' Valma chimes in, laughing

at the memory. 'Even if he said a few words he'd tack it on the end.

'Oh, he was the cleanest man,' she sighs. 'He and Tom'd be working on the truck—Max wouldn't shirk any work—grease … didn't matter what it was, he'd be into it—and they'd finish up: Tom'd be covered in grease, and Max wouldn't have a mark on him. It was always like that; you'd never think he did anything. He was so clean.'

'He was a great betting man, Maxy,' Tom continues. 'And a great card player. He'd think nothing of staying up all night hoping to get four sevens. And he was pretty hard to beat. By hell, he was. He was most energetic, Maxy. A total non-drinker, too. He'd go into a pub and shout all round but never, ever touched alcohol in his life. He was a devoted sugar drinker, though. If he had a cup of tea … hell, he'd have that much sugar in it …'

Neither Max nor any of the other drivers who succeeded Monty had the same kind of profit-sharing partnership arrangement—they were strictly Tom's employees, although all day-to-day transactions went through Valma. She was in charge of the business side of the mail operation and the Shell agency in Marree, as Tom was completely absorbed in his dam-sinking and earth-moving activities and was rarely home.

It was a busy life for Valma, caring for the children and the business. As far as spending time with her husband, the new regime was worse than the mail days. She usually saw him once in four to six weeks, in between jobs. Though Tom wasn't around much, she devoted a lot of time to him. Once a fortnight she'd have a load of supplies for him to go up on the mail truck with Max—the former mailman now receiving his own daily necessities via the Birdsville mail. Cooking tray upon tray of biscuits, baking cakes, stuffing butter into tins and wrapping it in wet newspaper, and including any spare parts that had come up from Adelaide at Tom's request consumed much of Wednesday and Thursday of mail weeks. In between, she would attend to the books, assisted by their accountant in Adelaide, and keep their fuel depot running. As the 1950s progressed and motor traffic on the Track increased, customers would arrive at any time of the day or night looking to fill their tanks. Responding to a knock at the door, Valma or one of the children would serve them by siphoning petrol from one of the large drums. Later on, the Kruses installed the first hand-pumped bowser in the town. Station customers wanting fuel would simply take a 44-gallon drum from the supply out the back.

What spare time she had, Valma filled with helping out at the nursing hostel and taking part in social activities in the town such as the weekly dance and playing tennis.

In the early dam-sinking days—when Helen and Phillip were small; Pauline was at school, boarding with family friends; and Jeffrey hadn't yet arrived—Valma used to go bush, too. She would take the two youngest and set up house in the desert with Tom for the three months or so that it took to scrape out a dam. She loved being with him and camping out, doing the daily chores—washing and cooking—in the great open spaces, and occasionally going into Birdsville on the weekly or fortnightly supply runs.

'I used to thoroughly enjoy it,' she says. 'I used to spend a lot of time up there before Helen and Phillip were going to school. And then later on there'd be school holidays and we'd all go up. We had tents for starters—live-in tents and a kitchen tent. Then we had the kitchen caravan. It had a nice wood stove and I used to cook in there.

'Apparently people used to say, "Fancy that poor woman out there, living in a tent," and that was me! But I never, ever remember once wishing I wasn't there.

'Tom'd usually have two workers with him. They'd do shifts, working till late at night and starting again early in the morning.

'The kids, Helen and Phillip, just ran around and played and fought,' Valma recalls. 'They were never asking, "What can we do?" And Jeffrey . . . I remember teaching him with correspondence lessons once, when we were away up on Pandie. I used to make runners for them—the briefest little pants. Or they'd be naked. If someone drove up they used to come running: "There's a car coming, put some clothes on us!"'

Helen remembers those times as some of the happiest of her childhood. 'We had really good times. We'd all have proper sleeping tents—Mum and Dad had their own, and Phillip and I had ours. I think they were army tents—really heavy canvas. Mum used to sweep the floor, wet it all down. Everything was clean and neat and tidy. And we had a kitchen tent with a wood stove and cupboards. Breakfast was always steak and gravy or something. Beautiful. I mean, you've got workmen, you've got to feed them. I remember Dad cooking, too. He'd go to bed early, and get up early. Mum'd make bread and do the washing with a pump-action washing machine.

'We had goats with us and we'd make gardens—we carted water from nearby waterholes and I remember we grew tomatoes and watermelons. Then you'd have to pack up and shift to another camp. Or when the really hot weather came, we used to come home then.

'We'd go into Birdsville once a week or so. We'd all just pile in the Badger and Dad'd drive. Our swags would be up on top and when we'd have to go to bed, Dad'd fix us up there and we'd go along looking at the stars—Phillip used to sleep-walk so he had to be tied down in his swag.'

Like the mail run, dam-sinking was an arduous and difficult job. The men out in the camps worked hard, but they also partied hard whenever they got the chance. They'd gather in the Birdsville Hotel and drink and entertain each other just as they had in Tom's mail run days. In the evenings, the women and a handful of men—the teetotallers—would gather at the AIM hostel for cards or table tennis. But most of the men were drawn to the hotel, where they'd imbibe five-shilling bottles of beer, or glass after glass of OP rum. When a bloke became argumentative and overly boisterous after a few too many, he'd be escorted to the 'blood room' and stuffed into a pair of boxing gloves to battle it out with his contestant amid cheers and yelling from the other patrons. Bob Gaffney was regarded as a good and fair referee. If there were only seven or eight in the bar of a night, the custom was that no one paid for drinks. The next day Mr Afford would count the bottles, divide the sum by the number of drinkers and work out the bill that way.

All the men had a special skill or trick they could do— something they had perfected to amuse themselves around the fire in mustering or droving camps. As evenings in the hotel wore on, spontaneous revues would erupt.

'Of a nighttime everyone could do something,' says Tom.

'Some of them'd be reciting poetry, or jumping, twisting and turning, buckjumping and scratch-pulling, all that sort of thing. Gordon Scobie, Monty's brother, he was most active. It was amazing. Gee, he could jump. No worries. And turn somersaults. Ah look, all the things that he could do. Wind his leg up behind his ear. Anything.

'I'll tell you what, if he had a few drinks and a little bit of coaxing he'd get up on the bar—at Birdsville there was a very high bar—he'd stand on the edge holding a butcher glass in his mouth, full of beer. He'd turn a somersault, land on his feet on the floor and the beer's gone. Hell, he was really great.'

Gordon's antics and those of other amateur gymnasts must have inspired Tom to comparable feats of athleticism. He retains a 2-centimetre scar on the flesh of his right thumb, a permanent reminder of one of his performances in the Birdsville Hotel.

'Hmmm, that was Gordon Scobie,' he says, fingering the scar. 'Ah, that was just mucking around,' he says coyly. 'Er, I can't really remember now . . .'

'Well, I wasn't there,' Monty divulges, 'but I heard how Krusey livened the place up a bit one time. He was having a few drinks at the hotel and he reckoned he was a buckjumper. He went down on all fours, and the deal was, if he bucked you off, *you* had to put money in the box for the Flying Doctor, and if you stayed on, then *he'd* have to cough up the money.

'So there he was on his hands and knees and all these blokes—ringers, you know, were getting on him. They couldn't ride him at all! He'd jump up as high as the table and they was all coming off. Well, then one bloke went outside and come back in with his spurs on! He landed on

Tom and hit him with the hooks! He ripped Tom's shirt about a bit but Tom threw him in the end. Then the policeman got his hat and went round the bar collecting money to buy Tom a new shirt. Ah, it was all just for a bit of fun.'

Monty's own act of showmanship was strictly an outdoors trick only: an animal-control technique said to be perfected by only the really tough guys.

'Cracking off snakes' heads, hell, that was Monty's thing,' Tom marvels. 'If there was a snake anywhere he'd track it and grab the snake in his hand and crack its head off.

'From Monty's side, unfortunately he had polio when he was very young, and still retains a little limp. But it doesn't affect him in any state or form because he could run. By hell he could move. He'd chase those snakes, no worries.'

'Oh yeah, I used to do that,' Monty confirms with a nonchalant shrug. 'Get around in front of him and let him go past. Then when he's walking away you grab the end of the tail and crack 'im. Like a whip . . . His head? Ah, his head flies off.

'When he's going away from you he won't trouble you much. There's only one I wouldn't touch and that's what we call a saltbush snake. Oooh, he's angry. He's lightning, that fellow. I wouldn't go near him. No, he's too quick. I reckon he'd turn around and bite you soon as you grabbed his tail. They're deadly, too.'

By the time Max Bowden joined the mail in 1955, Tom had expanded his collection of vehicles to include a British-made AEC Matador—an ex-Army four-wheel-drive with a 7.7-litre diesel engine—that he'd bought for 1500 pounds. Despite being four-wheel-drive, in Tom's opinion, the Blitzes he had bought earlier were not up to the task of replacing the Badger, but the AEC was a worthy challenger.

'When the AEC came along . . . the Badger . . . well, give her a rest,' he says. 'We took her dam-sinking. The Badger was our reliable wagon to go here, go there, get water. No, actually, she was very worn. At the same time, the old AEC . . . look, if you're in heavy sand it was like being in a DC3. It was just a matter of pulling the bloody lever up . . . four-wheel-drive, and away you go. That's dead right.'

Along with the Badger, the Matador became a perennial favourite. It had air brakes, an excellent transmission and, unlike the Ford Blitzes, was never known to overheat. Tom would often hitch up a four-wheel trailer to the Matador to cart additional freight up the Track. It was always called 'Maxy's trailer' because Max Bowden had made it from four-wheel-drive differentials and the tray from a Leyland Beaver. If the ground became treacherous the driver would uncouple the trailer and employ the Matador as a bulldozer, forming an initial track through the sand or mud, then return for the trailer. Tom liked the Matador so much that he eventually bought another, the cab of which now sits in the yard at the Mungerannie Hotel.

'We had two AECs,' he explains. 'The other one, the original one, is in the graveyard at Marree. When I say graveyard . . . well, we had several graveyards: one at Clifton Hills, one at Marree and one at Coober Pedy. In fact, the Blitz seen in *The Back of Beyond* went into the graveyard at Clifton Hills.'

When Tom talks of graveyards he thinks in the context of mechanical remains—work-worn and abandoned old trucks. However, several of the stations that line the Birdsville Track have their own lonely little cemeteries for youngsters who didn't survive to their teens, or men and women who had fallen victim to a life lived hundreds of kilometres from the nearest doctor—like Ken Crombie's father, William, buried at the family homestead, Mungerannie.

When Tom's counterpart, Ken Crombie, had begun driving the Birdsville mail, first with his brother-in-law, Harry Williams, and then as a driver for Harry Ding, he carried on his father's tradition. William Crombie had run the mail back in the horse-and-buggy days of the late 1800s—when it took a week to travel between Hergott Springs (Marree) and Birdsville, Crombie's home-made buggy covering at least 80 kilometres a day. At each of the ten or eleven horse changes he had only one helper. Often, he had to catch, yoke and harness the half-wild colts himself. He was so short of horses that he frequently had to break in a colt as he travelled.

Young Ken, one of ten surviving Crombie children, was only a lad of thirteen when his father died in 1926. William Crombie was buried at the foot of a sandhill behind the homestead next to the grave of his three-year-old daughter who had died tragically from severe burns.

Fortunately, by the time Tom settled in the area, radio was being introduced for the people of the outback, creating the 'mantle of safety' envisioned by the instigator of the Royal Flying Doctor Service, the Reverend John Flynn. Happily, the graveyards that Tom refers to are the final resting place of his usurped trucks, not the sad little burial grounds of bush pioneers like William Crombie.

•

When Tom got his second AEC Matador he installed a new cab at the Lelliot Brothers engineering workshop in Port Adelaide. His brother-in-law, Stan Lelliot, co-owned the business and Tom was granted permission to use their facilities to do major repairs or modifications to his trucks when necessary. In 1948, soon after buying the mail contract, Tom had made use of the workshop to do some major work on the Badger, completely discarding the Leyland chassis and replacing it with one of his own design.

'That old chassis, under there . . . weak? . . . look, weak as water!' he exclaims. 'Weak as water! All cracked, and holes drilled in it; I tell you, there was more bits of bloody weld and iron packed in underneath . . . even had plates welded with two bolts through it to stop it from cracking further— that type of thing. Look, she was already on her last legs when I bought her from Harry Ding.

'Stan Lelliot said, "Right, we knock off at five. You fellows do whatever you want of a nighttime." May've taken us . . . I don't know how long . . . It wasn't done in a couple of days. There were a lot of holes to drill.'

Tom planned to give the old Badger a new lease on life by completely revamping its undercarriage. He made his new chassis from rolled steel joists and strengthened it with cross members of railway iron. Using a rachet-system hand-drill like the railwaymen used, he painstakingly and tediously bored through the thick iron to form all the necessary bolt holes.

'Railway iron. Plenty of railway iron. Heavy? No, not that much heavier . . . No heavier than saying, look, put a pin through your hair to keep your hat on. It was really number one. No further trouble.'

Tom's new chassis was incredibly strong. Different parts

of the truck continued to deteriorate around it, however, slowly but inexorably succumbing to the abuse they were expected to withstand. After another five years of overloading, the Badger's characteristic knock-kneed appearance—its front wheels leaning inwards under the strain of its load—betrayed a bent and severely weakened front axle. Tom solved the problem by shoving a solid steel bar up into the centre section of the I-beam that constituted the axle, and welding it in place.

By this time, very little of the original Leyland vehicle remained. Both gearboxes and the whole back end was Thornycroft; the chassis was now a home-made invention; only the engine and accessories such as the cabin instruments and controls, the fuel and water pumps and so on, were Leyland. The Badger was now a peerless Leyland-Thornycroft-Kruse one-of-a-kind design.

Tom took his beloved Badger out bush and left the Blitzes, the AECs, and various other vehicles that came along later—such as the ERF, the Hippo and a procession of Landrovers—to his mail drivers. The Badger could still carry an impressive weight and at first Tom used it as a makeshift dump truck, filling the tray with excavated rock that he'd blasted away to form a tank depression and offloading it by hand at the rim. When he obtained a tractor and more suitable earthmoving equipment the Badger was relegated to the role of water truck, tripping out to nearby waterholes and returning with 24-gallon drums filled with drinking water.

The Badger, however, was feeling its age and the effects of a long life of toil. In 1958, after innumerable breakdowns and subsequent crafty bush repairs, a single nut came loose and spelt its final demise.

It happened while the Badger was being towed in the distinctive manner that characterised the Kruse outfit moving camp. Tom would hitch up all his vehicles, one behind or on top of the other, and haul them along like a big articulated snake or a modern-day camel string, slowly labouring to the next campsite at 20 kilometres per hour. Travelling in such a way he'd economise on fuel and drivers. On this occasion he was out the back of Pandie Pandie station dragging the Badger and various other gear behind the D7 tractor over a series of sandhills.

'We always used to put her in gear coming down a hill, otherwise the thing would jack-knife,' Tom explains. 'We were going over these damn sandhills and coming down one hill the nut came off the tail shaft . . . and o'course she crashed into the back of the truck in front.'

The loose nut in the Badger's tail shaft had allowed the input shaft in the worm drive axle to move, causing trouble in the front drive differential. Furthermore, the radiator was irreparably damaged in the collision.

'Look, if she hadn't hit the radiator she was still sort've driveable,' Tom maintains—a rather optimistic assessment. But then again, if anyone could keep a vehicle on the move it was Tom. It has been said that as a bush mechanic he could get a bucket of bolts going. 'Even when we left her there she was still quite a good goer, excepting you couldn't put water in the radiator. I think we did at one stage put a 44-gallon drum on the side but you wouldn't have to go very far and you'd have boiling water.'

Tom parked the Badger at a site called Gilpininna, where he'd been contracted to build a new dam for Pandie Pandie. The tray was still sturdy and he used the truck as a stationary platform on which to store fuel drums and suchlike while he was scraping out the dam. After a while a small Kruse depot grew up around the Badger and it became a central point for Tom's operations in the area.

'It was in no-man's-land. But it was an area that was easy to go to for us. We used to go backwards and forwards quite a bit. When we were working for Delhi we left quite a few of our old caravans there. And we had at least 100 empty fuel drums there at various times.'

But inevitably Tom's work took him further afield and eventually the Badger succumbed, gradually sagging down onto the desert floor. The truck that had served Tom for almost all of its 22 productive years was abandoned at Gilpininna Dam on Pandie Pandie station. A Cub was similarly discarded nearby and Tom moved on for the final time . . . the two forsaken Leylands standing sentinel over the empty gibber plains.

Back on the mail run, Tom had a parade of temporary, fill-in drivers after Max Bowden finished up and struck out on his own. Often his employees would overlap and alternate between driving the mail and driving tractors at dam sites or helping to cut tracks through the desert under the road-building contracts that Tom had started to gain.

'Kingy—"King of the Road"—drove the mail for quite a while. Matter of fact he did a lot of miles in the ERF,' Tom recalls. 'Actually, he was a bit of a worry for Valma—if he was on the bottle he was a pretty hard man to handle. He drove the D7 for a while, too.

'He used to swear a bit, ol' Kingy, 'specially when he was doing things,' Tom adds. ''Scuse me saying it, but if something dropped on him, he'd say, "Forty thousand bastards! Forty thousand bastards!"'

Tom's older brother, Ben, helped out on the mail, too, as did the wild Irishman Allan O'Brien—or Seamus as he was commonly known; Fred Jennings, who, it was rumoured, wouldn't sleep on the ground in case the dingos grabbed him; Ray Bell, aka 'Ding Dong' (no relation to the Bell family of Dulkaninna); and young Billy Wilson, whom Tom had known since Billy was a babe in arms. Occasionally some of the customers would be disgruntled with the variety of drivers jumping from the truck with the mailbags or chaperoning passengers up and down the Track.

'Ah, some were a bit colicky,' says Tom. 'They'd say, "Your man don't sound pretty," or so and so. With Billy it was, "What's this? . . . pulling up with a bloody schoolboy behind the wheel."'

By the time the 1960s rolled around Tom was finally on firmer ground financially. He had a fleet of dependable vehicles and a loose-knit team of workers. He had earned a solid reputation as a capable and reliable earthmoving contractor and big jobs were starting to come his way as oil and gas exploration burgeoned in the area. He was happy working in makeshift camps all over north-eastern South Australia and western Queensland and checking in on the mail run and his Shell agency during intermittent trips home to Marree. But the new decade also ushered in a new era on the home front.

By 1963, three of the four Kruse children were boarding in Adelaide, leaving Valma and eight-year-old Jeffrey alone in Marree. Pauline was at teachers' college; Helen was boarding at Immanuel secondary school; and having just started at technical school, Phillip was staying with Tom's brother, Uncle Reg. Valma missed her children. In a few more years, Jeffrey would be gone, too. From her vantage point on the dusty back verandah of a small corrugated-iron house in Marree, Valma's picture of the years ahead took on a long and lonely hue.

She was also feeling renewed pressure from her own family to move down south and establish a new home in Adelaide. Her parents were facing health problems and begged her to join them. They had never wholeheartedly approved of Valma being so isolated in Marree, with Tom living the peripatetic life of the bush. They counselled her that now was really the perfect time to join civilisation again.

Valma's parents, Gordon and Ruth Fuller, owned a roomy stone house on a large block in suburban Cumberland Park. They had just finished building a neighbouring house on the same block and at its completion they presented their plan to Tom and Valma: that they should relocate to Adelaide and take their house, the larger of the two, and the Fullers would move into the new place next door. Although business for EG Kruse Ltd, Earthmovers and Carriers, was on the upswing, Valma's parents knew that the couple could ill-afford a house in the city; thus they presented them with a solution they were unable to refuse.

Obviously, it was difficult for Tom to contemplate a change to an urban lifestyle. After lengthy family deliberations he somewhat reluctantly put the word out that the Birdsville-to-Marree mail contract was up for sale. He'd had the contract for fifteen years, in which time compensation for the service from the Postmaster-General's Department had risen from 396 pounds in 1948 to 1000 pounds per annum in 1963. But running costs increased in tandem and the mail run was still a business that relied on freight haulage for a profitable return.

It was Pat Smith who eagerly stepped forward with an offer to run the mail service. He was a carrier from Quorn, south of Marree, who had regular business contact with the Kruses. When seismic exploration in the outback had first started Pat had won the contract to cart fuel from the Shell depot in Quorn to Tom's depot in Marree. Now he was anxious to capitalise on the opportunity to take over the mail contract and thus have a continuous line to his northern fuel customers. Pat's offer was accepted. And so the Tom Kruse years on the Marree-to-Birdsville mail run drew to a close.

In November 1963 Tom drove the Birdsville mail for the final time, making the last run himself before handing over the business to Pat Smith. Rather than the lumbering truck that he'd captained on his first run and most thereafter, Tom stripped down to a minimalist Land Rover. It was just him and the mailbags for 500 kilometres: no awkward sticks of furniture or cumbersome windmill heads; no heavy drums of fuel or perishable cans of butter. He did, however, have two passengers with him: two well-heeled ladies from Canberra who wanted to experience the end of an era.

When they made their trip at the end of 1963, the Diamantina was still trickling past Birdsville. Most of the Track across Goyder Lagoon was traversable but the Pandie homestead was on the wrong side of the river.

'I remember George Morton getting on the radio and saying, "When you bring the mail, come up to the homestead and have a cup of tea," Tom recalls. '"Come on the inside road and I'll send the kids down to row across and pick you folk up," he said. Righto. So the three kiddies are there to meet us; David—I s'pose he was eight or nine, the little daughter and one other.

'We finally get over the river and there's this army jeep waiting on the other side. Well, o' course then there's a bit of a bloody fight, a bit of a scramble between the three kids—who's going to drive their vehicle up the banks and back to the homestead.

'They're grabbing each other by the hair and stuff, and having a bit of a box on—who's gonna be the driver. Anyhow, David finally wins the seat. We're in the back. We start to go up the bank and all of a sudden, this lady, she started laughing. Hell, she's screaming! She thought I was going to drive, see. And there're these kids, hanging on, going up the bank. 'Course David can't see over the windscreen, he's hanging out the door to see where he's going. He had to look down the side to put his foot on the bloody clutch. And she couldn't get over it!

'Well, to be quite truthful, she spoke with a plum in her mouth. She was a lady . . . a proper lady. Hell, now she's screaming and laughing. Anyhow, this little David finally looked around and said, "What're ya laughin' at, ya bugger!"

'When we were back in the home at Pandie having our morning tea or whatever, she burst out laughing again. George said, "What's going on?"

'"Well," I said, "look, these little tigers, they had a bit of a scrap, you know, who's going to be the driver. Pulled out a lump of hair and so and so. That's what she's laughing at." Hell, it was the highlight of her trip.

'Look, speaking of kids . . . Doesn't take 'em long to pick

up the lingo of what's going on,' Tom continues. 'Funny thing, this other little chappy, young Jeffrey, he was having a dental check with Dr Olary, the flying doctor. Olary, he was a bit of a hard case. And young Jeffrey, he's weeping, trying to get in behind his mother. He was only about this high. Anyhow, after Dr Olary had pricked his arm—whatever it was—he looked around . . . the doctor wanted to give him a lolly or something. And this kiddie thought he was going to give him another needle. "No! No, don't!" he cried, "I'll set my dog on to you, you bastard!"

'O'course, the Sister, she nearly dropped dead. She'd never, ever heard that language,' Tom guffaws.

When Tom returned from his curtain-call trip in November 1963, he strode into the Marree post office with the mailbags for the very last time. While he was away Valma had packed up the house, arranging all their belongings into three piles: things to be disposed of; clothes and essentials that she would pack into the car and take with her to Adelaide; and all the large, bulky items that Tom would bring with him later when he followed in one of his trucks. Harvey, their dog, was left in the care of Allan Crombie—Valma couldn't bear the thought of a dog who had had the run of the town suddenly being denied his country freedom in a suburban backyard.

Then she and the children piled into the car and left Marree for good.

'I can't really remember,' says Tom, when asked to describe the move to Adelaide. 'Valma would've come down in her car—the Ford Zephyr . . . Oh, no she didn't. That's right, I sold it. I sold it to a young fellow. Never ever got any money out of him. Four new tyres on it, too. I think the price was 250 pounds. I sold it and never ever . . . '

'Mmmm,' said Valma, never one to scold or deride Tom in public. It was her only comment on the matter.

11

Dam-sinking and Earth-moving Days

Reconvening in Adelaide, Valma and the Kruse children settled into their new house in Cumberland Park. However, it took another twenty years for Tom to give up the nomad's life and join his family in the city, subconsciously compromising his planned relocation by making sure that he was too busy with work 'up north' to seek a job closer to home. He called in on his wife and children on a loose monthly basis, but throughout the 1960s, '70s and early '80s, as he had done in the '50s, Tom roamed the inland. With his work taking him back and forth across the top end of the State he left an ever-increasing string of broken-down vehicles, truck bodies and spare parts behind him. The Badger was not the only one to be left where it lay.

'As a matter of fact, rather a strange thing,' Tom muses. 'A chappy rang me the other day. He said, "Look, you left a string of gear on our property . . . you know it's twenty years ago."

'"Ah, Douglas," I said, "How's the old Hippo going then?"

'"Well, the tyres are all flat. And I think there's about . . . well, actually I counted them the other day, there's about 50-odd wheels out there. They're all flat . . ."'

The outback was Tom's big backyard. His used-up trucks lay scattered about the desert like discarded childhood toys. But, like a teenager who has moved on to other pursuits yet still casts a sentimental eye over past playthings buried among the weeds in a forgotten corner of the yard, Tom knows exactly where all his possessions are and reflects fondly on the past triumphs and downfalls of each. He can account for every rusted truck cab and broken-down chassis as if he had conducted a stocktake just yesterday. In barren country of wide-open nothingness, Tom can drive straight to a truck that was abandoned 20 or 30 years ago in an uninhabited corner of a 17 000-square-kilometre cattle station such as Roseberth or Clifton Hills. Navigating by dirt tracks, stony outcrops and isolated stands of trees, he knows this country like he knows his own face.

Tom built his first dam in 1952, using Bert Griffiths's old earthmoving plant which he had bought from Celcie Morton. The dam was on Celcie's property at a site called Moorayepe, 130 kilometres due south of the Roseberth homestead, where all the little creeks from Cordillo flowed down and pooled at the base of the sandhills. No-man's-land, Tom called it. Out among the stones.

'The very first dam we did. What excitement! . . . Look, from my side, I knew nothing about a tractor,' he says. One of Tom's nephews who used to drive tractors offered to show him the ropes and it wasn't long before he had mastered his new line of work. The necessary skills for dam-sinking were those that Tom had in abundance: mechanical aptitude, patience, fortitude and commitment.

It was the landowner's prerogative to name each dam and Celcie christened this one Moorayepe Lake. Many years later, Tom was sinking dams on Todmorden station, out along the Oodnadatta Track, and was honoured when the owner, Gordon Lillecrap, named the first one for Tom.

'Very first dam we did for them they named it "Kruse". That's a fact. I might say, Gordon, he was a tall man—a big strider. I know from my side, the boys always used to giggle 'cause I had to trot to keep up with him.'

Tom also fondly recalls 'Rainbow', which was completed at Todmorden just as Rain Lover won the Melbourne Cup in 1968, and 'Moonland', named for the lunar landing in July 1969.

The second and third dams Tom built were at 'The Planet' outstation on Arrabury station. They were bigger and deeper than the first: excavated squares 10 metres deep with 100-metre sides. Tom scraped out 27 000 cubic metres of earth for each dam and was paid in the customary manner, by the amount of soil shifted. The earth taken from the hole was piled up around the edge to form a bank 2 to 3 metres high.

Tom and his two workers—an energetic New Zealand lad named Jimmy Callis and Freddy Scott, who liked his tea so strong you could stand a spoon in it—toiled on rotating shifts long into the darkness. Tom would usually take the late shift, from 8 pm till 10 pm or midnight, then start again at 4 am and go till breakfast at eight or nine. In this way, they slogged around the clock, stopping only on Saturday evenings to listen to Bob Dyer's 'Pick a Box' on the wireless. It took them three months.

Tom knew that it was the way of the outback to pile the pressure on a bloke to see what he's made of and then to back off slightly once he had proved his worth. 'Give 'em a bit of a hammering for kick-off and then ease off a bit,' as he describes it. Tom wanted no doubts in any station owners' minds about his abilities as a dam-sinker so he strove to complete the dam as soon as possible. His enthusiasm, however, was no compensation for inadequate equipment.

'Three months was about the time for us, initially, because we had a lot of breakdowns,' he says. 'Actually, the first one was over three months 'cause we struck a lot of rock—had to blast it out. Fred was quite up with it 'cause he'd done a lot of blasting at Leigh Creek. Then we carted all the rock out with the old Badger. The banks were steep—three in one. But she could do it, having a low-ratio gearbox.

'Then again, a person'd never do it now . . . even if I was able to. Fancy loading these stones up by bloody hand and carting the buggers out and tossing them off. You'd say you gotta have a tip-truck. But anyhow, I won't go through that . . . We did it.'

During the '50s Tom had constructed multiple dams for Celcie Morton and his sons who eventually inherited his stations, and for Brooks at Clifton Hills. He had amassed more suitable machinery, gradually building up his stable to include a D6 and a D7 Caterpillar crawler and a couple of scoopmobiles. He also became adept at picking dam sites— judging where the water would naturally accumulate and then searching for an area with a clay bottom to hold it there. Dam-building was work that he would continue for the following twenty years while pursuing other jobs in between.

In the early '60s, EG Kruse Ltd, Earthmovers and

Carriers, began working for oil exploration companies Delhi Santos and United Geophysical, bulldozing roads, or 'cutting tracks' as it was known by those in the trade. He forged exploration lines over the Strzelecki and Stony deserts: six weeks on and ten days off for four pounds an hour—a sum from which he had to pay his own men and provide for their upkeep. On one job he spent fifteen months blazing a 100-kilometre trail across the Sturt Stony Desert from Damperannie on the outside route of the Birdsville Track to the oil and gas fields of Gidgealpa, 65 kilometres west of Innamincka.

Cutting tracks was more than simply forging two wheel ruts through the scrub. Sandhills needed to be lowered at strategic points, then overlaid with clay to allow vehicles to negotiate them with relative ease. Four-wheel-drives were now ubiquitous—the days of steel plates and coconut matting long gone—but obstacles remained that would defeat drivers lacking the natural savvy of Tom Kruse. It was his job to ease their passage.

As with anything else, there was a knack to claying roads. 'We did a lot of claying in the desert,' says Tom. 'There's plenty of clay out there if you can find it . . . and there's nothing to buy. Look, wherever you find good clay, you take it up, then dump it and spread it where you want it. Smooth it out wide. But you don't want to make it too smooth. If it's too smooth the water wants to run down the hill—washes the clay off. You try to put a slope on it, so instead of running down, it runs away to the sides.

'Matter of fact, the first bit of claying that was ever done was done by old Bert Griffiths up at Cluny, 120 mile up. Actually, we finished up with that scoop—years later of course. Bert Griffiths was there with all his gear to do dams for them at Cluny and it rained and he couldn't get out to the stockyard to start work on the dams. The stockyard was behind a big sandhill. If you wanted to get over there from the homestead you had to go seven miles down, round the point and then go back up to the yard. Anyhow, Bert Griffiths was getting pretty itchy. He says, what about claying the hill and going over the top. And that was the first bit of claying that was ever done. In five minutes they could be over at the yard.

'Matter of fact, the boss cocky of the Lands Department went up to have a look [at the claying] . . . No worries, you can drive over; don't even have to have four-wheel-drive. That really was a sample of what could be done with quality clay.'

It was a prescient advance—road improvements heralded a new era of accessibility for all. For some of the oldtimers, though, it forever changed the spirit of outback travel.

'Later on o'course, they started on the Birdsville Track. I reckon Monty was still driving the mail when they did the first little bit of work on it. I remember him saying, "People travelling, anyone coming up, would always make a point of pulling up and speaking to you. Now the buggers are going past you like flies."'

Delhi Santos also contracted Tom to move their work camps when they so desired. Tom would hitch up the workers' caravans, the drilling rig and all the associated paraphernalia in his customary manner and drag it to the next spot in the company's endless quest for oil.

Early in 1963, Tom was approached by French Petroleum to take on a big track-cutting project for them. They wanted a line across the Simpson Desert to facilitate their own search for oil. They'd heard about Tom's work for Delhi and believed that he was the man to lay it for them. Unfortunately the timing was all wrong since he and Valma were talking about selling the mail run and moving to Adelaide at the time. It would have been foolish to take responsibility for such a long-term, large-scale project when his future in the north was somewhat uncertain, so he reluctantly rejected the offer.

The project got underway without Tom but it wasn't long before they were calling on his services anyway. The company was working on its second well site at Dalhousie Springs, and the road contractor they had hired was having trouble carting materials from the Pedirka railway siding out to the site. The area was crisscrossed with creeks and the 50-kilometre run rapidly turned into a big boggy mess. The boss of the operation appealed to Tom for help and flew him out to the site for an assessment.

'We went up in an aeroplane . . . at a well site the first thing they do is put in an airstrip. It was awfully hot. Hell, it was hot,' he recalls.

'They were most hospitable . . . come in and have a meal, have a drink—they all seemed to drink a bit of alcohol. You gotta look out, too many will put you off the beam. Once a person gets on the outside of a bit of drink . . . Really, there's nothing worse than seeing a man hanging onto the blades of grass.

'Then the cook came in and says, "How d'ya like your meat done?"

'"Look, long as I can see a bit of blood in it, I'll be happy," I said.

'Anyhow, this meat came in, sliced about an inch thick. Lovely. Beautiful. O'course they used to eat different to what we do. In those days, horses were being shot and they were all eating horsemeat. Their order would be for two horses and half a bullock. That was the first time I ever tried it. It's really number one.'

Tom agreed to assist the exploration team and began work at the Dalhousie Springs site, carting materials to and from the railway siding. In the school holidays, his son Phillip came up to help. Phillip's return to Marree at the end of this stint produced one of the rare occasions on which Valma lost patience with Tom.

'We were doing some of the rough stuff,' Tom remembers. 'Cement, pyrites—everything had to be handled by hand. Phillip must've been thirteen or so, I s'pose. Anyhow, he was strong, because those pyrites bags were a little bit less than a hundred weight [51 kilograms].

'Funny thing . . . the time came that he had to go back to school. A message came up from Oodnadatta through the railways saying Valma's getting worried about Phillip coming back.

Tom sent a message back, saying, 'No worries, Phillip's on his way.'

'How'm I gonna get home, then?' the boy asked his father.

'You'll have to take the Land Rover. Don't call in to Oodnadatta; the police down there'll grab you. Just keep going and take a pretty wide sweep.'

So Phillip did as he was told—without fuss—and set off on the 531-kilometre journey; driving himself back to Marree down the Oodnadatta Track.

'Are you talking about when Phillip drove the Land Rover back?' asks Valma, walking into the room upon overhearing Tom's account. Tom glanced at me as his eyes slid away to the floor. He lowered his head in mock disgrace. 'Mmm, I was *cross* about that,' she scolds. '*Oooh*! He was twelve years old and on his own. I had no idea that it was supposed to happen like that! Just as well I didn't know. Really! I mean, fancy sending him off on his own like that. He could've broken down anywhere and no one would ever've known.'

It took Phillip two days to get home; two days in the relentless sun—as the Rover had no cabin—skidding and bumping over kilometres and kilometres of rough bush track; sleeping in the seat when he needed rest.

'He got down all right,' Tom says proudly. 'No worries. The road from Marree to Oodnadatta those days . . . very little traffic. At least he did as he was told: Don't go into Oodnadatta because you'll get picked up . . . No licence.

'And Valma?' Tom hesitates, glancing towards the kitchen with an impish smirk. 'Well . . . she didn't have a smile on her face when I got home . . . No, actually she wasn't very happy.

'Fact is . . . Phillip used to do quite a bit of driving. He used to drive old Jack Clarke around Marree. Jack didn't know anything about motor cars . . . well, to tell you the truth, I don't know that Phillip knew much more . . . But he'd tell Phillip, "I'll drive out of the town and you take over from there." He used to have to go up to Finniss Springs. Oh, only 40 miles up. He was a bit of a caretaker round about and it was Phillip that he'd always love to take him.'

But to Valma there was no denying that a 65-kilometre jaunt with Jack the Dogger was something quite different from a 500-kilometre solo journey down the Oodnadatta Track.

Helen, too, remembers her brother's pre-teen driving odyssey, but at the time it seemed nothing out of the ordinary to her. Phillip's driving incident probably left her unaffected because she'd had first-hand experience of her brother at the wheel.

'One time we went out to the Cooper with Dad in Jack Clarke's old vehicle—a little truck thing,' she recalls. 'I don't know why, but Phillip and I were sent back. Phillip got it going and drove for a while, and I'm sitting up there happy as Larry. Next minute he says, "You have to drive now, I'm gonna have a sleep."

'Well, that's all right. But you could hardly see where you were going over the dashboard. It was sandy. And I seem to remember that he'd got [the truck] going to the fourth gear. He said, "If you see something coming, just keep on your side."

'We must've been only about ten or twelve. Dad was very trusting,' she concludes with a shrug.

Trusting he may be, but Tom is certainly not ignorant of the hazards of the bush. He'd had his share of grisly experiences: accidents and tragedies accentuated by the isolation and primitive conditions of the outback.

Several drownings occurred in the first year of the Cooper floods, and Tom grimly recalls other terrible episodes from his mail-run days. One fellow swelled up and died on the back of his truck from eating poison berries; Tom racing to get him to hospital. Too late. A helper once laying fencing wire beneath the truck's wheels was struck by the buckling strands and lost an eye. Another lad lost much of the use of an arm to shenanigans on the back of the Badger.

'This young fellow—he would've been fifteen or sixteen—he used to jump off the load onto the ground,' Tom recounts. 'The Badger was fully loaded—about 16 foot high.

I remember saying, you'll finish up driving your legs up through your body, you know.

'Well anyhow, we pulled up to have breakfast at this waterhole and this young lad jumped off, and of course he had a ring on his finger and he got hooked in some wire . . . Pulled the sinews right out through his hand. Torn from his shoulder . . . Right through, and down . . . it was all on the ground and the finger was on the end of it,' Tom says in a low voice. 'I can remember it really well . . . Hell, what an episode.'

'Poor old Jack Gaffney, he fainted . . . ' Tom continues gravely. 'Oh, he fainted. He couldn't stand it. I might say, he was sort of weak for that sort of thing.

'I remember I asked old Jack Clarke if we had anything to wrap it up.

'"I've got clean singlets in me swag," he said.

'"Right. We'll toss the load off and try and get him into Birdsville if we can," I said. We were 90 mile out and it was just starting to rain. We put most of the load on the ground and headed to Birdsville as quick as possible. He didn't even pass out, poor little fella. Matter of fact, it was a shame because the pain . . . Oooh it was bad. Poor little beggar. Hell, it was awful.

'Anyhow we got him to Birdsville and the flying doctor plane came out from Charleville.'

Away from the relative civilisation of the Birdsville Track, the men in the dam-sinking and line-cutting camps faced the potential of even greater calamities. Tom was instrumental in saving the life of one them.

'Seamus and Freddy, they used to always fight—argue

over nothing,' he says. 'You wouldn't let them work together . . . always make certain one's over here and the other's away over there. And when they'd had a few drinks it was worse. Well, off they went into Birdsville. They got held up at the pub and were a bit slow getting back so I got on the radio to Birdsville.

'"Hello, Sister, good morning," I said, "happened to see the red Rover running around?"

'"Why, yes. They're heading out your way today."

'"Good. Okay."

'That night, no one arrives,' Tom continues. 'I said to [one of my workers] Rossy, "I think we should really go and have a bit of a look around, 'cause those two fellows, they do a fair bit of arguing over which way the sun rises and sets."

'So we're just about to leave, and who should come staggering along . . . it's Fred.

'"What's happened?" I asked him.

'"I don't know . . . the Land Rover . . . I walked miles . . ."' Fred gasped, sinking to the ground.

'"Where's Seamus?"

'"I don't know . . . He was walking that way . . . had the crank handle . . ."' Fred's eyes were bulging and he was on the verge of collapse.

'It was early in January,' Tom goes on. 'It was hot weather, really hot. "Right," I said to Rossy, "let's go." Look, every man for his trade. Rossy wasn't a tracker, he was a tractor driver. But he could track a flea on a windy day on a stony bit of ground. Fair dinkum.

'We finally got the tracks of the old Rover. In a little while Rossy said, "He's using the crank handle as a walking stick." Then we finally picked up the crank handle. Hell. We're driving around. Next thing, there's a man lying under a bush. It's Seamus. Hell, he was . . . well, I won't go through that,' Tom says quietly with a grim look. 'Rossy wouldn't touch him. He couldn't go near him.

'Well, when you're perishing, the first thing you want is water. We had plenty of water, but tell you what, it was an awful job just to give him a sip. Mouth all swollen . . . tongue hanging out. Hell. I took my singlet off and laid it over him, threw a bit of water on him. Gave him a little bit more of a sip. By that time he started to come round.

'It took him several days to recover. Look, it was only something simple with the vehicle, too. But then again, when people start to argue and fight . . . stupid.'

Although Seamus was saved from certain death on this occasion, he met his untimely end a few years later at the talc mine near Lyndhurst. Apparently, Seamus attempted to climb over the back of a moving truck and lost his footing on the devilishly slippery white powder. He fell under the wheels and was killed. He wasn't yet 40 years old.

Despite his wife and family being comfortably ensconced in a cool, stone home in the Adelaide suburbs, it soon became clear that Tom wasn't ready for city life just yet. He continued sinking dams, cutting tracks and doing heavy haulage while Valma, serene and steadfast as always, established a life in the city. They fell into a familiar routine. Instead of stopping in Marree, Tom would now regularly pass through the town en route to Adelaide to visit his family. In fact, Valma feels that she saw more of him *after* the move to the city, than she did before. For Tom, the new arrangement also made it easier to purchase spare parts, workshop manuals and equipment.

Valma could buy things and send them on at Tom's request rather than the old way of relaying messages to a third party down south. Or Tom could shop for himself in Adelaide. He soon became a regular visitor to the spare parts counter at the local Land Rover dealership.

Valma would still join him up north when she could. Like Tom, she had not lost her passion for living in the great outdoors. But once she became involved in city life, opportunities for jaunts to the bush were few and far between. She took up golf, enjoyed her new proximity to her family, and devoted time to the activities of her teenaged children.

Valma's husband, though, mostly stayed north of the city. Tales of Tom from people who worked with him or met him on their travels through the outback create a map of his whereabouts in later years.

In the mid-'60s he was working in the mid-north of South Australia doing earthwork at Dlorah and dam-sinking on Ballara and Tepco, sheep stations out along the Barrier Highway between Yunta and Broken Hill. Dlorah was one of the properties owned by Byron Macdonald's father, who was a strong proponent of harnessing water to redirect it where it was needed. He commissioned Tom to divert a creek so it flooded onto an alluvial plain and brought up feed.

Byron remembers his father commenting that big Tom's usefulness extended beyond his construction abilities. 'If ever a scrap would break out, he'd look to see where Tom was, and if Tom was about, he'd fix it,' Byron says. 'Tom'd never fight; he was very placid. But if he said, "Stop doing that"— if someone was being a bully or something—they'd stop when Tom told 'em to.'

Derrick Cheer, who was the overseer at Ballara station in 1965, remembers Tom as a strong, hard worker with no laces in his boots. As usual, Tom and his young assistant worked long hours and camped out during the time it took them to dig three dams on the property. But sometimes Tom found time to socialise with the overseer in the evenings.

'Tom used to enjoy a beer and a game of cards with us at night in the homestead,' Derrick remembers. 'He was a pretty shrewd card player. We'd have a friendly game of euchre . . . not for money. He had a massive hand on him and he'd bang the table. Oh, it'd make you jump when you weren't expecting it. But he was very placid. I've never seen him get overexcited.'

Ballara was a sheep station that also ran a few vealers—eight- to twelve-month-old cattle. Tom was living on mutton and so gradually found himself yearning for a good bite of steak. One day he approached Derrick and mentioned that he'd like to have a bit of beef for variety.

'If you can kill it, you can have it,' Derrick told him.

'Right,' said Tom, running a greasy hand through his hair. 'No worries.'

'I'll take you out in the ute, if you like,' said Derrick. 'How're ya gonna kill him?'

'You just get me close enough and I'll get it,' Tom replied.

'So I took him out there; found this vealer,' Derrick recounts. 'And Tom jumped out and hit it on the head with an axe! I couldn't believe my eyes! He had to get out of the ute and grab it quick. Gee, he could move pretty fast for a big fella.'

Tom was still working at the station when Derrick's friend Ron Smedley came for a holiday. Ron enjoyed watching this man, about whom he had heard so much, digging out the big, deep holes with his bulldozer. He took photos—including one of Tom's kitchen van parked at the campsite—and remembers how Tom spoke of it as his pride and joy.

Tom had made the kitchen van himself in Marree in the late '50s. It was a 10.5 by 3-metre unlined, galvanised-iron hut on wheels. It was fully equipped with a wood stove and a gas stove, a gas deep freezer and two fridges. Saucepans and frying pans hung from the walls and a 44-gallon drum filled with water sat in a corner. Up the top was an old bed with drawers in it that served as a mechanical supply cupboard. Any new hydraulic hoses, seals and suchlike, Tom stowed 'up top'.

'Inside, we had two tables. Look, nine of us could get in there and all sit up to the table at once,' Tom says proudly. 'It was a good width. The main table had a tin top. Beautiful. Used it for cooking and eating and just washed it down . . . There was a stove at the end of it—a Gifhorn number two. It used to make the meat taste beautiful. Fair dinkum. Then again, the plates . . . don't clean 'em down too well . . . you'll take the flavour off!

'It's amazing, this old van . . . a lot of people used to laugh at it, but it was really number one. Look, you could lift the windows up—we used to have a couple of old tin doors over the windows and in the daytime you'd prop them up for a bit of shade. Lovely. When we worked on Kenmore Park, you'd even say to Hugh MacLachlan: "Mr MacLachlan, do come in and have a cup of tea or coffee if you'd like one." We had very fine insect netting to keep the flies out. How delightful.

'Well, it was a galvanised-iron caravan with all the

windows knocked out of it,' Des Thompson says bluntly. The former Shell rep had visited Tom several times at his campsite and dined in the Kruse kitchen van.

'I tell you, it was rough. He had an old wood stove . . . and dust! He had dust instead of pepper and salt,' Des exclaims with a laugh.

But Tom heard none of this. He was enchanted with his kitchen van.

In 1968, Tom was offered a job building dams on Kenmore Park—a cattle station in the Musgrave Ranges near the Northern Territory border. He had happened to meet the owner, Hugh MacLachlan, at Yunta. Mr MacLachlan told Tom how he had a full-time man searching for underground water on his northern property but it was coming up much too salty. Tom suggested that he build a couple of dams rather than drilling for bore water and, before he knew it, he was pencilled in for a formal interview.

'We've got other contractors giving us quotes,' MacLachlan said. 'If you feel that you can do it, you be down in my office at eight o'clock on Monday morning. If you're interested at all be at my office Monday and we can discuss the conditions then. I'm saying eight o'clock. Monday morning.' Tom didn't know Hugh MacLachlan, but perhaps Mr MacLachlan had heard of Tom and his cavalier regard for time. He was on his way back to Adelaide for a break, but returned to meet Mr MacLachlan Monday morning as promised.

'I didn't know anything about Kenmore Park,' Tom

admits. 'I told him we'd done a few up around Birdsville, a few here and there, and just completed a big tank at Tepco.'

'We want at least 50 000 yards,' MacLachlan told him. 'Why don't you go up and take a look around. See what you think. And when you get back we'll talk about the rest of the job.'

'So we took up a bit of gear . . . put down a few trial holes. Hell, what easy country. They all came up with white clay on them. When we got back, Mr MacLachlan told us to start immediately.'

Tom back-tracked to Tepco station to collect his heavy equipment, which he routinely left unattended at each work site until it was needed for the next job, and loaded up for the northward trek.

It was a long, slow journey up the Stuart Highway to the Northern Territory border. Tom's Leyland Hippo was the prime mover, hitched up to a low-loader carrying the 25-ton Allis Chalmers crawler tractor, and towing the Moore scoopmobile, the 3-metre-wide kitchen van and a string of other gear behind. They inched along at 15 to 20 kilometres per hour. Tom's trucker colleagues took every opportunity to poke fun at him as they repeatedly passed him on their way to Alice Springs and back.

'It was in the summertime,' Tom remembers. 'As soon as it was light enough to see, we'd be on the road—and as soon as it was dark we'd make a point of pulling over. We used to do longer hours than the Alice Springs boys because they could go faster . . . you know, they mightn't start till about seven or eight o'clock in the morning and then they'd catch us up. I think I was on the road for about ten days, going up to Kenmore Park. If we could do a hundred mile in a day I was happy.'

Part-way into the trip, Tom lost almost a full day's travelling time when he had the fright of his life and needed a day of rest to compose himself and gather his wits again.

'I tell you what, it was the closest thing ever,' he says. 'It was at Lake Hart . . . where the railway line goes around the lake. Well, the low-loader, you had a job to see daylight under it, that's how low it was, we used to have to drive on sleepers—raise her up—to get over the railway lines.

'[One of my workers] John Berry's outside putting marks on the ground. He says, "She's right now, I can just see daylight under her . . . er . . . hang on . . . I think I can hear a train coming. I think there's a train coming. There's definitely a train! I can't see it, but I can hear the rumble. Get back!"

'Hell! We're halfway across the railway line!' Tom continues excitedly. 'I threw it into reverse. And of course the old Hippo used to jump out of reverse. I'm hanging onto the stick . . . pushing it up against the what's'name. Hell! She's stalled. I jumped out of the cabin, and it was, run! Run! Run!

'And I tell you what, the only thing—we had road signs: "Long, wide load following" and this sort of business—there was a bolt sticking out an inch [at the front] . . . and that's the only time it hit, touched about the middle of the train.

'And . . . 'scuse me saying it, the bloody train . . . I think it would've been doing 60 miles an hour—an express. I might say, I've never had such a rotten shock in all my life. The thing of it is . . . just imagine . . . the truck being halfway across the line, and this passenger train . . . Hell, it would've derailed the train . . . and who'd've been at fault? It was hair-raising! I tell you, it was awful.

'It was about five o'clock in the morning. We hadn't had breakfast, yet. Well, from my side, I said, "Ah . . . we won't go any further today."

'No, that was hair-raising. I can always remember that.'

Tom built eight dams during the job at Kenmore Park, each one 15 000 cubic metres. He returned some time later and built several more before ownership of the property was eventually handed over to the Yunyarinyi Aboriginal community several years later.

Ken Warriner was the manager and John Handbury the overseer when Tom first went up to Kenmore. One of John's jobs was to deliver piping to the dam sites in an old Bedford truck. He was impressed with the organisation and teamwork apparent in Tom's camp.

'He had one bulldozer pulling the scraper and another old International bulldozer pushing it,' John remembers. 'He was a man of excellent skills in the bush and could fix anything anywhere.

'I remember going into Victory Downs with Ken Warriner one night while Tom's team was on Kenmore. One of the young blokes working for Tom upset Ken Warriner to a degree where Ken took him outside and a fight developed. I remember Tom being a bit upset that Ken had slightly damaged one of his workmen. But he was more upset that he was going to lose two days' work because of it.'

Tom doesn't recall this incident but he remembers one absurd scenario at Kenmore—riding calves into the homestead sitting room—that obviously appealed to his roguish sense of humour and affinity for bush antics.

In between stints at Kenmore Park in the late 1960s, Tom sank dams with John Berry at Todmorden on the Oodnadatta

Track, and at other properties in the area such as Welbourne Hill. This work continued during the 1970s, interspersed with many line-cutting jobs. He bulldozed kilometres of tracks through the outback for companies such as Delhi Santos; Stockdale Prospecting, whose main camp was at Barton on the Nullarbor Plain; Meekatharra Minerals, in the Coober Pedy area; and the Japanese outfit searching for uranium on Mulgathing station, between Coober Pedy and Ceduna. He clayed sandhill after sandhill in the Simpson Desert for French Petroleum, constructing the French Line from Dalhousie Springs east to Poeppel Corner, and cutting tracks on old Kalamurina station west of the Birdsville Track. He laid survey lines for the new Ghan railway line north of Tarcoola and he was the first person to forge roads for the Moomba gas fields.

When earthmoving work was scarce, Tom turned his hand to carting wheat at Ceduna—using his International V8 to carry grain from the surrounding farms to the storage silos—and carting water at Coober Pedy: pumping water from outlying waterholes and delivering it to the thirsty residents of the underground mining town. His innovative water-carting operation flourished into a lucrative business that he ran with his son Phillip.

'Look, water was their worry,' Tom says. 'Hell, more value in water than what there was having a lump of opal in their hand.'

To begin with, Tom rented natural waterholes from Charlie Kunoth, who owned Mount Clarence station, 52 kilometres northwest of Coober Pedy. Charlie was unhappy with local miners plundering his waterholes and wanted a more formal arrangement for this precious resource. Charlie knew Tom from years before. In fact, he, too, had driven for Harry Ding in the past. He offered Tom water rights and, in return, Tom improved the waterholes and worked on additional dams for him.

'The miners were giving Charlie a fairly horrible time,' Tom explains. 'Long Hole and different other waterholes on Long Creek and Mabel Creek—where he'd probably think he had three months' water or six months' water for sheep and that sort of thing, he'd find he'd come along a fortnight later and the hole's dry. From Charlie's side he was getting awfully sick of this.'

Charlie had researched the legalities and learned that if improvements were made to a waterhole and a commercial agreement was in place, the waterhole was no longer 'natural' and miners were prohibited from using it indiscriminately. He and Tom staked out warning signs and it wasn't long before the miners got the message.

Charlie asked that certain waterholes remain untouched, but the rest were Tom's domain. Tom had gained for himself an abundant supply of a precious commodity, now he needed customers to whom he could sell it.

He put on his most winning smile and door-knocked around the town. 'I used to do a . . . like politicians do, a house call. I'd go out first thing in the morning. Funny thing, I knocked on one door . . . "We'll be carting water here very, very shortly," I said. "Perhaps we can sign you up?"

'"But I'm a water carrier," the bloke replied.

'He took a very dim view . . .' Tom recalls. 'Anyhow, that's how we first cracked off.'

After the hot, dusty work of line-cutting, water-carting was a welcome change. 'Pumping water . . . hell, the engine's doing the work and you're keeping the flies out of your eyes,' he says.

All the residents of the town had their own water storage tank mounted up high. Tom would pump the water from the waterholes, truck it to town, 45 000 litres at a time, and pump it into their tanks.

As the operation got underway, Phillip joined Tom in Coober Pedy and father and son expanded the business, gathering water from bores and waterholes up to 130 kilometres away. They forged a road from the opal town out to Mount Barry station when they won water rights on that property, and eventually built a dam on the outkirts of the town.

The business was in competent hands under Phillip's management and Tom gradually returned to his dam-sinking work. By the early '80s Tom was back in the Oodnadatta area. He was sinking a dam on Macumba station in 1983 when his dear kitchen van came to a sad yet highly spectacular end.

'It was the most awful thing that ever happened in a person's life,' Tom says gloomily. 'We were doing a bit of work just north of Lake Eyre. I'd been away for a while—settling some bills and tripping around—and I got in at night.

'About five o'clock in the morning, the boys had the kitchen stove going and the little gas stove going, cooking a bit of breakfast. Reg said the deep freeze was running low. I'd brought back four new bottles of gas from Oodnadatta and I put one on . . . it was a leaker.

'"Hell!" I said "I can hear the gas, let's get out!" And all of a sudden, up in the ceiling was all alight. "Get out! Get out!" And as soon as we did—we got about four or five metres away—Bang! The sides went out the caravan. Then the deep freeze fell out.

'The money and all my clothes were in there—I'd just bought a new set of clothes for the winter and $1100 I'd just collected in cash—it was all in there in one of those ice-cream shippers I was using as a suitcase. And all my brother's pennies—Ben was a great collector of bloody pennies, had a great pile. They all melted together. It was terrible. Everything burnt to cinders.

'Next thing, on the radio: "What's happened?" About 60 mile away they could see it—see the smoke. Then, on the wireless, they're saying, "Old Tom's caravan's burnt. He's terribly upset."

'The only thing we got out of it was the hot water—we had a [44-gallon drum] standing right in the middle of the caravan, and it was as hot as you could ever get it. Everything else was destroyed. Nothing. And that was the bloody end of the caravan.'

The demise of the kitchen van signalled the end of Tom's time in the desert. A lifetime of dust and flies, stark winter cold and searing summer heat finally brought him to Adelaide in 1984 at the age of 70. He sank his last dam on Allandale station, 16 kilometres from Oodnadatta.

Australia's best-known postie, that great man of the bush, Tom Kruse, Esquire, MBE, hung up his rag hat at home in Cumberland Park and endeavoured to make the transition into urban retirement.

12

Saluting the Carrier
Called Kruse

By the mid-1980s, Tom's working life in the outback may have been at an end, but a new phase of the Kruse saga was about to begin—in the form of public recognition and unsolicited accolades for the man who had quietly and humbly given a lifetime of toil to the people of northern South Australia.

Two years after Tom officially retired and moved down south to Adelaide, South Australia had her birthday. It was 1986. The State was celebrating 150 years of existence and official 'Jubilee 150' events to commemorate the occasion were in full swing. Most involved town parades and fairs and organised activities in the capital. The only event planned to salute South Australia's outback heritage was an old-fashioned trail ride from Port Augusta to Birdsville via the Birdsville Track. The so-called Jubilee Overlanders—two

South Australians and a Texan—would ride the Track in addition to a shorter distance across Texas later in the year to honour early pioneers and to promote the shared sesquicentenary of both states. The riders would lead a plant of packhorses from Mungerannie station and camp out in the open, sleeping in swags.

Dave Burge, a safety officer working for the Electricity Trust of South Australia at the Leigh Creek coalfield, wanted to see greater representation of the State's far northern region in the 150th birthday celebrations. He also felt that too many of the planned events focused on explorers and heroes long gone. Dave knew that there was a legend of the outback living under their very noses. This was the perfect time to commemorate the exploits of the carrier called Kruse, who had spent a lifetime traversing the rutted gravel tracks of outback South Australia. He decided that he would organise a Jubilee 150 re-enactment to honour the pioneer drivers of the Birdsville mail. His mate, Tom Kruse, would be the guest of honour.

Dave had first met Tom in the mid-1970s, when he was 26 years old and living in Lyndhurst, driving road trains up the Track and roundabout. Tom, as usual, was blanketing the bush.

It was at the William Creek gymkhana, where Dave was eating crabs from the back of a friend's ute, when a bloke strolled up and asked if he could join them. When the newcomer was introduced as Tom Kruse, Dave nearly fell out the back.

'Tom Kruse! Well, it's kind of like young guys would be these days with the new Tom Cruise,' Dave says.

Dave had seen *The Back of Beyond* as an impressionable seven-year-old, gazing avidly at the screen in the old Sunday school hall at Port Germein. He had been affected by the film ever since and was now awestruck to meet the great man himself. The two went on to become friends, seeing each other on and off over the next ten years. Now Dave saw the Jubilee year as the perfect way to pay homage to the person who had inspired him so much.

Dave began planning the re-enactment, scheduled for May of that year. He envisioned it as a re-creation of the run depicted in the film and he wanted it to be as authentic as possible. He arranged for Tom to drive a representative mail truck—a Chev Blitz—loaded with station supplies, as it would have been in the 1950s. Dave had bought the Blitz from the District Council of Wudinna and planned to present it to the township of Marree at the completion of the run. He borrowed a second Blitz and a 1949 Chevrolet to complete the official convoy.

The event would open in Marree with a street party, then Tom would lead the convoy to Birdsville, stopping at stations along the way to emulate his original journey. Overnight camping in the Cooper Creek would include a communal campfire where participants would be entertained by country music and story-telling. The re-enactment would conclude in Birdsville and everyone would make their own way home from there.

Early in the year, as Dave made final preparations and began alerting the media to the event, he checked in with Tom to confirm his participation and ensure that he would be in Marree at the appointed time—if Tom turned up a day or a week late, as he was wont to do, the celebration would be a dismal failure. As they chatted, Tom suggested to Dave that the contingent go out and take a look at the old Badger while they were up at Birdsville. Perhaps an audience with one of the authentic, original mail trucks would fit in with the overall theme of the event?

'The Badger? . . . *The* truck?!' asked Dave.

'Yes. Sitting by a dam on Pandie,' Tom said casually.

'The one from *Back of Beyond*?' Dave asked again. He was incredulous.

'Right, Dave . . . the very same.'

'In all my preparation for the mail run re-enactment I had never considered that *that* old truck might *be* somewhere,' Dave admits. 'It staggered me! When Tom told me where it was, I knew right then that we had to include it in the trip.'

A visit to the Badger became the jewel in the crown of Dave's re-enactment plan. A small team would make an excursion from Birdsville to the site on Pandie Pandie station where Tom's two abandoned Leylands languished in the desert. If found fit for retrieval, the Badger would be towed back to Adelaide for restoration and, eventually, museum display. It was an ambitious undertaking but Dave was fired with enthusiasm and eagerly sent letters to reporters, outlining the planned proceedings. His passion proved contagious.

A brief announcement describing the upcoming event appeared in the *The Advertiser* on 31 March. It caught my father's eye and immediately piqued his interest—he, too, had seen *The Back of Beyond* and been captivated by Heyer's poetic portrayal of the Birdsville mailman and his taxing run. My father, Neil Weidenbach, had first seen the film in the mid-'50s when he was a fresh, young teacher at the Kingston School in South Australia's southeast. For him, the film's magic had lingered ever since.

After seeing the note in the paper, he promptly wrote away to Dave Burge for further details and upon receiving a warm response and an open invitation to join in, he alerted his colleagues at the Military Vehicle Collectors' Society of South Australia, who were interested in the kind of Blitzes that Tom used. He urged them to take part in what he was convinced would be a memorable journey.

Aynsley Rowe, an avid inland traveller, learned of the upcoming event from his Marree mate, Wally Davies. Aynsley had been generously offered the use of Wally's oxy torch in 1977 when the little cart he'd pulled along on his solo walk from Darwin to Adelaide needed running repairs en route. There was no garage in Marree, so when Aynsley arrived with trolley troubles he was immediately directed to Wally's place. 'He's got everything up there,' Aynsley was told.

'Yeah, Wally had it all right,' Aynsley remembers. 'But it took about three-quarters of an hour to find the oxy bottle and put it alongside the acetylene, and then find the torches and then find the hoses and put it all together and make it work.' Aynsley chuckles at the memory.

Together they repaired the cart, and from then on, once or twice every year when Aynsley passed through on his way to or from his outback adventures, he dropped in to see Wally.

Aynsley would also make a new friend at the re-enactment: a like-minded individual named Bob Bilton. Bob was a diehard bushie who'd travelled from his home in Melbourne to take part. He'd been regularly touring the inland since buying his first Land Rover in 1953. His love of the outback had been fostered in childhood, through many hours of reading the field journals of early explorers such as

Burke and Wills, as he lay slowly recuperating from the loss of a leg following a motor accident at age eleven.

South Australia's Jubilee 150 Birdsville Mail-Run Re-enactment was scheduled for May 17–23. 'Birdsville "Blitz" mail will roll again', read the headline in the 23 April edition of *The Advertiser*.

It was a motley collection of old vehicles that trundled into Marree for the official start of the re-enactment: the two red Chev Blitzes with 'EG Kruse, Marree. Royal Mail', painted on them and loaded up with a cargo of swags and typical outback station supplies—fencing wire, hay bales, bags of chaff, wire rope and tyres; a red Chev camp truck; a jeep carrying Military Vehicles Society newlyweds (as my father noted, the groom, with a proper sense of priorities, cut short his honeymoon and brought his wife along in their jeep); a GMC; the red 1956 Austin tow truck that the Weidenbach family were driving on the 2400-kilometre return trip; and a green and yellow Blitz sporting 'Matilda' the boxing kangaroo on its side driven by Leigh Creek local Peter Ware.

The opening celebration was in full swing that night when Dave Burge felt a broad hand come to rest on his shoulder and heard that familiar soft voice in his ear.

'Good evening, David,' said Tom.

Dave swung round with a stubby in his hand and a big, relieved grin. Tom! At last! It was 8 pm and he was begining to think that the naysayers, who'd repeatedly told him the big man wouldn't make it, had been right.

Officially retired, Tom had returned to the north by special request to clean out a dam near Oodnadatta. It was an old paved dam that had proven too much for the local contractors and the owner had called Tom begging for help. Reluctantly, he agreed to take the job, which meant first travelling all the way up to Pandie to retrieve the scoop from his former depot at Gilpininna Dam, before back-tracking to Oodnadatta to begin work.

He had spent a couple of months camped on the outskirts of the town working on the old dam, finishing just in time to assume his guest-of-honour duties in Marree.

Tom moved through the crowd clapping people on the back, shaking hands and thoroughly enjoying himself. At one point a familiar figure emerged, a man in his early sixties clad in army-green shirt, pants and hat. He advanced on Tom with a smile and thrust out his hand.

'G'day Tom, how are ya,' he piped up in a distinctive high-pitched voice. 'You remember who I am?'

'Yes, Bob. Hey, how marvellous. Good to see you.'

Tom and Bob Bilton had first met Christmas Eve 30 years previously in the Great Northern Hotel in Marree. A few days later Bob inadvertently gained a reputation as a mail truck thief when he made off with one of Tom's Blitzes after his own Land Rover had broken down. When Bob and his companions eventually returned the vehicle undamaged, Tom forgave the miscreants—even dissuading the Marree policeman from hustling to the Cooper to take the men into custody immediately. But as a result of the debacle, Tom was stranded at the Cooper and had to make the journey from there to Birdsville—370 kilometres—sitting on Bob's bonnet.

'Oh, well, look, it's a ride,' Tom says dismissively of the episode.

After this dubious start to their relationship Tom soon became happy to count Bob Bilton as a friend.

On Sunday, 18 May 1986, the Jubilee 150 mail run re-enactors assembled at the head of the Birdsville Track. By now, the number of participants had grown to several hundred. To Dave's delight, about 80 vehicles joined the northbound convoy, far exceeding the fifteen or so that he had originally envisioned.

The drivers had a slow, two-day journey ahead of them. Two television crews were in attendance and they both wanted shots of the two mail trucks struggling through strategic patches of sand and circling around with people clinging to the top of the load—the way passengers had done 50 years before. For Tom, driving one of the Blitzes, it was a return to his movie-star days—patiently taking direction and repeating each action until the cameramen were satisfied. For the re-enactors, what began as an interesting spectacle gradually dissolved into a series of mildly irritating delays while the filmmakers gathered their footage.

At Pandie Pandie station the mail trucks remained on the west side of the Diamantina overnight so that the TV crews could film them crossing the dry riverbed and climbing the sandhills in the morning. The onlookers also assembled the next day, seeking a good vantage point to watch Tom's progress. But they were repeatedly ushered away from the watercourse and shepherded back behind the video cameras. The demands of the TV crews and their constant instructions and directions to stay out of the shots finally became too much for one man. He turned toward a reporter sporting a big, bushy beard and yelled frustratedly: 'You're not the only one with a camera, Father Christmas!'

By 11 am the convoy had covered the final 27 kilometres into Birdsville. There was little time for relaxing, however. For the diehard fans the run to Birdsville was only the preliminary leg. The real excursion was just about to begin: The expedition to rescue the Badger.

Gilpininna Dam is 50 kilometres southeast of Birdsville on the very edge of Pandie Pandie station where it borders Roseberth, between Lake Etamunbanie and Lake Short. It was mid-afternoon by the time the small group of volunteers had picked their way through the vast expanse of packed red gibbers—polished by windblown sand and gleaming in the sunlight—to the dam site. Cresting a gentle rise, they saw two small, dark humps appear in the barren middle distance before them. There the two old Leylands— the Badger side by side with the Cub—had stood defiantly against years of blazing heat and sand scour, occasional rainstorms and human opportunists, the only objects breaking the horizon in an infinite yellow wasteland. It was an awe-inspiring moment and the drivers paused to take it all in.

Upon closer inspection, it was immediately obvious that the Badger was too decrepit to move. The whole truck had sunk to the ground. There were tyres on each side on the front, but none on the back. The left-hand door was attached, frozen tight to its hinges, with the yellow lettering 'EG Kruse, Marree' faded but still clearly visible. The driver side door was gone. There was no seat in the cab nor running boards to mount it. There were no cab roof panels. The bonnet was detached and lying nearby on the ground. The metal sidecovers over the engine were gone—however Tom had discarded these himself years before, when the Badger was still running, to help prevent overheating in the baking conditions of midsummer.

The steering wheel, gearstick and rusty radiator remained, and the casing of the Lord Nelson lamp was miraculously still perched at the front on the driver's side. There was glass in the driver's side windscreen but none on the passenger side—either in the windscreen panel or the door. The skeleton of the tray was there—the metal supports across the width of the truck and a cross member running its length. But the wooden decking was reduced to a few derelict planks of timber poking up from the ground at odd angles.

In short, it was a complete wreck; 'a proper wreck', as Tom would say. The volunteers quickly ascertained that the Badger's remains would not survive being towed the 50 kilometres or so back across the gibbers to Birdsville. There was nothing to attach the towing equipment to, nor axles on which to mount the spare wheels they had brought. Only one of the four driving axle half-shafts remained. The Badger's body had been reduced to a fragile corpse of wood and metal. It would simply disintegrate if they tried to drag it from its bed. The rescue would have to be postponed.

After all the anticipation, though, Dave Burge did not want his crew to return empty-handed. He switched his attention to the petrol-driven Cub. It was in slightly better condition and deemed to be towable. The salvage team was not at all discouraged—they enthusiastically fell to and started work immediately.

In short order, most of the Cub's wheel nuts were turned free or the studs oxy-cut away, and the replacement wheels the crew had brought with them were on. Someone checked and found adequate oil in the diff, and someone else disconnected the tail shaft. In the space of two hours the Cub was coupled to one of the Chev mail trucks and ready for towing.

'It was amazing. We were all there, digging things out of the dirt. I've never seen men work the way they worked,' my father recalls.

Meanwhile, Tom, was happily poring over the Badger like a long-lost relative. From under his narrow-brimmed canvas hat, which he wore low on his forehead such that the shadow line cut straight across his cheekbones in a black stripe, he peered into the cabin and poked around in the engine well.

'She's got the dinkum oil in her,' he announced, playing to the camera for the ABCTV 'Countrywide' crew, who were there in the hope of filming the Badger's retrieval. 'Look here,' he said proudly, reaching down and pulling out the dipstick, smearing his thumb in the thick black oil that clung to it. 'She was never hungry on oil. Look at that. And they reckon Shell oil's no good. No, I tell you what, if I was here for a couple of hours I'm quite sure I could start this thing,' he smiled. And, having heard tales of his prowess in bush mechanics, no one ventured to doubt him.

He paid little attention to the efforts going on around him to get the Cub mobile. The other Leyland held no interest for Tom. He'd bought it purely as a cheap alternative to transport a piece of earth-works machinery from Adelaide up to one of his work camps.

When it had served its purpose he abandoned it at the Gilpininna depot with no regrets. It held no sentimental value for him. But each time he tried to point out that the men were wasting their efforts on the wrong vehicle he was gently but firmly dismissed.

'I remember there was a couple of us scratching our heads about it. Look, you boys are . . . you've got the wrong vehicle . . . You've got the wrong sister. "Look we know what we're doing," they said to me, "Keep out of it." Right.

'Then we walked over to the Badger. I remember pulling the dipstick out and walking round the damn thing. Actually, I'd been back there lots of times. The last time I was there was seven or eight years before, I'd say—easy. It wasn't so dilapidated then. The seats and everything were still there. Someone had taken the back axle out and the wheels had been taken off, but they were still there.'

The Badger had deteriorated rapidly in the eight years since Tom had last seen it and he was a little dismayed at her condition when the re-enactment convoy arrived in 1986. There were also signs of unwanted visitors to the site and it was obvious that the abandoned truck had been repeatedly plundered of anything of use.

'If the Diamantina was ever in big flood, in order for people to get to the outside road they'd go up to the Bluff and around,' Tom explains. 'The Badger really was only about six mile off that sandhill road, and people see tracks and they have to follow them. So they knew it was in there. Matter of fact, the grader drivers used to go in there to camp 'cause it was on a flat bit of ground and there was a dam there for water. I think they took the wheels off it and something else. And that's how tourists started going in there as well, 'cause there were tracks going in there. Now it's all closed.'

Each time he'd seen his old truck over the previous

decade or so there had been more things missing from it. His pity was all the more poignant now because he maintained the belief that, but for the damage to the radiator, the Badger was 'still sorta driveable'.

With the Cub hooked to the Blitz and ready to roll, Dave's crew were anxious to return to Birdsville and parade their prize. Tom Kruse's Leyland Cub had been wrangled from the desert! The labourers, thrilled with their efforts, shouted 'Hooray!' as the replacement wheels turned and the Cub slowly moved from its resting place. The volunteers, filmmakers and spectators climbed back into their vehicles, tired yet elated, and made for Birdsville. The Cub gradually disappeared over the horizon. The sun sank low in the sky, the dust settled, and the Badger sat in silence again.

13

THE COPLEY AFFAIR

'Tom! We've got the Badger!'

'Er, just say again, please?' Tom asked.

'We've got the old Badger . . . at Copley. We went up to Pandie and picked 'er up and she's back down here at Copley,' said the delighted voice at the end of the telephone line.

'What? Ah . . . I'm not quite clear. Look, tell me again, who am I speaking to?'

It was seven o'clock on a Sunday evening, and the call came to the Kruse home completely out of the blue. Tom was having a little trouble comprehending this sudden turn of events. No one had consulted him about another trip to Pandie, let alone any talk of moving the Badger. And now here was some bloke on the phone, obviously pleased with himself, and expecting some expression of gratitude from Tom.

'Well, what the hell do you think you're going to do with it?' Tom enquired

'Ah . . . right . . . well . . . that's something we've got to ask you about,' the man replied.

It was 1993, seven years after the jubilee re-enactment and the public expedition to investigate the remains of the Badger. After the thrill of being toasted for his twenty years as the Birdsville mailman, Tom had returned home to Cumberland Park ready to face household chores and odd jobs. He was gradually becoming used to the leisure time retirement afforded and was settling into his twilight years with customary Tom Kruse style and grace.

The experience of visiting the truck's grave site had kindled a flame in some of the re-enactment participants, though. These men had returned to their homes reinvigorated by the story of Tom and his truck. They waited expectantly for further news.

My father was under the impression that firm plans had been laid for the rescue of the Badger. The Cub had been taken to Adelaide the day after it was towed from Gilpininna and he had expected the Badger to follow suit. He assumed that its restoration was already underway somewhere.

Dave Burge, on the other hand, believed that George Morton, the owner of Pandie Pandie station, intended to transport the Badger to Birdsville. But he never followed up with George and nothing had happened. The Badger remained where it was.

Tom, himself, had thought intermittently over the years about bringing his old truck in from the bush but so far had done nothing about it. It was something he had talked of with friends, but the desire to retrieve it had not yet coalesced into the momentum needed to go and fetch it. He knew, of course, that the Leyland the team had worked so hard to rescue in 1986 was the wrong truck. The Badger was the favourite, with a pedigree and history unmatched by any other. The business of actually venturing out to get her, however, seemed for Tom, to remain an unattainable dream.

'Ah well, we talked about it,' he says. 'But then again, a person'd been talking like that for 40 years!'

Over cups of tea or glasses of beer in his sunroom in Cumberland Park, Tom and his neighbours idly kicked around a plan: They would get the Badger, fix her up, and go for a spin around Australia. Charlie from over the road was going to come, plus a neighbour from down the street and a couple of other blokes from round about. But as time went by, the impetus for the trip began ebbing away. The technical side of the operation seemed almost insurmountable. Inspiration, too, withered, as one by one, Tom's potential travelling companions slipped away.

'The fellow down the street died. He used to love to get away from his wife, if you don't mind me saying. He'd come down the back here, with a packet of cigarettes. I'd get him a couple of bottles of beer. Oh, and he'd suck away,' Tom reminisces. 'But he died. The old chappy up the road, he's passed on. And, old what's'name . . . just over the fence here . . . he's among the flies now, too. They were all gonna come, see.'

But Bob Bilton, far away in Melbourne, was one who would not give up. Although he had never seen the famous Badger, he was enthralled with the idea that it was sitting out there . . . just waiting to be collected. He was determined that *something* should be done. For his Christmas holiday in 1991, he and his wife, Jan, went up to Gilpininna to see the Badger for themselves and gauge the chances of bringing her in. He promised to report back to Tom on what they found.

After five more years in the desert the Badger had deteriorated still further and Bob was alarmed at her state of decay. The weather, time and vandalism had taken their toll. The old truck existed now merely as a decrepit assemblage of wood and metal; a rusty skeleton almost unrecognisable as the automotive star of *The Back of Beyond*.

Upon his return Bob hammered Tom about the disservice being done to the Badger. It was slowly crumbling away, he told him. The unrelenting heat and sun were drying the non-metal components into dust, and people who came across it were blithely helping themselves to bits and pieces of any use. 'If you don't go and get it soon,' he implored Tom, 'there'll be nothing left.'

Under the onslaught of Bob's constant urgings, Tom was eventually stirred into action.

'He was always saying, let's go and get the Badger,' Tom confirms. 'I'd been putting him off for too long and then I said, "Well, we will." I had a couple of old trucks that were still quite roadworthy, and Bob was going to bring his Toyota. We had it all worked out. Then . . . well . . . it never happened.'

The phone call from Copley came instead. It was Peter Ware on the other end of the line.

'We've got the old Badger. It's unloaded and it's in Copley,' he said.

'Well, I know he realised from my tone of voice that they were doing the wrong thing,' Tom says. 'I know I spoke sharply. I was totally dumbfounded.'

Tom had no idea of any rival plan to retrieve the Badger.

The last he knew, it was still sitting at Gilpininna where he'd left it, and where Bob Bilton had seen it two years before. Now he waited for an explanation as to what had become of his truck.

Peter filled him in on the events that had transpired since 1986.

Seven years previously Peter had taken part in the re-enactment journey, forming part of the convoy in his green and yellow Blitz. It was his interest in Blitzes and old trucks and cars in general, that had drawn him to the event and on the side-trip from Birdsville he had eagerly assisted with the rescue of the Leyland Cub.

Some time later, returning from a trip to Kakadu, Peter had stumbled across the Badger again. At that point, he was operating an outback tourism business from Copley in the northern Flinders Ranges, just 4 kilometres north of Leigh Creek. Flooding had closed the Birdsville Track, so he took his group down the old stock route through Pandie Pandie station. Wending his way over the sandhills he happened upon the wreck of the Badger, lonely and forlorn at Gilpininna Dam. Back at Copley, he mentioned his find to a couple of friends and the idea of rescuing the old mail truck was bandied about.

After frequent discussions about the merits of mounting a recovery mission, they finally decided that another look was warranted. The Birdsville races were approaching—they could combine the reconnaissance trip with a jaunt to the famous outback race meeting. Peter, his mate Dave Mills, and John Cooke, the owner of a garage in Copley who could possibly lend some mechanical expertise, composed the team that ventured north.

They returned to Copley with a formidable list of requirements that would have to be met before moving the old Leyland could seriously be considered. Foremost among them was a low-loader upon which the Badger could be transported, and a truck able to tow it. The Badger was far too fragile to be towed over any distance at all on its own chassis, and there were axles, wheels and all other kinds of essential components missing. In addition to suitable tyres and rims to fit to the Badger to make it mobile enough even to mount the low-loader, the team would also need ropes, jacks and a mobile oxy-welding set.

There was by now a specific group of five—christened 'the Copley Crew'—committed to the project: Peter Ware, Lizzie Dodd, and Dave Mills from Copley; Phil Smith from Adelaide; and John Pengilly from Leigh Creek.

During 1992 and early 1993 the group slowly gathered the resources and equipment they would need and began planning the trip. Tom Agnew, self-styled 'Mayor' of Copley and an old friend of Tom's, agreed to lend them a gooseneck low-loader for carting the Badger, and they were able to obtain an old Dodge truck with which to haul it. Lizzie's ute would be the back-up and supply truck. Specialised equipment for moving the Badger was procured in case the old truck's diffs or axles were rusted solid or otherwise immovable. They tried to prepare for every eventuality.

In June 1993 they set off for the recovery mission, heading north to Birdsville, then east to the Gilpininna site. There was no road to speak of once they left the Track so it was a slow journey across scrub and gibbers, navigating as best they could. Sand and creek beds were a nightmare to negotiate with the gooseneck low-loader; progress hampered further still by the fact that the brakes of both truck and trailer failed during the first day. In some places it was faster to walk than drive.

Once the five had located the Badger they set up camp under the only trees they could find in the vicinity—5 kilometres from the work site—then began work on the truck immediately. It had started raining in a constant drizzle and the crew worried that the mission would have to be aborted for fear of bogging if the rainfall got any heavier.

It was backbreaking work in the hot, humid weather, but finally they succeeded in lifting the wreck of the old truck onto the low-loader by shoring up the front of Lizzie's ute and using it to push the Badger along doggedly. It was an interminable process and many tinnies were dispensed with while the Badger crept slowly forward. There was much rejoicing when it was finally in position and strapped down; the low-loader hitched to the Dodge and ready to go.

It was a three-day homeward journey from Gilpininna with the old truck and trailer both feeling the strain. Besides the lack of brakes, the truck's headlights failed, requiring the driver to fiddle constantly with the wiring to keep them illuminated, and the gooseneck trailer struggled to support its load, forcing frequent minor repairs along the way. Thus it was a relieved quintet that crawled into Copley with their precious cargo. They unloaded the Badger at Tom Agnew's place and toasted the success of their mission.

It was sometime later that Peter finally phoned Tom and told him what had happened.

'I was totally dumbfounded,' says Tom. 'Well I was, because when I got off the phone, Valma said, "What's happened now? You seem to be a bit upset with who you were speaking to—you spoke to him pretty sharply.'"

Tom, naturally, was taken aback by this sudden development. The Copley Crew had not asked him—the rightful owner of the Badger—for permission to remove the truck, and ill feelings developed all around. Members of Tom's family were indignant about the unauthorised removal of the truck, and various charges surfaced among some of Tom's supporters that the truck had actually been stolen by the Copley Crew—it seemed that some of the Copley folk preferred that the truck remain there for restoration and were reluctant to see it disappear from under them after all their efforts.

The recovery crew protested that they had done Tom a favour by retrieving the truck and had embarked on their mission with only the best intentions. They failed to see that it was the lack of consultation beforehand that had upset Tom and riled his friends and family.

The Badger sat in Tom Agnew's yard, meanwhile, as the interested parties continued negotiating and debating its future. He, too, was keen for the Badger to stay in Copley, thinking it would become a bit of a tourist drawcard for the town.

Possible homes for the recovered Badger at the Wadlata Outback Centre at Port Augusta or the National Motor Museum at Birdwood were considered. Restoration by a private firm was also proposed. Jim Crawford, the managing director of Commercial Motor Vehicles (CMV) had expressed interest in Tom's Leyland Cub and he was also a potential contender for restoring the Badger. Several years earlier Jim had restored a 1935 Diamond T three-ton tray-top, which the company had sold new to a farmer at Melrose and bought back from him 50 years later. Crawfords (the precursor to CMV) was the company that had originally sold the Badger new to Harry Ding in 1936 and company seniors were obviously interested in seeing the vehicle preserved.

The disputed Leyland was at Copley for about 18 months in the end, before eventually being trucked to Adelaide. It was Tom Kruse who decided to bring it back, and once the decision was made there was no further argument from either side.

Over time, any hostile feelings gradually mellowed or were set aside for the greater common goal of getting the Badger back on its feet. 'We did it . . . not for the glory, but because Tom had long talked about getting the Badger down and we decided that no one else seemed to want to put their words into action,' says John Pengilly, one of the original Copley five.

Looking back, Tom readily admits to being glad that someone else pitched in to get the ball rolling. 'A person gets older and older, slower and slower, crankier and crankier, and once that happens . . . hell, all I know is if it had been left to me it'd still be out in the desert.'

And so, with the arrival of the Badger at a trucking storage yard at Gillman, near Port Adelaide, at the end of 1994, the book was closed on the episode of Badger history forever after referred to as 'the Copley Affair'.

14

THE LEYLAND BADGER
RESTORATION GROUP

The Leyland Badger Restoration Group came to life in a
serendipitous and convoluted way, full of coincidence
and happy circumstance. The core of the team, my father,
Neil, Aynsley Rowe and, of course, Tom, had all attended
the 1986 re-enactment mail run, but none had known the
others then. My father had been introduced to Tom, as had
almost everyone taking part at some stage or another, but he
generally kept a low profile at the time. He had not the
faintest idea, at that stage, that the Badger would evolve into
a project that would consume four years of his life.

In 1993 the Badger was still at Copley when Tom
wandered into the Historic Military Vehicles Museum in Port
Adelaide for a look around. It was only by luck that Neil
was on duty that Sunday. He was delighted to meet Tom
again and they nattered happily about Blitzes and old trucks
and the fate of the Badger. Tom told Neil how the Badger
had been brought in from the desert and that he was

ruminating on the possibility of restoring it. Over the next two years, their friendship blossomed and the kernel of an idea germinated.

Tom was obviously eager to see the derelict Leyland brought back to life and if he was determined enough to embark on such a mammoth project, Neil was willing to pitch in. He had recently retired and this was a worthy task to occupy some of his spare time. Already a fan of *The Back of Beyond*, he had now been captured by Tom's personal charm and wanted to help him fulfil his ambitions in any way he could. At Tom's home in Cumberland Park they had a serious discussion concerning exactly what Tom hoped to achieve and what the project would entail.

Valma remembers that pivotal conversation: Tom was adamant that this would not merely be a 'put-up show', a term he reserves for an artifice—doing something for the sake of appearance. He wanted to drive the Badger around Australia. The old girl would be roadworthy again, not a veneered and impotent museum piece.

My father was more realistic. While Tom entertained images of the Badger 'pushing out smoke' while he sat behind the wheel with a twinkle in his eye, Neil pictured the hours and hours of work ahead of them to get the truck into any kind of driveable condition, not to mention finding rare parts, helpers and the money to pay for it all. Even then, he underestimated the effort involved. But Tom's excitement was contagious and this truck was a treasure. There was only one Leyland-Thornycroft-Tom-Kruse film-star truck and it deserved to be saved. The two men agreed: the Badger would live again. My father gave his word.

By this time the Badger was back in Adelaide. Throughout

1995 Neil wrote letters and made enquiries, trying to find a permanent place to house the vehicle. Tom, meanwhile, began spreading the word, informing his friends and supporters of the proposed plans and seeking helpers and sponsors.

Bob Bilton was delighted at the prospect of some Badger action at last. On a visit to Adelaide he introduced Tom to his mate Aynsley Rowe. Like Neil, Aynsley had been part of the jubilee re-enactment but to Tom they had both been anonymous participants. Bob felt that Aynsley, a qualified motor body builder who had done his apprenticeship at Lawtons in the 1940s, could be a handy addition to the restoration team. Bob discreetly orchestrated a meeting between the two and while Tom sat lamenting the fact that rebuilding the Badger's chassis and motor would be incomplete without a decent overhaul of the cabin, he watched Aynsley willingly step into the void.

Aynsley was not in the habit of freely offering his services for vehicle restoration projects but he, too, recognised the historical significance of the Badger. He was honoured to have a part in it. Re-polishing his old skills would be fun— meticulously shaping the timber to form the cabin interior and carefully following his contours with metal cladding for the exterior. It would be a journey into the past for him.

Tom was overjoyed. Aynsley reckons Tom's grin was so wide at the end of that afternoon that he could hardly fit through the door.

With my father and Aynsley on board, the critical people were in position. Between them, they had the Badger's body, undercarriage and mechanics covered. Tom would repair the engine in his backyard shed at Cumberland Park, Neil would rebuild the chassis and drive mechanism, and Aynsley would construct a new cab. When the South Australian Urban Projects Authority offered a shed to house the Badger in early 1996, the final piece fell into place. The shed was on an allotment of land slated for a new housing development at Northfield, a suburb on Adelaide's northern outskirts 8 kilometres from the city. It was one of several vacant sheds that stood on a rise in the north-eastern corner of the property. Spacious and peaceful, and with a panoramic view all the way to the sea, it was perfect.

On 30 March 1996, Tom and John Clifton, a friend of his with a trucking outfit, loaded the Badger onto a low-loader trailer and towed it to Northfield. Ten years after the abandoned truck was 're-discovered' at Gilpininna dam, the Leyland Badger Restoration Project finally crawled out of the starting gate.

At its new home at Northfield the hull of the old truck rested inauspiciously in the gravel yard while Neil and Aynsley set about making the place presentable.

My father was never one to work in disorderly surroundings. A shed must be clean and tidy and properly equipped—not a place, as some might imagine, simply to stuff old tyres, discarded toys, cobwebby gardening tools and random household junk. To be sure, there were some of those things in Neil's shed at home, but everything had its place and there was an order to it all. Tools hung from gaily painted shadowboards, lending them an artistic style. Axes, long-handled crowbars and a variety of mallets stood to attention in every corner; welding masks, safety glasses and goggles hung from a multitude of hooks; and 'the Clementine

Chamber'—the pit, which bisected the length of the shed and extended out into the yard—was covered with strong wooden planks. Originally these planks were connected into metre-long panels but over time the fastenings had failed, allowing the wooden boards to move individually, popping up and down in sequence as a vehicle's tyres ran over them, creating the disconcerting effect of a giant wooden xylophone.

My father's shed at home was a comfortable mechanical retreat and the Badger's shed at Northfield would be equally organised and functional. He and Aynsley set up the air compressor, an oxy-acetylene welding station and three strong wooden benches with sturdy metal legs. Over the following days, Neil continued shaping his shed away from home. Additional benches and a water tub were installed; hooks and brackets were fixed to the timber frames of the walls; weeds were cleared; the floor was cleaned; and tools were transported from home, including a three-quarter-inch rattle gun, sockets, crowbars, chisels, jacks and an arc-welding machine.

Two weeks passed before a hand was laid upon the object of all this preparation. In the style of all great chroniclers, my father had furnished a logbook in which to record daily events at the shed. A slim leather diary for 1996 was the first of four volumes of logbooks in which every step of the Badger's rehabilitation was duly noted.

Monday April 15, 1996
IN AT 11.00 AM. INSTALLED HOOK, REMOVED LOOSE CAB TIMBER, STARTED FREEING CAB FROM CHASSIS. OUT AT 1.30 PM.

Thursday April 18, 1996
IN AT 8.15 AM. REMOVED NEARSIDE DOOR &
STEERING WHEEL & KEY. OUT AT 10.05 AM.

Friday April 26, 1996
IN AT APPROX 11.00 AM. REMOVED RIGHT-
HAND GUARD & THROTTLE LINK. BRAKE
PEDAL & DRIVING LAMP TOO HARD.
CLEARED WEEDS EAST END. OUT AT 4.20 PM.

Saturday April 27, 1996
IN AT 11 AM. REMOVED BRAKE PEDAL &
DRIVING LAMP. REMOVED LEFTHAND FRONT
WHEEL & MUDGUARD, ALSO BOTH FRONT
(TRIANGLE) CAB BRACE BRACKETS. OUT AT
4.00 PM.

Tuesday April 30, 1996
IN AT 9:45 AM. FINISHED RELEASING CAB
MOUNTINGS. COULD NOT REMOVE
GEARSHIFT LEVER. OUT AT 3:30 PM.

On 1 May 1996, Neil, Tom, Aynsley and a handful of helpers
gathered at the shed to lift the cabin from the body of the
Badger. Then Neil used the crane on his Austin truck to move
the Badger indoors. It was the first time the truck had been
undercover since it rolled out of the factory 60 years before.
'Our best day yet,' my father recorded with satisfaction.

The cab went home with Aynsley. 'By the time I got it,
there was virtually nothing left,' he says. 'Every time you
touched the body more fell off, and I hardly got much of it
[back to my workshop]. But you could sorta picture what it

used to be like, and we did have some photos that gave a bit of an idea. And the main thing—I had one full door and that's what I built it from.

'I couldn't quite get the shape of the roof because the bows were all cracked and there were bits missing. But I had the cant rails—those two shaped panels that go from the top of the door up to the roof. They were the only two panels that were original from the truck and they are the only two pieces of the old body that's on there now—the cant rail panels.'

While Aynsley cut lengths of Australian oak in his shed at home for the interior-lining of the cab, work at the Badger shed progressed steadily. In those early days, Frank Eckert was my father's only consistent helper. The two had met through their mutual involvement in the Military Vehicles Collectors' Society and had become friends. Frank is garrulous and cheerful, compensating for his deteriorating hearing with boundless conversational enthusiasm. Not being a natural mechanic, he made himself a willing apprentice and Neil gratefully guided him in stripping down the Badger.

Together they removed the tail shaft, centre bearings and brake pipes from the old truck. Both hydrovac units, the gearbox and the four rear hubs were progressively removed and the only remaining original drive axle was eased from its housing. Some things came apart easily; others required much patient coaxing before nuts, bolts and screws that had doggedly held their position for years would release their grip. Neil gave directions loudly and Frank adapted with intuition when hearing failed him. As autumn turned towards the short, grey days of winter, the Badger slowly disintegrated under their hands.

●

The automotive mosaic that the truck had become during its lifetime, combined with the abuse it had suffered over twenty years of harsh outback conditions made repairing it a slow and challenging task. Even before the group reached the repair stage there were some unconventional construction elements for the restorers to contend with.

Separating the two rear drive axles and their four supporting leaf springs that composed the Thornycroft rear bogie from the chassis that Tom had made in the 1940s was a difficult job that took several weeks to complete. Some of the pins connecting the springs to the chassis had been fixed by weld, which had to be cut. Others were corroded in place. Long bolts securing the bogie frame to the chassis were wedged into blind holes, so they couldn't be simply hammered out backwards from their housing. Makeshift grips had to be welded to these bolts so they could be extracted like giant teeth.

Often Neil worked alone at the Badger shed; his logbook sprinkled with the entry 'no helpers today'. Tom popped in regularly but he was devoting most of his spare time to the engine, spending contented hours in his little shed at home, patiently dismantling the motor, calmly cleaning and mending. Neil was careful to keep Tom informed of the progress on the chassis and didn't make any major decisions without consulting him.

By the end of June the naked chassis was sitting on a temporary frame so that workers could attend to it at a comfortable waist-height. Tom's homemade chassis was extremely strong but it had few cross members to stiffen it. Over time, as the suspension sagged, great gouges had appeared in the structural steel where the trunnion bearing pins at the ends of the springs constantly rubbed. All of these scrapes and holes had to be filled with weld and ground until smooth.

The four rear suspension springs were also in various states of disrepair. Some of the ten individual leaves that formed each spring were cracked or broken in half and had to be welded back together. All of them needed the rust knocked or ground off and general cleaning.

Once all the components were cleaned, repaired and painted, and Neil and Frank began putting the first spring back together, another problem revealed itself—two special seats for the U-clamps were missing. 'No worries,' said Tom. He devised a clever method to bind the first three spring leaves using two temporary ligatures of sheet steel. Widely recognised as a master of bush engineering, Tom's ingenuity still bubbled, even in suburban Adelaide.

More physical evidence of Tom's outback inventiveness came to light as work on the Badger progressed. The pipe that carries fuel from the tank to the filter and into the fuel injection pump was a masterpiece of innovation. Constant vibration had chafed the pipe to such an extent that one day all the fuel simply leaked away. Tom fastened the two sections of pipe together with fencing wire and secured it with bronze he melted from a .303 cartridge shell and dribbled over the join.

'Tell you what, 303 bullets . . . if you go up and down the road there . . . there used to be tons,' he says. 'A cartridge case or a bit of bronze rod . . . same material. Hell, the casing's better than a welding rod 'cause you didn't need the flux. And there's thousands and thousands of the damn things lying around. Driving over them, sometimes you'd find the bloody cartridge stuck into a tyre.

'They wanted to exterminate the horses, see,' Tom says, explaining why so many spent bullets were strewn around the Track. 'Hell, that country used to be full of them, absolutely thousands and thousands of them, especially on the inside road. A mob of brumbies . . . might be twelve or fifteen in the bunch . . . two and six a head for the ears. Big dollars.'

Another of Tom's make-do fix-it jobs was called for when the petrol pump failed in his Land Rover. He bypassed the fuel pump and made a gravity-fed system by mounting a can of petrol on the roof, making a hole in the bonnet and running a hose to the carburettor. He drove for kilometres this way, petrol trickling down in a stream in front of him.

By the end of September, the Badger's rear springs were finally reassembled, refitted to reclaimed yokes, and then reattached to new trunnion pins. Neil's logbook entry conveys some of the frustration and the tedium that the four-month job had entailed:

Thursday, September 26, 1996

IN AT 9:30. TOM ARRIVED ABOUT 10 AM. BY 2:30 PM WE HAD FITTED THE LAST OF THE DREADED BOGIE SUSPENSION PINS SO NOW ALL FOUR REAR SPRINGS AND BOTH REAR AXLES ARE ASSEMBLED. (PHOTO TAKEN) OUT 6:10 PM.

This short, simple entry belies the hours and hours of welding and grinding and tireless rebuilding that went into the reconstruction of the springs. And this was just a fraction of the time and energy expended on the Badger's back end. It was all work that would be invisible on the final product and sometimes my father couldn't help wondering if it was all worth it. Could it be wasted effort?

'I wasn't sure we were even going to drive the truck. I didn't know whether we'd live long enough to ever finish it,' he confesses. 'But I thought, if we work on it as long as we can, if we have to give up, at least it's reached a stage where people won't take it to the dump . . . That we'd pass a point where someone surely would be interested in going on and finishing it and it wouldn't be scrapped. That was my hope.'

As the rear bogie neared completion and winter turned to spring, members of the restoration team began turning their attention to other Badger work. Neil and Tom broke down the front and rear differential units, dismantled the brakes and began restoring the front springs. Machining and reconditioning jobs they couldn't manage between them or their helpers they farmed out to local automotive businesses.

Tom had recently begun spending more time at the Northfield workshop, working on the Badger's wheels and front axle because his work on the engine had slowed to a halt, held up by the constant scavenger hunt for parts.

The truck's original wheels had all vanished out in the desert. While the Copley Crew had used a rag-tag assortment of wheels to get the Badger mobile enough to move it from Gilpininna, the restorers elected to fit Blitz wheels on the Badger's Thornycroft hubs. It was a straightforward substitution, and one that Tom would have done if he were undertaking the repair himself in his backyard in Marree. Tom had preferred the Blitz wheels when the truck was in service because they were strong and because they separated into two halves, making roadside tyre replacements easier. The Blitz wheels were held together by ⅞th inch bolts, the same bolts railway workers used to join sections of rail together. This fact further bolstered their desirability in Tom's eyes—there was a plentiful supply of those bolts going begging in the bush and, what's more . . . they were free.

Removing truck tyres from rusty rims can be an almost impossible task but Tom had done it many times before and displayed the trick he'd invented with wedges to budge the recalcitrant tyres. The wheels were then sandblasted to remove rust, and painted black before they received a set of second-hand, hard-to-come-by 9 × 20 tyres.

Whatever the task for the day, whatever difficult job needed doing, Tom was always the first to step forward. My father watched him manhandle and wrestle with heavy, rusted axles or rims, then spend hours standing, immobile, at the workbench, completely absorbed in a tiny shim or seal that needed minor tweaking. He admired the enthusiasm and stamina of his older workmate.

'For a man of 85 Tom was doing amazing things,' he marvels. 'Restoring trucks is not like restoring your car—the parts are heavy—and in this truck, very heavy. We did a lot of disassembly, a lot of lifting, and Tom never let up . . . The heaviest job, he never shirked anything . . . Manhandling gas cylinders, bashing tyres off old rims with a sledgehammer . . . I've seen him lying on his back, drilling big holes in the bottom of the chassis with hot metal chips falling over him. He'd be oxy-cutting with the oxy torch and there'd be hot sparks and molten metal flying. He doesn't wear glasses and quite often he'd have no goggles or any protection when he was doing these things—that was always a worry to me. I s'pose he's got away with it for so many years that he feels that he always will. But nothing daunted him in the slightest. He was a marvellous inspiration.'

In November, George Maze, a sales manager from Leyland Motors in England, toured the Badger workshop. He had heard about the mail-truck project through one of his Adelaide agents and was keen to see this remarkable 60-year-old vehicle for himself. Tom was excited by his visit because George offered his help in trying to find a timing chain for the engine. The timing chain was a particularly unusual one and Tom had had no luck trying to locate one in Australia. George left promising to send one out.

Many months passed with no word from George, so Tom became rather anxious. He couldn't reassemble the engine without the timing chain. Polite enquiries to Leyland UK revealed that George was just about to commission one to be specially made, when he happened to stumble upon a motor dealer who had an original Leyland timing chain still sitting in its box. This was a marvellous stroke of luck.

Almost a year after George's visit the chain finally arrived, complete with original instruction leaflet. It was a satisfying day for Tom when he watched Neil wind the chain between sprockets and snake it around the water pump, generator and fuel injection pump.

In the weeks approaching Christmas, Tom, Neil and Frank continued cleaning, repairing and fitting tyres, tubes and wheels. They worked on hub seals and bearings; axle seals and collars; and brake shoes, hubs, and back plates.

With the temperature rising to 34 degrees Celsius the

galvanised-iron shed where the men toiled on grew hot and airless. Tom was oblivious to the heat; he'd endured worse—changing tyres and repairing broken parts in furnace-like conditions with the sun beating at his back, flies in his eyes and dust in everything. Out there, in the middle of Australia, it wasn't like this at all. There was no shade for relief from the sun's fiery glare; there was no fridge for cool refreshments or electric kettle for ready cups of tea; there was no company or friendly conversation from interested onlookers; and there was no smooth cement floor to catch errant nuts or bolts that slipped from one's fingers. Out there, a dropped component was beyond retrieval in seconds, lost in the burning sand for good.

Friday 20 December was my father's final logbook entry for 1996. The first year of the Badger's resurrection was behind them. Neil and Tom and their helpers had made a solid start on reclaiming the Badger's back end; Tom was making headway with the engine; and Aynsley had the cabin in hand. Five days before Christmas, it was time to take a break from the shed.

Labouring on the front and rear bogies, the wheels, hubs, axles and brakes, the two diffs and the engine consumed most of 1997. Tom finished reassembling both diffs and the restorers mounted them in position and began connecting them to the front and rear axles.

The engine was also nearing completion. Neil, along with Eric Deer, an old friend of his who had become a regular member of the restoration team, helped Tom with the finishing touches, and they transported the finished motor back to the Badger shed. Within days, the gaskets, oil filter and exhaust manifold were fitted and the diffs and engine were filled with oil. Tom was eager to test his handiwork and see his engine run.

'Tomorrow is likely to be a working day at the Northfield shed,' my father wrote to me on 1 January 1998. 'We will soon be starting the diesel engine, God willing.'

It was an exciting time for the Badger restorers. Tom and my father were hopeful that their work of the previous few months on the old mail truck's motor would soon see it operational. Tom had spent many hours bent over the engine in his small, backyard workshop, and he and his helpers had devoted several days to fitting the injection pipes and modifying the drive couplings. Hearing it finally roar to life was a reward they anticipated eagerly.

On 2 January, Neil was back at the shed as expected. He spent the morning skimming the weeds that had accumulated over the Christmas break, sweeping the floor and attending to general housekeeping chores. He then turned his attention to the Badger—specifically to her engine. The original Leyland Motors timing mark was set at exactly 28 degrees. He meshed the pump as best he could to achieve 28 degrees injection timing and, tentatively, hopefully, tried starting her up. 'Smoke but no firing,' he noted in the logbook.

A week later there was a second attempt to get the old girl to go. Tom, Neil and Reg Donoghue—a diesel expert who had helped Neil in bending the thick-walled, high-pressure fuel injection pipes into their required intricate shapes—gathered at the shed on Friday morning. Neil made a new pump drive coupling while Reg and Tom used a grease gun to squirt a litre or so of oil into the engine oil gallery.

Then they gave it a whirl. The engine wanted to fire; it almost fired, yet stubbornly refused to turn over. 'We found gas leaking from injector copper washers so next attempt will be after replacing these with correct ones,' my father entered in his logbook.

On Monday morning, 12 January, they congregated at the shed once more.

'When the engine started—for the first time in about 40 years—there was 80 psi oil pressure and a good supply to the rocker gear. No rattles or oil leaks,' the logbook entry read.

This was a restrained recording of the day's events. The men were thrilled to hear the engine rumbling along steadily. The sound of the Leyland motor springing to life seemed to bring the reality of the Badger's resurrection one step closer.

'The sound of music,' Tom says. 'No it was. Errr, Errr, Errr . . . and away she goes. No that's right. Fair dinkum. Totally unbelievable. She had the same beat. They had a sound of their own, Leylands . . . a real humming. I think it was a shrouded valve. If you heard a Leyland coming in the distance, you could pick them. You'd say, I bet that's a Leyland. I remember it really well.'

With the engine operational the restorers began to focus on the Badger's transmission. Tom had been working intermittently on the two gearboxes at home and now Neil joined him for a couple of weeks to complete the job.

The Thornycroft joey box was in a poor state of repair. The extent of the damage glaringly revealed that the Badger, effectively, had had no low range in its latter years. Tom used to keep a strap around the gearstick to prevent it from jumping out of gear when in high range but the system wasn't failsafe and eventually the teeth were stripped back to their base. Eight teeth on the gearwheel had been reduced to stubs, and had to be rebuilt by hand with arc-welded steel. The end of the gearshift lever was also worn away so Neil painstakingly built it back to size with layers of molten nickel bronze.

While the tasks of patiently bending and fitting brake pipes and overhauling the steering box continued at the Northfield work site, the Badger's refurbished radiator was taking shape at Cumberland Park under the experienced hands of Tom's yodelling English neighbour, Charlie. Although they were different in many ways, Charlie Stevenson and Tom were of the same vintage and they had become good friends. Charlie often popped into the Kruse home, looking to lend a hand with any odd jobs on the go. He had built a new letterbox for Tom, and put his coach-building skills to good use refurbishing the interior of Tom's station wagon when it burst into flames one night in front of his house. Tom was unconcerned with the sooty damage. 'I said to Charlie, look here, don't worry about it. Leave it as it is . . . keeps the mosquitoes away.'

In his tiny home workshop Charlie worked for months, carefully clamping bits of metal in place and delicately tapping them with a rubber mallet, diligently shaping all the thin metal flanges and heat deflectors that formed the Leyland grille. Once the radiator was finished, he began making the Badger's bonnet and engine cowlings, moulding the shapes from a photograph and a single piece of the original metal panelling. He was thrilled to be part of the Badger's restoration and to have the opportunity once again to display the metal-working skills that had earned him first prize for the whole of Surrey at the age of thirteen.

With some of the major jobs such as the back end, the engine and transmission behind them, the restorers began to focus on the myriad smaller chores, such as the fuel tank and bash-plate; the engine fan, muffler and exhaust system; the running boards, front fender and mudguards; and the cooling system. Days and weeks were consumed in endless benchwork as the autumn days diffused into an Indian summer. Each part was important and necessary in its own right, but Tom was anxious to give the Badger a test run. He was itching to leapfrog some of these cosmetic jobs and see if the old girl would go. Had all their work been successful? Would she hang together?

Tuesday 14 July 1998 was the day the Badger ran under its own steam for the first time in 40 years. Tom was in his element. He sat tall atop an upturned, yellow plastic milk crate and gleefully guided the naked chassis down the driveway. While my father motored sedately during his turn at the test drive, gingerly double-declutching, carefully braking and accelerating, Tom whirled the Badger's undercarriage round the yard in a joyful cloud of smoke like a kid riding an overgrown go-kart. He was gamely undeterred by the contraption's uncertain ability to come to a halt—the Badger's brakes had always been feeble at best—he was simply completely thrilled to be driving it again. His delighted expressions confirmed for Neil that all the effort to date had been worthwhile.

'Well. Totally unbelievable,' Tom says, his blue eyes opening wide as he relives the moment. 'We made up a bit of a seat for kick-off, just to see how she'd perform. She was a bit heavy in the head, o'course—hard to steer. But she always was, without a load . . . especially in sand—she'd wanna sink. We used to say, "Going down, Sir. Going down."'

After the exhilaration of the Badger's first test run, it was back to the usual routine for the remainder of July. Throughout winter and spring, Neil and Tom worked on the hand-brake assembly and the starter motor, and sought out door locks, windows and other hardware for Aynsley, who had almost finished the cabin.

They also entertained some important visitors to the shed. A trio from the National Motor Museum came to inspect the Badger, followed by a visit to Aynsley's house to view progress on the cab. By the end of the day the vehicle's future was assured. The truck would reside at the museum in Birdwood in the Adelaide hills when restoration was complete.

Neil was relieved to know that someone else would be taking responsibility for the Badger's upkeep; that she would be undercover and on display for everyone to admire. However, it was ultimately Tom's decision as to where the Badger would end up. It was his truck and he had largely paid for its rehabilitation. But he, too, was happy with the offer of housing at Birdwood. There, the Badger would be in an appropriate place for everyone to enjoy it. This vehicle was now much more than Tom's favourite truck; it had grown into a national icon and Tom recognised that it should be accessible to all. It needed to be located where *The Back of Beyond* fans, Leyland afficionados, history buffs and Australiana connoisseurs alike could all share in it, not to mention the restorers themselves, and Tom's own friends and family. The opportunity to display the truck at the motor museum deftly resolved the quandary of how to satisfy all these interests before it became a gigantic headache for him.

By the end of the year the new cabin was on, resplendent in a coat of rich green with yellow signwriting across the doors. With the cab repositioned on the chassis frame the truck began to resemble the Badger of old. Aynsley had done a wonderful job in constructing the cabin—so good, in fact, that it risked putting the rest of the truck to shame. Neil and Tom's handiwork was neat and presentable, but most of that would be hidden once the entire truck was assembled. Of the highly visible components, Charlie's radiator grille was outstanding and Aynsley's cabin was impressive—but the Badger's replacement tray was an eyesore.

Long ago, Neil and Tom had procured a rather decrepit ex-Ford tray for the Badger, but now, with the rest of the truck looking so glamorous, Tom began to second-guess their decision: a new tray would look so much nicer.

Aynsley, too, was considering the topic of the tray. He was a little reluctant to have his handsome new cab followed by a raggedy, hand-me-down tray-top. It seemed a shame to pair the one with the other.

'It looks nice, doesn't it, with all the new paint, and that,' Aynsley remarked, critically circling the Badger's cabin after the painting was complete.

'Totally lovely,' Tom agreed. 'Look, bit of a pity about that old tray . . . a total waste . . . with the cabin, you know . . . like giving fruit salad to pigs.'

'Well a tray body's not much. You get me the timber and the iron and I'll build you a new one,' Aynsley quickly responded. Constructing a tray was a much simpler task than the job of fabricating the cabin with all its accoutrements.

If Aynsley was willing to do it, Tom needed little persuading. He took Aynsley's measurements and requirements to a timber yard and secured a quote of $1100 for materials. Within a month the Badger had a new tray.

During the first half of the new year, 1999, my father and his helpers worked on the brake and throttle linkages, installed the accelerator pedal into the floor frame, and designed the hand-brake lever mounting. The hand-brake was fashioned from scratch using Blitz parts—since the hybridisation with the Thornycroft in 1939 the Badger had managed without one. He and Tom also worked on the bonnet latches and began making brackets and fitting lamps to the tray. They installed the steering column and started painting and wiring the rear combination lamps. Sometimes Aynsley joined them at the shed, working on interior furnishings such as the cabin floor, seat, windscreen and doors.

The restorers were also informed that the Badger could stay at the Northfield site until July 2000. By tremendous good fortune their initial one-year lease had stretched to three years and would see them through the entire restoration project—until the revamped Badger was safely ensconced at the Birdwood museum.

In June 1999, a visitor from Newcastle arrived to do the Badger's wiring. Don McNair had spent his working life as an auto-electrician—wiring buses during the Second World War, when everything had to be made by hand. But Don's real passion was botany. During one of his plant-collecting forays into the outback he had met John Hammond, the proprietor of the Mungerannie roadhouse hotel and custodian of an old AEC Matador. When Don learned that the AEC was one of Tom's, he offered to do the necessary rewiring—he'd done hundreds of them before and would be pleased to do it for an original Kruse truck.

Like many Australians of his era, Don knew the Tom Kruse mythology. He had loved *The Back of Beyond*, and he also remembered reports of Tom's expedition to recover the Badger in 1986. Once John Hammond had told him about the Badger restoration project underway in Adelaide, Don decided to drop by for a gander.

Back in September 1998 when he had first visited the shed, the Badger was still merely an engine on wheels. But once Don saw the quality of the restoration in progress he immediately offered to return in the future to do the wiring.

There began an exchange of letters between kindred spirits. It was wiring by remote control. Don wrote from Newcastle requesting dash panel measurements. Neil replied with his calculated wiring distances. Don sent designs and wiring paths, and Neil pasted them on a board in the shed for easy reference. The two men were like-minded, meticulous souls and enjoyed their auto-electrical correspondence.

When all was ready, Don came to Adelaide and he and Neil crawled all over the truck, attaching the wires and connecting them up. After so long communicating by phone and letter they took great pleasure in their face-to-face working camaraderie. For Don, his time with the Badger restorers was precious. 'It was one of the greatest seven days I've spent with men in my life,' he says. 'They were all gentlemen. No matter where you turned there was someone there to help you or to talk about it—from your Dad, to the man who built the cabin, to the gentleman who did the radiator. It was really a dream.'

Soon after Don reluctantly returned home, the Badger had its first road test. With new licence plates attached and the special registration decal in place, Neil and Tom were able to take the Badger onto the street for the first time. Tom took Valma and Helen for a ride the next day and from that moment on, the floodgates were open. Every shed visitor hoped for a private ride in the Badger with the mailman of the Birdsville Track.

At the same time, general interest in and excitement over the old truck had started to escalate. Word was spreading that there was to be another re-enactment—the ultimate re-enactment: Tom and the Badger together again on the Birdsville Track. The promoters pitched it as the *pièce de résistance* of the Badger's restoration.

Once again, Dave Burge was in the driver's seat. Since the Jubilee 150 re-enactment in 1986 he had maintained sporadic contact with Tom, stopping by his home whenever he was in town. Dave knew that the Leyland had been rescued from Gilpininna and was supposedly being restored somewhere, but he'd lost touch with the specifics. In early 1998 he popped into the Northfield shed for a look and an update. It was the first time he'd seen it since 1986 and he was, as he says, 'gobsmacked'.

From then on, Dave monitored the progress more closely. 'Tom, you know we're going to have to do another trip when it's finished,' he told him after viewing the latest advances in the Badger's rebirth.

'Right, Dave. You dream up a so and so . . .' Tom replied.

He was keen to take the Badger out for a spin when she was finished—sort of a last hurrah for both of them—but he didn't have any definite ideas about what should be done or any real inclination to orchestrate a big public event. And anyway, in 1998, going for a trip in the Badger still seemed a long way off. It wasn't Tom's style to rush into anything.

But now, a year later, with the Badger nearing completion, it was clearly time to put some plans in place. A film crew from Melbourne had homed in on the Badger's story and the thought of competing interests stirred Dave Burge into action. After receiving a vague go-ahead from Tom he formed a re-enactment committee, drew up a schedule of events and announced a date: Tom and the Badger would drive from Birdsville to Marree on the Labour Day long weekend, 2–4 October, 1999.

The announcement startled my father. Suddenly there was a deadline. The Leyland Badger Restoration project that had trundled along steadily for three and a half years in serene isolation now had to be ready for a grand public unveiling in just five months' time. The comfortable, unencumbered, companionable little world that he and Tom had inhabited was suddenly invaded by television crews, event planners and other organisers. At the shed there were still many small jobs to contend with. The frequency of general visitors increased, too, as excitement about the re-enactment and the Badger's unveiling spread.

Monday 2 August 1999 was the official completion date of the restoration of Tom Kruse's 1936 Leyland Badger. 'The most exciting day of the project so far,' my father wrote in his logbook. Installing the new wooden tray onto the resurrected truck's waiting chassis was the last major task in the Badger's rehabilitation and 30 or so workers, supporters and media people had congregated at the shed for the occasion. Aynsley's tray had been propped up on petrol drums until the Badger was ready to receive it: today was the day the old Leyland would proudly shoulder its load.

The men surrounded the wooden platform and fourteen pairs of hands reached for a hold. Gripping the black metal railing around the edge, they shuffled forward under its weight and carried it inside the shed to where the Badger stood in its customary spot in the centre. They carefully guided the tray forward and slid it onto the truck's metal frame, where it settled easily in position. It was an inspiring moment. With the gleaming, polished planks on its back the Badger sprang to life.

Six weeks later Neil placed the Lord Nelson lamp in position, high on the Badger's cab on the driver's side. It was one of the very last pieces to be installed.

Of all the trucks Tom had driven during his years as the Birdsville mailman, this one was special. He reflects on it fondly, like he would a firm mate or a loyal dog. When he first drove the Badger it was only a year or two out of the showroom. When he last drove it, it was little more than a relic . . . a workhorse on wheels that he eventually used as a stationary loading platform, and finally abandoned altogether in the desert 50 kilometres from Birdsville.

Tom thought of how the old Leyland had metamorphosed in the years he had known it—from the shiny, red Badger fresh from the factory to the rangy, green mongrel that he'd gradually adapted to service by adding and modifying parts;

and finally to the sunburnt and rusted carcass that had been hauled in from the desert.

But now here she was, back on her feet and sparkling like a new pin. What a challenge it had been to bring her back to life, Tom thought to himself. What a thrill!

He gazed at her admiringly, stuffing his cloth hat in his pocket, resting his hand on the front mudguard and quietly soaking up the hubbub and excitement generated by her rebirth.

The new Badger was not a restoration of the original truck that had rolled out of Lawtons more than half a century before. It was a chimera of original and rebuilt and newly fashioned components, suffused with the spirit of Tom's old mail truck. Over the years that Tom had had the Badger he had modified the Leyland and Thornycroft parts and cannibalised bits and pieces from other trucks at whim. The restored Badger was simply a bona fide extension of the Kruse guide to the mechanical arts—if you can't get the original part, cobble together something that will do the job.

The new Badger had wheel-bearing seals that Tom had shimmed at Northfield from the lid of a biscuit tin; it had the original gearbox from a Thornycroft wrecked in 1939; it had wheels from an old Blitz—the Badger's frequent understudy truck on the Birdsville Track; it had the genuine Leyland radiator, gussied up with traditional craftsmanship; it had a brand-new Leyland timing chain imported from England; and it had a starting handle that Tom had created from a lump of steel he'd found in his backyard shed. It definitely was *not* Harry Ding's original Leyland Badger . . . But it most certainly *was* Tom Kruse's authentic Birdsville Track Badger. And Tom was delighted to make her acquaintance again.

15

THE MAIL RUN RE-ENACTMENT

With the Badger complete and ready for its final run, my father spent the last few days prior to the big event preparing her load. An array of empty 44-gallon drums, wooden crates, wheat bags and swags created a convincing rendition of the Badger cargo that people fondly remembered from *The Back of Beyond.* An armchair and dressmaker's dummy, just like John Heyer had arranged for his film back in 1952, completed the effect.

The schedule of events called for the Badger to be trucked to Birdsville and offloaded a few kilometres south of town in order for Tom to motor in to a hero's welcome on Friday 1 October, the first day of the official event. After a day in town sorting the mail and festivities that evening, the official re-enactment convoy would depart for Marree on Saturday morning with Tom once again at the wheel. The party would camp the first night at Mungerannie and the second in the bed of the Cooper, where celebrations would include an auction to raise money for the Royal Flying Doctor Service, music, fireworks and a screening of *The Back of Beyond*.

The Badger was not expected to drive the entire length of the Birdsville Track. Tom would captain it at certain strategic points, but the remainder of the time it would be carried on the low-loader, for it would be a slow journey following the Badger all the way down the Track. The restored truck had been carefully overhauled but no amount of loving attention would succeed in getting her engine to exceed its traditional top speed of 40 kilometres per hour. Furthermore, there was no need to risk damage to the truck by having it drive more than necessary. The sturdy little vehicle that epitomised the beginnings of the road-transport era would spend much of its time being chauffeured on the back of one of its modern-day counterparts.

A herd of brumbies gazed from the side of the road and the dusty plain slid by in a neverending continuum as the re-enactment contingent travelled to Birdsville. A tour bus company had been engaged to ferry Badger fans from Adelaide to Birdsville and back. Tom and Valma were onboard, along with my parents, Neil and Jennifer Weidenbach; Aynsley and his wife, Cynthia; Charlie and Olive Stevenson; Frank and Yvonne Eckert; and many other members of the restoration team. Passengers ranged from those directly involved in the event, such as Tom and the restorers, through Kruse family members and relatives, to interested Australians who had heard about it through the media and were keen to take part in the Badger's final run. I had joined the outback cavalcade, travelling in the family Toyota Landcruiser with my brother, Julian.

Tom relaxed in his bus seat, letting the views of his cherished outback wash over him once more. Every now and then he pointed out a landmark to those around him—the site of Mrs Morley's drovers' store at Mirra Mitta bore, for instance—gesturing confidently toward a stretch of desert that looked as nondescript as any other to his city-dwelling companions. As the bus approached the south-eastern outskirts of Birdsville he reminisced about the times the Diamantina was in flood and how he'd had to negotiate his way into town by boat, slapping away the snakes that tried to find purchase on the oars and climb aboard. The old culvert of the original crossing point was now abandoned in favour of a smart new bridge. In the dry times, Tom would have crossed the river at Goyder Lagoon and entered the town from the south-western side, the post office and hotel his first signs of habitation.

It was late afternoon on 30 September 1999 when the buses transporting the participants drew into Birdsville—a cluster of houses, a handful of small businesses and a sprinkling of short, wide streets. In a far cry from Tom's mail-run days when twenty or so residents gathered to greet the mailman, 120 people now called Birdsville home. Adelaide Street—what once had been a mere continuation of the rutted, dirt Birdsville Track—was now a sealed road transecting the town from east to west. A dusty airfield abutted the north-western end of the town. Light aircraft sat with their noses pointing across the road to the famous Birdsville Hotel. We all headed toward the Diamantina River billabong, pulling into the Birdsville Caravan Park where the next day a big, red banner proclaiming 'The Mail Truck's Last Run', would hang over the entrance.

That afternoon, sitting in the back seat of our car in the visible cloud of dust that had breezed in through the Toyota's gaps and worn door seals, I'd suddenly realised why Tom has such a distinctive squint; why a glimpse of his vivid blue eyes is such a rare surprise. His facial expression had adjusted to constant besiegement by sand and dust and flies and settled into a permanent peering squint. Even against the fierce glare of the sun, reducing his eyes to slits and pulling a hat down low onto his forehead were his only defence. Sunglasses, tinted glass, *windows* even, were deluxe accessories that Tom Kruse had no call for. Under the influence of the outback elements the smooth, chubby face of Tom's wedding photo— a dimple in the centre of his chin and an unlined brow—have gracefully weathered to a tanned, careworn visage—hooded eyes, skin of surprisingly few wrinkles, and a permanent expression of unflappability and peace.

The next day, Friday 1 October, Tom was to drive the mail truck ceremonially into Birdsville. The Badger was offloaded by the racetrack on the outskirts of town and the large, maroon tarpaulin whisked from its back to reveal the higgledy-piggledy load. Atypically it had begun to rain, a soft, warm drizzle that didn't interrupt proceedings but was anomalous to the weather we had expected to encounter on the fringes of the Simpson Desert. The small posse of helpers surrounded the truck, their shirts growing damp from rain and sweat as they untied ropes and bundled up the tarp.

Tom pushed the starter button and the Badger fired with the familiar bursts of grey smoke that emanated from the exhaust pipe exiting behind the cab on the passenger side. With a couple of enthusiastic cranks of the horn, Tom was off. Four-wheel-drives converged and overtook the Badger from both sides as my father, Dave Burge, Tom's son Phillip and the other men hurried back to town to join those waiting to greet Tom and the Badger.

The cars and utes soon disappeared ahead, as the Badger ambled along at a cruising speed of 30 kilometres per hour. It was still spitting. Small jets of water shot up from the road as the new 9 × 20s rolled along. The windscreen wipers swung like pendulums from the top of each window, moving rhythmically across the panes. The Brunswick Green bonnet steamed down the road like a stately ship, Charlie's grille gleaming regally in front. Tom's contented smile, reflected in the driver's mirror, was spotted with rain drops.

The truck passed over a cattle grid on the edge of the settlement, entering the more concentrated stretch of houses and single-storey buildings that signalled the centre of downtown Birdsville. Parked cars lined the main street, and small knots of people stood on the footpath and on the median strip in the centre of the road, smiling, clapping and waving at Tom. He acknowledged each wave with a sound of the horn. At the service station, a group of 100 or so fans cheered his arrival, giving the famous man and his truck a rousing reception. All the key players were there: Bob Bilton; Aynsley Rowe; Eric Deer; Frank Eckert; my father; and Charlie Stevenson, with tears streaming down his face and 'a lump in his throat the size of an orange'. The little tin shed that used to be the Birdsville Post Office was now an odd-looking, pale-blue plaster-board appendage to the fuel station. Tom made his grand entrance by sounding the horn a few dozen times and drawing to a halt beside the petrol bowsers. The Badger's motor sputtered to a stop.

During this scheduled rest day in Birdsville the re-enactment participants were left to entertain themselves. People strolled up and down the main street and walked over to the Birdsville Working Museum. If you were in the right place at the right time, the Badger appeared, running errands, and people were able to inspect the truck or perhaps hitch a ride from one street to another. Each time one caught a glimpse of the Badger it had figures clinging to it like an army of sticky bush flies. People scrambled over the load and found precarious perches among scratchy wheat sacks and sharp-cornered wooden boxes. Always, one quick-footed passenger would triumphantly gain the summit and be seen riding in style in the armchair on top of the load. One or two others would wave out the window from the wide bench seat inside the cab.

The Badger had carried a couple of precious cargo items from Adelaide that now had to be distributed in Birdsville. Aynsley's daughter-in-law, artist Suzanne Brierley-Westall, had painted Tom's portrait and the painting had to be unloaded for display during the evening celebrations. Tom had bequeathed the two remaining pieces from the Badger's original cabin—the passenger-side door and the nameplate from the head of the cab—to the Birdsville Museum and these, too, had to be offloaded and delivered. John Menzies, the museum owner and curator, was eager to display the original Badger pieces alongside his other historical items. Harry Ding's two children, Eric and Jenny, and Eric's son Ellis, posed reverentially with the battered section of cabin roof from their father's old truck. The yellow lettering 'HE Ding Yunta' could still be seen clearly, along with traces of the original red paint showing through the green.

While the Badger and its various drivers were occupied with delivery chores and filming commitments, a fleet of volunteers at the post office was busy sorting the mail. When the old Leyland truck left Birdsville the next day for the very last time it would once again be carrying the official 'Royal Mail'. Via announcements in the media, members of the public had been invited to send a self-addressed envelope to Tom, care of Birdsville, where it would be franked with a commemorative post-mark and returned to them with a postcard picture of Tom standing beside his portrait and a letter from him describing the restoration and seeking donations for the Royal Flying Doctor Service.

Approximately 8000 letters had arrived over the past few weeks, via the regular airmail delivery that now supersedes the roadmail delivery of Tom's day. Each one had to be opened, and the self-addressed envelope retrieved, stuffed and stamped. The six- to ten-person crew formed a happy team inside the small hut and by the end of the afternoon they had filled two big, fat, heavy Australia Post mail sacks, which stood at the door ready for loading the next day.

That night, it was Birdsville's chance to put on a spread for the out-of-towners. The Community Centre was filled to capacity as 400 to 500 Kruse fans and Badgerites dined noisily. In a perspex box on the stage, a large golden seahorse caught the lights and gleamed. It was the trophy presented to John Heyer at the 1954 Venice film festival, specially polished and on loan from the Shell company for the occasion.

Then it was time to screen the film that started it all: to see the movie that had brought the legend of the outback mailman to an Australia beyond the isolated inhabitants of

South Australia's north. The film that had introduced the men in this room to the story of Tom Kruse and inspired the re-enactment and restoration and re-re-enactment that followed. The entire Badger story since 1986 had been fuelled by these men's fascination with John Heyer's images of a fabled man and his truck.

The lights went out and the reels of the old 16-millimetre movie projector whirred in the centre of the room. The familiar music trumpeted and the cultured voice began narrating the introduction: 'Central Australia, a vast flat wilderness; as large as Europe and a thousand miles from anywhere . . . ' Then the sound of an engine became discernible and gradually grew louder. It was the same throaty beat that everyone in the hall had heard around town that very day. Forty-seven years later and the restored Badger sounded identical. Then the truck loomed over the crest of the sandhill and they were off . . . viewing *The Back of Beyond*, with the leading man himself, in attendance.

Just like in 1954, the audience applauded when Tom's face came into view through the driver's window and they cheered when Valma appeared onscreen calling Tom in for his dinner. A murmur went through the room when the dressmaker's mannequin first appeared, as people anticipated one of their favourite scenes. They clapped heartily as Tom bounced toward her on his toes and took her as his dance partner on the sandy banks of the Cooper. They laughed when he fell overboard from the *Tom Brennan* and fell silent when the haunting mission scene unfolded.

Tom seemed to enjoy the film as much as everyone else. He laughed along with the crowd when he saw himself fall from the boat, and he and Valma smiled when he danced with the dummy. It was a treat to watch the film in these circumstances and soak up the inclusive, comradely atmosphere. It was a long time since he'd taken so much pleasure in viewing *The Back of Beyond*. 'I always say it's a great chance to have a bit of a snooze,' he chuckles.

Not that he doesn't like the film . . . just that he's seen it too many times; like the Shell employee who took it around the country back in the fifties. The PR man, Bob Jolley, showed it for the first year or so, then Wally Smith took over. He knew it word for word and would often fall asleep until the flapping of the last piece of celluloid flicking onto the full spool woke him at the end, an hour later.

Des Thompson, Shell's northern representative, often travelled with Wally in the late 1950s through Woomera, Commonwealth Hill station, Coober Pedy, Oodnadatta, Marree and Birdsville, Des in his Holden station wagon and Wally in the fully equipped Mobile Film Unit van.

'Wally'd take out the movie camera and screen and set it up with the big spools of film,' says Des. 'We'd be in a town hall, or church, or station homestead . . . At Coober Pedy we showed it in the open. At Marree the hall was full, up to about 100 people, I'd say, and they were absolutely thrilled.

'All around the north it was virtually the only film that was shown. Everyone wanted to see *The Back of Beyond*.'

On Saturday morning, after the success of the previous night's gala, Tom slowly walked through a crowd of spectators to the side door of the service station that served as the post office, and emerged with a bag of letters. Helpmates followed with the two large, canvas Australia Post mail sacks. Together they stowed them on the back of the truck, then the mailman of the Birdsville Track climbed into the cab and departed with the mail. The crowd gave him an enthusiastic send-off as he drove to the end of town to take his place at the head of a snake of almost 100 vehicles that would follow him down the Birdsville Track.

The Badger led the procession for about three hours; Tom and Neil bumping and chugging along in the noisy cabin till lunchtime. Tom revelled in sounding the klaxon horn at every opportunity: errrrrah, errrrrah he made it warble to the delight of each overtaking motorist. He waved out the window and lifted both hands off the steering wheel in animated conversations with my father. He seemed completely at home in command of the Badger, as if it were only yesterday that they had last negotiated the ruts and bumps of the Track together.

So far, the revived Badger was performing well. It started easily and ran smoothly, and fuel consumption was good. Riding in the truck, Neil and Tom both focused on sensing any peculiarities with the Badger's engine or drive components, easily ignoring some of her inherent quirks and characteristics that those less familiar with the truck found alarming.

'The vibration on that steering wheel was atrocious!' Aynsley exclaims. 'I was amazed when your Dad was driving it when we were coming back from the causeway up in Birdsville. It was corrugated along there, and the movement of that steering wheel was absolutely *horrendous*. Your Dad could hardly hold it! The thing was going like this, up and down,' he says, jiggling his hands in front of him. 'And I was thinking, God, Tom used to drive like that for hours!'

•

In the afternoon the Badger was loaded onto the trailer once again and the convoy was given its head. The drivers, relieved to finally motor at modern-day cruising speeds, pushed on to Mungerannie to prepare their campsites. Tom was scheduled for another television interview.

By now, the bulky video camera and the long, fuzzy microphone on a stick were a familiar presence hovering around him. In addition to the documentary film crew a three-man team from the ABC was following the story, shooting a segment for their rural affairs program, 'Landline'. Although they joined forces to lessen their demands on Tom, the media duties created a gruelling schedule. As Tom was such an energetic and accommodating 'celebrity' it was too easy to forget that he was still a man of 85. He was never one to complain or call out 'Enough!' so it was up to his family and minders to ensure that there was sufficient time for rest and recovery, and for him simply to enjoy himself.

By the time Tom arrived in Mungerannie and joined the camp, it was dark and there was no doubt he was tired. It had been a long and demanding day, but one filled with joy and unexpected pleasures. On the road between Birdsville and Mungerannie, when Tom's interview was over and he was ensconced in the cab of the prime mover with driver Mark Metzger—the Badger onboard the low-loader behind—the CB radio crackled to life: a member of the transport crew whose job it is to maintain the Track wanted to say hello. The truck duly pulled up at a lonely roadwork depot so the woman, who remembered Tom from her childhood, could renew his acquaintance and offer her congratulations. Word spread over the radio and a few kilometres on, the truck drew to a halt again, hailed by a crew driving a fleet of scrapers, tractors and bulldozers that had rolled out of the desert to admire the Badger and pay their respects to a comrade of the outback.

Soon afterwards another salute buzzed over the CB: another roadworker who remembered Tom from long ago, wishing to send his regards. 'The last time I saw you was on the back of a camel with your mother,' Tom's voice returned to him over the airwaves. 'I'd like to congratulate you on a lovely smooth road. OK, OK,' he signed off, conversing with the ease born of a lifetime of radio transmissions.

It was a short hop the next day to the Cooper Creek crossing, where another elaborate celebration was planned. There would be another—open-air—screening of *The Back of Beyond* and Tom would be serenaded with songs written in his honour.

Monday 4 October, was the last day of the official re-enactment. The campers packed up at a leisurely pace and drove the final 150 kilometres from the Cooper back to Marree. Tom arrived in his old hometown in the late afternoon to a conquering hero's welcome. Hearty cheers rang out from the crowd assembled on the main street in front of the old post office building—a stone's throw from the pub, and the tiny outback town glowed with toasts to Tom and the Badger.

Tom was overjoyed to have completed the re-enactment in such style. He sat there in the cab, chortling the horn and beaming; waving out at his admirers, almost as if he didn't want it all to end. In front of him and all around, people cheered and clapped and grinned. It was a perfect finish.

For Tom, the best part of the event had been the opportunity to catch up with old friends. This re-enactment had been a much bigger affair than the 1986 trip and people with ties to the Track had gathered from all over Australia.

There were people there whom Tom hadn't seen since he gave up the mail in '63 and left Marree, 36 years before.

'Really, the best thing was meeting so many different folk,' he says. 'It was great to shake Monty's hand at Mungerannie; and some of the Afghan boys who used to live in Marree; and some of the Aboriginal folk around there—I knew them really well as kids. They used to ride up on the back of the truck and come and help . . . "Mr Kruse, Mr Kruse can we help you?" . . . No, it was really great.

'Look, there were some folk I hadn't seen for 35 or 40 years, and it was really great to shake their hands . . . have a bit of a chit-chat . . . remember so-and-so and so-and-so. Well, from my side, there were lots of things I did remember and lots of things I couldn't remember. One chap said, "Well you still owe me five shillings."

'I said, "Have you got a bit of paperwork on it?"

'Look, driving into Birdsville again—we came from a different end—but I tell you what, it was totally unbelievable. When I first went to Birdsville I really feel there wouldn't've been more than twenty people there . . . I think there might've been about six or eight white people . . . The other day, look, when I say hundreds . . . well, there was . . . up and down the street.

'And the night at the Cooper . . . well, totally . . . totally . . . when I say totally . . . It was! Could've been as many as 300 or 400 people there,' he comments in amazement, 'and waving . . . as though a person had won a lottery. Really exciting, I thought. The fireworks and so on—

like a Christmas party! No, I thought it was really excellent. Wonderful.'

A few days later, Tom drove the Badger into Adelaide to the GPO to officially hand over the mailbags. The Lord Mayor, Dr Jane Lomax-Smith, came out of the Town Hall across the street to congratulate Tom on a successful journey, while postal manager Trevor Holm took charge of the mailbags. Then it was on to Birdwood, where the Badger itself was officially handed over in the presence of South Australia's Governor, Sir Eric Neale.

It really *was* the end of the Badger's last run. Now the 1936 Leyland would ease into comfortable retirement and see out her days as a dignified museum piece.

The re-enactment had been a grand spectacle and everyone who'd taken part was gushing about its success. At every opportunity Kruse fans had applauded and saluted him. They lined up to slap him on the back and shake his huge hand, and pushed forward to swap tales of the outback or to tell him how much they enjoyed 'his' film and the effect that it had had on them. It was warming and energising to see how much admiration people had for this humble man who sometimes seemed a little bemused by the amount of reverence bestowed on him.

For Tom and Valma the official handing over of the Badger was the culmination of a momentous week. They returned from the trip with warm memories, a pile of mementos—commemorative programmes, shirts, hats, photos—and a bundle of more than 600 letters. These were notes and personal letters for Tom that hundreds of people had spontaneously included with their self-addressed envelopes for carriage on the Badger's last run. Each evening over the following months, the Birdsville mailman and his wife settled into their lounge room to read through pages and pages of congratulations and tributes—some from anonymous well-wishers, others from long-ago friends—all saluting Tom as an Australian icon.

Everyone was eager to contribute to the Tom Kruse mythology and each person had a special story about the man from the back of beyond. Letter-writers from across Australia wanted to share the moment when they rubbed shoulders with big Tom. No matter how brief the meeting or inconsequential the exchange, Tom's charisma was such that those involved cherished the time they experienced a little bit of the old Tom Kruse magic.

'Hey! Totally amazing! . . . A pile of letters so high a camel couldn't jump over it,' Tom exclaims. 'Oh, we haven't gone right through them yet. Might do two or three dozen of a nighttime.

'No, I tell you what, it was actually amazing, because there were people sorta from past times—fellows that worked for Lelliot brothers, and a bloke that worked for Harry Ding—there's not many of them around these days . . . Folks from Queensland—look, honestly, there would've been more from Queensland and Victoria than South Australia. Better get Valma on to it,' he says, looking around for the large folder filled with letters.

'There's an old bloke . . . he's 94, I know. He was a highly educated fellow and being an old truck driver he'd treat you like a black snake. Queer, but I tell you what, it was nice to get a note from him . . . And I know Hans Mincham, he wrote too.

'There was a lot of letters saying . . . Look, they must've thought a person was on the bread-line. "Please, here's $20, $50." No, it's awful because I should've had the audacity to reply and thank them. But then I said, look you reply to one and then . . . well . . . a person's got a job to write their own name let alone a letter.'

Some letter-writers, such as Hans Mincham or Monty Scobie—' . . . hope the Badger gives you a trouble free trip. I don't think you will need a long handle shovel or plates'—were clearly old friends of Tom's, writing to offer their formal congratulations on the restoration and the re-enactment. Others simply seized the opportunity to remind him of a one-off meeting years ago that they had never forgotten, asking 'Do you remember me?' 'I met you once', 'You probably won't remember me but . . . ' Anyone whose life had brushed up against Tom's, however fleetingly, took pride in their association with Tom Kruse.

The publicity surrounding the Badger's last run brought back childhood memories for Margot Baker of the time she travelled on the Birdsville mail truck. Don Durant, son of 'Ray' (Sam) Durant who was Tom's childhood friend from Waterloo, wrote to say how much he had enjoyed hearing about Tom in stories from his father. Jim McDiarmid wrote a letter to remind Tom that he had met him at Lyndhurst in 1952 when Jim was a postal clerk in the Leigh Creek coalfields post office.

Keith Edwards, another correspondent, had met Tom when he was mining opal in Coober Pedy. 'I knew him and his young son Phillip—Ooh he's a big bruiser, too, wouldn't want to get on the wrong side of him. They had the water trucks and young Phillip used to cart the water. The old water works, that's what they used to call it,' Keith remembers. He had written to congratulate Tom on the re-enactment journey. 'I hope you have a safe trip down. Don't let those big road trains give you a hard time, just show them who's the "King of the road".'

Peter Watters, who had stumbled across the wreck of the Badger in Tom Agnew's yard at Copley in 1994, confesses that he couldn't believe his ears when he heard that the restored truck was back on the road. 'Bugger me! I was listening to Macca on Sunday—yesterday—and heard that you are going to take the old girl on her last mail run from Birdsville. So I just had to write this letter. I wish you well on the trip and I wish I could be there.'

Heather Beckman spent four years of her childhood in Marree in the late 1940s when her father, Tom Atkins, was in charge of the PMG Repeater Station and a section of the Overland Telegraph line. 'I think all the Marree children (school population 28) hero-worshipped Tom K,' she wrote in her letter. 'We would have a wonderful time watching the truck being loaded (several feet high, with the passengers and helpers often sitting on top of the load) and taking off along the track. Tom, to me, was a genial, gentle man who would go out of his way to give a helping hand to anyone. I have always believed that the part of my childhood spent in Marree has had a huge impact on my life and Tom was part of that impact.'

'The Ghan came twice a week, and the Marree Mixed,' Heather remembers. 'When the trains came that's when Tom would be packing up. I have a photo of his truck outside the post office. It seemed to be metres high, packed up quite densely. People would order groceries and green groceries from Quorn or further south—you'd always be picking up a box of vegetables from the train. Library books for the school came up on the train, as well. And there were lots of troop trains going up and down, through to Alice Springs.'

Laurel Prunster wrote from Western Australia to reminisce about the year she and her family spent living in Marree. 'My husband, Leo Prunster, was the Commonweath Railways Roadmaster stationed in Marree and he was responsible for a long, long length of the railway track both north and south of the town,' she wrote. 'We lived there, right in the station yard, in 1960.

'I was a little like Mrs Kruse in so much as my husband left home Monday mornings to go "up the Track" but unless something untoward happened he did return Friday evenings, whereas Tom was away for a fortnight. Even then he was a legend and we would hear stories of his everyday adventures.'

Another correspondent, Anne Calliss, remembers Tom from when she used to live at Lyndhurst, working in Brazel's store in the early '60s. 'Tom was quite an icon around the bush—most people got to know him around the place,' she says. 'He'd come in to buy groceries and things when he was passing through. I was about sixteen years old at the time and I always remember this huge man coming in. He filled the whole doorway! A great big man with a soft, gentle, little voice.'

While many of the correspondents referred to isolated incidents that now escape Tom's mind, he had had more extensive dealings with a few of the letter-writers and their notes conjured up familiar faces and triggered memories of the past.

'Do you still remember May and I?' Allan Franks enquired. 'We worked at Marla Bore, 1983, where we became very friendly with you, which gave us many happy times together.'

'Hey, yeah,' says Tom. 'When the gas fields first started he had a truck up there.'

Tom particularly remembers Allan from a conversation they'd once had on the merits of Queensland versus Northern Territory water.

'I've got three daughters and I'd still like a son,' Allan told him.

'Well, you drink Diamantina water,' Tom declared. 'I know a man with four sons and he drinks Georgina water. I'll get you some.'

Many years later the two met up again. Allan did some kind of a favour for Tom and Tom wanted to buy him a meal in return.

'No way,' said Allan. 'You sent me that big drum of Georgina water years ago and now I've got a son twenty years old!'

Colin Need, Tom and Valma's lifelong accountant, also sent his formal congratulations to Tom: 'Congratulations on the recognition of your wonderful service to the Birdsville Track and the faithful delivery of Her Majesty's mail and so much else,' he wrote.

'I've known Tom forever, seems like,' Colin says. 'I worked in the Peterborough office of my boss and mentor, Max Cope, and he did all Harry Ding's accounts in the 1930s. After the war, I left the army and got a job back with Mr Cope in the Adelaide office, and I started doing all the books and accounts for Tom's carting business on the Track.

'Tom was reasonably casual about putting his bills in and getting paid, but with the station owners there wasn't very much delay. Occasionally there'd be an argument about the measurement of dams or that sort of thing—Tom got paid by the cubic yard of soil that was shifted. The earthmoving business was much more profitable to him than the mail run. On a scale of one to ten from poverty to wealth, the mail run would've been a four or five. It wasn't ever a big money-spinner. But they got by.'

'We were like the Ten Commandments,' Tom says when reflecting on his mail-run years. 'Always broke.'

In addition to the letters from friends and casual acquaintances carried on the Badger's last mail run, there were hundreds of letters from anonymous well-wishers. They showered Tom with praise, congratulating him for a life well-lived in service of the outback; thanking him for the joy his story brought them, for representing the true Aussie spirit, and for instilling in them a sense of pride in being an Australian. People who had never met Tom nor had any personal connection to him wrote to express their joy at hearing that Tom and the Badger were reunited and to convey their admiration for the outback hero. Some remembered seeing *The Back of Beyond* in the '50s or '60s, others were hearing his story for the first time in the media reports that surrounded the mail run re-enactment. Either way, they instinctively knew that Tom was a piece of living history. People wanted to write and personally salute him as an Aussie icon.

People, such as Robert Spriggs, for whom letter-writing was 'as rare as a bottle of Grange Hermitage', wrote to say how they remembered seeing the film 40 years ago and have admired Tom ever since. 'Your story is one of the magic of the outback,' he was told.

Writing to Tom even became the subject of school projects. Inquisitive eight-, nine- and ten-year-olds asked Tom about his life as a postman, some illustrating their letters of enquiry with spidery drawings of Tom and the Badger.

Margo Wilson's class of year-fours (nine- and ten-year-olds) at Highgate Primary School in South Australia had been learning about Australia's early development in their history and geography lessons. When the teacher heard about the re-enactment trip she shared the story of the Badger's restoration with the children, and they watched *The Back of Beyond*. 'You are now a celebrity,' Ms Wilson wrote. 'The children have written letters to you and admire you greatly.'

With her letter, Tess sent a lovely graphite drawing of the Badger cresting a large sand dune. The truck was loaded with petrol drums and wheat sacks and with Tom at the wheel it was coasting right over the top of the sandhill, no problem at all.

Paris-Anne, another of Ms Wilson's students, drew many comparisons between Tom's trips and the way her family travels. 'You must have driven from Marree to Birdsville a lot of times. Have you always travelled with people or did you once travel alone? I like travelling by car but since I have a little sister, we now travel by plane, because she doesn't behave very well on long trips. I wonder if you have any pets? Sometimes when my family travel, we take our dog, Honky. It must be very handy to know how to fix your Badger. My dad has to call the RAA to come when his car breaks down and he has to call them at least an hour or two before they come. Just imagine if you had to call the RAA. That would take a very long time! You must have made many good friends over the years on your trips. I wonder if you will keep in touch with all of your friends. I hope you don't miss your job too much. Warm Regards, Paris.'

Students from Highgate and other schools wondered what Tom's life was like. They asked whether he still had his music box, and 'how he had the strength to travel in such hot desert'. 'How old are you?' they wondered and, 'If it isn't too personal, how old is your truck?' 'If someone like me was about to do something like you did, what advice would you give?' young Jake enquired. 'How many journeys have you had?' and 'Have you broken down 200 kilometres from anywhere?'

'I wish that I could see your Badger and yourself,' Adel wrote wistfully, while Dom was more pragmatic: 'I bet you've got a few cups of tea in your stomach,' he surmised.

Back home in Cumberland Park, Tom and Valma slowly waded through letter after letter, humbled and overwhelmed by the outpouring of public adoration. People wrote to say how they admired the 'guts and fortitude', of 'Australia's greatest mailman'; how Tom was 'a legend to inspire future generations of Aussies'; how his 'lifelong achievements' made him 'a credit to be called an Australian' and 'a living part of Australian history'; how he epitomised the 'Aussie spirit which can get the job done, against all the odds'. 'May we prove that we deserve the great accomplishments of our pioneer generation, and the courage and success of such a splendid man as Tom Kruse!'

'Congratulations for a life so courageously and usefully lived.'

'Ride well big fella and God Bless.'

EPILOGUE

It is a Tuesday afternoon in spring when I arrive for one of my weekly chats with Tom. The front lawn is a neat, trim square; the cement path and driveway swept clean. Roses hang over the low front fence in a colourful parade. Across the street, all is quiet at Charlie and Olive's place.

Walking down the side pathway to the back of the house, I squeeze past Tom's old cream Ford station wagon. The front seat and both passenger side doors have been removed—bashed in from an accident a couple of months before from which, thankfully, Tom escaped with only a scratch on one knuckle. Valma hopes it might be an appropriate time to send the station wagon to that great jewel box in the sky but Tom quietly and surreptitiously sets about fixing it. He's scanning the papers for a couple of second-hand doors, otherwise he says he'll rivet a length of tin over the two doorways.

'You can't drive around with a piece of tin up instead of doors,' his daughter Helen tells him, 'you'll get pulled over by the police. It'll attract too much attention.' But Tom brushes her aside, saying, 'Hey, ah . . . no worries. Piece of tin to keep the weather out . . . bit of paint . . . lovely.'

At the back of the house more roses bloom. Vines and shade trees create an inviting corner at the rear of the garden. Pot plants hang along the verandah. The grass is lush and green. I pull open the back screen door to find Valma on her own in the sunroom, Tom's customary chair empty. We chat about the weather and mutual friends and swap family news, until Tom appears from his workshed down the back. He makes it just inside the doorway before cupping his hands together in front of him, assuming a characteristic pose.

'Kristin, ah lovely, good to see you,' he says. 'How's ah, Julian? Did you see the little whatsaname? . . .'

I had told the Kruses I was going to meet my brother's dog, Devo, for the first time.

'Hey . . . ah, talking about dogs,' Tom continues, 'I'll tell you what, Harvey . . . eh, Harvey . . . look it's amazing how people . . . in Marree for argument's sake, all the old chappies after their evening meal, they'd all poke down and sit on their stools in front of the shop—go down and have a bit of a yarn. And it's funny how these old chaps used to fight. Argue about so-and-so. Well, then there's this chappy, Ernie . . .'

'Take a seat, Kristin,' Valma says, 'I'll put the kettle on.'

I stand with Tom just inside the doorway, my heavy work bag hanging over my shoulder.

' . . . Ernie, he starts going on about our dog, Harvey. The other fella, Mick, used to always tell him about a white dog that they had at Deep Well. Oooh, it could kill, he's saying. Any dog that could beat that dog in a fight . . . he was tremendous . . .'

'Kristin, take a seat,' Valma urges, stepping back into the sunroom for a moment. 'Tom, sit down. Let Kristin sit down.'

' . . . Well, it so happened that this Harvey, *by hell*, I tell you what, he was a good fighter. No, he was. He was a big strong dog . . . '

Valma leaves. Tom keeps talking. It would seem so rude to turn away.

' . . . Anyhow, Ernie and Mick, they finally get stuck into a really heated argument about the white dog and the black dog. Ernie's saying how this black dog—that's Harvey—how he tore a dog's shoulder off the other day—round town there's big dogs, you know. O' course it finally gets to a stage where Mick says, I'll get the white dog down from Alice Springs and show you. Right, I'll bet you 50 pounds. Put your money down. The white dog against the black dog. Hell . . . this is in the main street in Marree . . . '

'Kristin, here, just take a seat,' Valma says, bustling into the sunroom once more. 'Tom!' she laughs, 'you can still talk just the same sitting down.'

'Valma, I've been doing it all my life.'

I drop my bag to the floor and pull up a chair. Tom remains in the doorway, standing in mid-sentence, waiting a beat until my eyes are back on his.

' . . . The white dog and the black dog. I reckon the white . . . honestly, I thought he had Harvey . . . had him over. Then I saw Harvey . . . all of a sudden Harvey was able to get his favourite grip, on his bloody shoulder somewhere. He had this poor bloody white dog . . . They had to get the broomsticks to get them apart. Harvey won the fight. Look, they loved to have a fight. It was their life . . . Yeah, Harvey, that's right . . . Then before that we had Bluey . . . '

'Tom, sit down!' Valma says, returning with tea and biscuits.

'I'm trying to grow good.'

'Well, you'll have to stand there a long time,' she teases him.

'Hey! You've been reading my letters,' he responds with a sly smile, finally moving to his chair.

'Did you always have a pet?' I ask.

'No, Bluey was the first one,' Valma replies. 'He was a lovely dog—a blue heeler.'

We sip our tea.

'Actually Ernie was a Dunn—Dunn, Dunn, all done . . . Old Jackie Dunn, used to be at the hotel in Lyndhurst. We were living at the hotel; 21 shillings a week, all paid by HE Ding. Me and Curly—commonly known as Apple Bill and Biscuit Joe—we were always eating apples or biscuits . . . '

'Right. Well, I'm going out,' Valma says, gathering up the cups and saucers. 'I've heard your stories so many times.'

Tom sings a ditty:

'She wore her silk pajamas in the summer when it's hot,
She wore her flannel nighties in the winter when it's not,
And sometimes in the autumn when the leaves began to fall,
She'd walk into my bedroom with nothing on at all!'

'Nah . . . ,' he sniggers, 'shouldn't be saying that . . . Jackie Dunn was always singing—that was one I can always remember.

'He was fat, Jack Dunn. And a great brandy drinker. Then when Jack died his wife, Emily Dunn, married a Pierpoint. Mrs Dunn/Mrs Pierpoint, she was like a mother, she was. Fair dinkum, she was. Well in plain words, she used to feel sorry . . . Fancy, kids coming up here working for this little bit of money. No, she was very kind, you could never, ever've got one sweeter.

'Then George Dunn—oh, you wouldn't know George . . .'

And so the yarns flowed, skipping across the years, each one spinning seamlessly from the end of another . . . sometimes stretching back to incorporate a loose loop of twine dangling from the middle of the tale, then weaving it forward into the fabric of the story. And just when you thought the thread was broken, irretrievably frayed at the edges and about to unravel, he would deftly knit it all together again, drawing it to a finely spun conclusion—as long as you stayed with him. The more time you spent with Tom and the longer you listened, the better you came to know the rich characters and stories of his life. On first glance the yarns may seem too fragile, too old, too much effort. But with motivation and patience the sideways references, the incomplete anecdotes and the endless raft of people and places meld into a shimmering narrative cloth that beckons you in and warmly envelops you.

After the excitement of the '99 mail run re-enactment ebbed away, people wondered what Tom would do. After four years, would the restoration of the Badger leave a void that the usual daily activities could not fill? If this was a concern that crossed Tom's mind he didn't let on. There was always something on the horizon.

In October 2000, Tom and the Badger made a guest appearance at the National 4 × 4 Show in Melbourne. A constant stream of visitors from among the 70 000 attendees visited the display, eager to see the Badger and to meet Tom.

Bob Bilton was there, sitting on a chair beside the truck. 'An honour to meet you, Mr Kruse,' a reverent fan said, approaching Bob with his hand extended.

'I don't know how many people come up to me saying, "Hello Tom, how are ya,"' Bob laughs.

'Hell, I hope he had his teeth in!' Tom exclaims upon hearing of the mistaken identity.

One loyal fan arrived far too early but waited patiently for six hours for Tom to turn up. Kevin O'Neil had spent six weeks making a slightly larger than shoe-box-sized wooden replica of the Badger and was determined not to leave before Tom had an opportunity to see and hopefully admire it, and maybe even sign it. Tom was enchanted with the model.

Krusemania continued in 2001 with the long-awaited screening of 'Last Mail from Birdsville', the television documentary about the Badger's restoration and the re-enactment. Tom and the restorers reunited in Adelaide in March for a private screening prior to the film's public premiere on Channel Seven's 'The World Around Us'.

The documentary inspired another wave of complimentary comments in the form of emails to an associated website, including: 'Onya Tom'; 'Tom, YOU RULE'; 'To Tom and the team of dedicated craftsmen who rebuilt the Badger I say thank you, it made an old tradesman swell with pride to see the results of your dedication. Smooth roads and well done to each and every one of you'; 'They don't make men or trucks like they used to'; 'From now on when I think of the term, MODIFY, ADAPT AND OVERCOME, I will think of you Tom'; and 'I think you are more herowick [*sic*] than Sir Donald Bradman.'

Dave Burge was thrilled with the documentary, announcing it to be one of the proudest moments in his life when he saw his face appear beside Tom's in the opening scene. He still found it hard to believe that he had become so intimately involved in a story that had first captured his interest 45 years ago. For him, it was a fitting conclusion to all that had happened to Tom and the Badger since *The Back of Beyond*.

At the beginning of October, a week after my previous visit, Tom hands me a piece of paper when I take a seat in the sunroom. It's a gas and electricity bill.

'Valma keeps on telling me, "Look, you don't do what you're *told*. Kristin's asked you several times . . . Please, answer . . . You haven't answered even one of her questions." Right. Anyhow, the thing is, the other day I was sitting here . . . If you could just read that . . .'

On the back of the power bill, under a heading 'Re Memories', Tom had written over the printed customer enquiry and account information, and filled the page with notes in scrawling black biro ink:

As kiddies we were keen on golf (Waterloo). Those days the golf course on the Slattery family land approx. 1 mile north of town centre, also the tennis courts adjoining. Re the Slatterys: three brothers; Dan, 3 children; Mick, 3 daughters; Bill (WJ), his eldest son also Bill, my age— school pals. After the primary school days Bill went to the Rostrevor College, Bob Gaffney (Robert Patrick) also there—his mother owned the Birdsville Hotel, store, post office. At times during the College holidays, I remember very clearly playing golf (one stick), meeting Bob Gaffney, his yarning about the late Harry Williams, old Dodges etc. (Little did I know one day I would have the pleasure of delivering mail Marree to Birdsville as a driver for HE Ding.) Bob those days, or a little later, became the shire clerk. Bob was on the verandah waving to us in Jan. 1936.

I thought of Tom's aversion to writing . . . the load of wood, the blunt axe, the high truck . . . and was infinitely touched.

'You've written this?'

'Yes.'

'I'm impressed. You don't like writing, do you.'

'No I don't. But at the same time, I just thought . . . It was sort of half raining the other day . . . What are you doing today? Well I'm keeping out of the way . . . I don't know whether you can read it . . . Look, there could be mistakes—commas and so on . . . No, I tell you what, I just . . . again, as Valma said, how will people know? . . . You leave that many words out . . .'

'Oh, I can usually join things together. I know what you're talking about,' I reassured him. 'But that's very nice. Thank you for writing that.'

'No, well, I just thought, give you a bit—look, you just read it . . . give you a bit of an idea about Bob Gaffney . . .'

Tom's notes provided an easy launching pad that day and we were soon in flight: me listening, Tom reminiscing.

'Yeah, I knew Bob Gaffney when he was at Rostrevor. He was always yarning about Birdsville and so forth.

Actually, I'll tell you what—I shouldn't be saying this, but I can always remember it really well . . . I had to do . . . I think it was an essay. I said to Bob, please . . . It was on sports. I can always remember these two lines: "Sports was one of the most important factors in the development of human body and character."

'O' course . . . Hell, whoever wrote this? . . . They queried me at school, see. Bob had written it all out very clearly. All I had to do was read it. Which I did. I always remember that bit about human body and character. But then he went on to say, how with sports you can overdo things, he spoke about the Romans, about how they overindulged . . . Anyhow it was long. So Bob Gaffney—between him and Bill Slattery— they got the old teacher down there at Waterloo a bit puzzled. We only had the same teacher all the way through. Mary Margaret Keane. She was a lovely old lady. I had a lot of respect for her.'

Despite the skulduggery, the kindly Mrs Keane put her signature to all Tom's school certificates: Certificate of Merit, Annual Examination, Grade 1, December 1921; Certificate for Excellent Work in Grade VI, 1926; and the Qualifying Certificate: Esmond G Kruse, Pupil of the Public School at Waterloo, having completed the Primary School course is qualified to enter upon a course of higher instruction, Education Department SA, December 16th, 1927.

'You know, I was just thinking the other day . . . Those things that you remember, that give you a thrill, the greatest moments of your life . . . Oh, that wouldn't be the word. But . . . I can remember very clearly our eldest brother—I must've been, I s'pose, five years of age—Brother Joe's welcome home—coming back from World War One. It was quite a common thing to have a welcome in the little hall at Waterloo. He'd lost all the lower part of his body—a lot'd been shot off . . . He still had one of his legs . . . Anyhow . . . But I do remember him waltzing with our mother. Might've been just one or two steps. But I can remember that very clearly.

'An English couple owned the hotel there at Waterloo. Mrs Withers, she said, if you milk my cows for six weeks I'll buy you a tennis racket. As kids we used to play a lot of tennis.

'Actually Skin was the best tennis player, *by hell* he was. And Vera was a good player, too. She used to swear so much, people'd say, well look, let her win.'

Later on, Tom's barefoot tennis-playing prowess was almost as legendary as his brute strength. The publican at Marree told Des Thompson that it was 100 degrees and Tom was playing tennis on an asphalt court with bare feet. He'd never seen anyone do it before or since.

'Oh, just got used to it,' Tom says. 'We could never afford shoes. If there were any stones you'd just pick 'em up and toss 'em off the court.'

One elderly lady, writing a letter for the Badger's last run, alluded to Tom playing tennis not only without shoes but without a stitch of clothing on at all:

'Hope you remember me, cos my thoughts now are of you playing tennis in the nude—NUDE—at Marree. Bright moonlight really showed me the colour of the balls. Really showed me what good form you was in.'

Tom, uncharacteristically coy, feigns a memory lapse and declines to elaborate.

'Er . . . can't remember . . . ah, anyhow . . . er . . .' he says, flicking through his mind for a new topic. 'Rats,' he announces presently. 'Valma, you tell about the bloody rats,' he calls out to his wife in the dining room.

'Well, it was only very rarely, they'd have a rat plague,' Valma picks up. 'But Tom used to tell me about the rats . . .'

'Look, during the floods you'll find that the rats will be walking over you,' Tom interjects. 'And the rabbits . . . one year they were that thick . . . Fair dinkum, driving along, crunch, crunch, crunch, crunch, crunch.

'Hey it was rather queer—Valma, this is no joke,' he interrupts himself, anticipating her likely reaction of, 'Oh, Tom' said in a gently chiding tone of disbelief. 'About 28 mile out of Birdsville, we shot a dingo and the dingo had just caught a rabbit. We had rabbit stew for dinner that night. No that's a damn fact. It had a rabbit only freshly caught— shot the dingo and got the rabbit. Valma, I'm not skiting,' he says, catching her sceptical look.

Valma just purses her lips. As always, she refrains from demeaning Tom in public. If it's true that she sometimes scolds him in private for the 'tallness' of some of his tales then it would be done in the same calm, practical manner with which she moves through life. And Tom treats his wife with the chivalry of a true gentleman. After a remarkable 60 years of marriage, they seem to delight in each other's company, enjoy each other's teasing and jokes; always at ease, solicitous, respectful.

'Look, now, I've put you off the beam,' he says to me. '. . . eh memories . . . Well, Dr Madigan. From my side it was quite a thrill to be associated . . . and I might say, one of the great memories was driving the old Badger out of the shed that first time. Of all the things in the world . . . Matter of fact I thought your Dad was going to drive it. He said, "No, no you get up in it, you've got to drive it." Yeah, that was one I always remember really well. Going out, do you think you can turn the wheel? Well, I'll try. But then she always used to be a bit heavy in the head . . .'

A few days later, an artist named Beth Roberts drops by to introduce herself to Tom and Valma and show off the quilted, poster-size wall-hanging she has stitched depicting the Birdsville Track. The restored Badger drives out of frame at the bottom; Tom stands nearby, his Badger-green official restorer's shirt forming a stark contrast to the orange desert sands; and motifs of the dog fence, the Cooper, the Birdsville Hotel and the abandoned truck are placed in their correct locations along the track, interspersed with embroidered emus, dingos, camels and snakes. The handiwork is magnificent and Beth Roberts is thrilled that the Kruses approve.

Tom admires the wall-hanging, then retreats to the sunroom. He reflects on the enjoyable weekend he and Valma had spent at Orroroo a couple of weeks previously when they drove up in order for him to officially open the annual show. A few nights later, a documentary about Lake Eyre screens on television—Tom is once again on TV, leaning over the balcony of the Marree hotel, describing his mail run days. In November 2001, he stands in effigy for two weeks with 5000 other life-size figures on the lawns of Parliament House, Canberra, celebrating Australia's Centenary of Federation. In July 2002, the Year of the Outback, he would fly to Arkaroola in the Flinders Ranges where he and the Badger would be guests of honour at the Legends of Outback Transport celebration.

In between, there would be birthdays and anniversaries, trips to the crash-repair shop, dinners with friends, working bees with the family and visits from overseas and interstate friends and relations.

Tom tilts his newspaper towards the window, pooling the sunlight on the pages of the *Stock and Station Journal*. Unaided by glasses, he carefully reads each column. The back door pulls back and Charlie's head appears. 'Ah, Charles . . . Come in out of the weather,' he says softly, folding his paper and stretching out his legs. 'Valma'll make us a cup of tea, directly.'

Tom's great-grandson Josh races in from outside and activates the little wooden Badger—handmade and presented to Tom by an admirer—that runs on a magnetic track through a diorama of the Birdsville mail run inside a glass case. The phone rings: 'I think it's nice to hear the telephone ring. You know you're wanted,' Tom remarks. Grandchildren and great-grandchildren dash in and out. The miniature Badger circles through the sandhills. Tom putters along quietly. Serenely. Taking everything in his stride. As always.

Appendix

1943: Riding the Birdsville mail

In August 1943, Florence Wade travelled with Tom in the Badger to visit her friend, Dorothy Brook, daughter of the Birdsville Hotel proprietor, Mrs Gaffney. Florence's father had just passed away and Dorothy suggested that a holiday with her would do Florence the world of good.

As this was Florence's first foray into the outback she eagerly described her experience in a letter to her sister. Some years after sending the twelve-page letter, Florence had come to repossess it. Before she died in August 1995 at the age of 92, she handed the letter to her Adelaide neighbour, Pat Rogers, whose family have cherished it ever since.

In her letter Florence gives a fascinating description of the country she passed through during her journey with Tom and provides an evocative sense of the social mores and conventions—both the good and the bad—of the times.

Note: This letter is reproduced in an abridged form to provide a contemporary account of the colour and flavour of the times.

It should be read in that context, bearing in mind that this is an historical document portraying prejudices that are unacceptable today.

C/- Mrs W F Brook
Adria Downs,
Birdsville,
Via Marree
11.8.43

My Dear Gert,

I had a good trip from Farrell's Flat to Terowie—then changed to a carriage which claimed by white chalk markings on the side that it was 'first class'—it wasn't really and no one took any notice of it anyhow, and in came a lot of rough looking, none too clean men that proved to be Italian internees from the Loveday Camp on their way to Alice Springs on Allied Works Council work. At first I was pretty sure I was in for an uncomfortable trip, thinking they would be as rough in their behaviour as their looks suggested, but they were really a most inoffensive crowd—gave no trouble at all . . . They were a very philosophical crowd—there was a war on and they must just put up with it until it blew over . . . It was rather ironical that at a wayside station a small boy got on with a tin collecting for the prisoners of war!! However these chaps all contributed.

At Quorn where we arrived at 6.15 pm we changed yet again and again for the worse . . . Eventually however we set off for the last stage of the trip to Marree . . . I was glad indeed to see Marree next morning somewhere about 9.30 or 10 am . . .

The mail truck is a Leyland Diesel truck of about 5 tons—loaded to about 6 tons with cement and chaff, fruit and vegetable, mail and all other possible requirements for the people outback.

The mail driver is a young married man—huge in size—wears the dirtiest old battered felt hat, khaki shirt with no coat and the biggest pair of greenhide boots I have ever seen, but as a driver a perfect wizard which indeed he needs to be—no roads in the bush, just track and very often not even that—and the things that that overladen truck was asked to do amazed me and do it she always did with the persuasion and perseverance of the mailman. He is a model of patience and nothing daunts him—when things break he just gets out and mends them somehow or other and when we came to what you would think was an impassable sandhill he just got her over an inch at a time by putting iron plates under the wheels.

Mrs Staples and her daughter were the two other passengers with myself and we all packed into the cabin of the truck—they were bound for Mulka about 100 miles from Marree.

The Mungerannie Station Truck with Mr and Mrs Oldfield, the owners, on board plus their two children and the dog at the back amongst a collection of miscellaneous purchases was travelling with us—they usually travel with the mail truck out here if going along anywhere near the same time—convoy idea—it seems that 120 miles to go and do some shopping is a mere nothing.

Things went along pretty well for a while—the only life we passed at all from Marree to Birdsville was on just leaving Marree a number of packhorses laden to the ground . . . and then later a handful of cattle this end on [Pandie Pandie] Station about 18 miles from Birdsville—the intervening distance without any living thing for miles except where we stopped at stations.

About 35 miles from Marree we came to what was my first taste of real bush track as it was a small sandhill—to get through it they have iron plates strewn along the way and it is marvellous the way they get these trucks up and over and around bends under the most impossible circumstances . . .

The first sign of habitation was Lake Harry Station . . . No one home here so we just passed by. Dulkaninna Station next—Mr and Mrs Bell [are the] owners, and with true bush hospitality we were asked to come in and have tea but were anxious to push on so just got out for a few minutes then off again.

It was here that I heard the first news of the pedal wireless. This is the most marvellous invention and a perfect boon to the bush. Certain times in the day all the stations within a huge radius talk to one another by means of this pedal wireless. You hear the call signs coming over and then away they go with all the news of the bush and it is a great help. Imagine my surprise when Mrs. Bell told me enquiries were being made for my welfare on the trip—my friends from Birdsville having been talking to her in the morning—reports are given from the various stations on the track of the progress of the mail and the welfare of those on it.

Canuwalkalanna [sic] was the next sign of habitation but as there was no one home at this station we just pressed on.

Next big thing to be got over were the Natarannie Sandhills [sic] but the mailman in his usual style got through.

The country is most interesting—changing all the time—

some times for hundreds of miles every way you look you see nothing but flat plains covered in what they call 'gibbers'—really small stones. There is very little vegetation on the whole trip—very few trees—you go hundreds of miles or so it seems and never see a tree or a bush, and naturally never the sign of bird or beast—you feel you are the only living creatures in the whole of the heart of Australia . . .

About this time we commenced to strike a little trouble—the mail truck was on ahead and it was about 8.30 pm and the mailman decided to camp in the bed of the Cooper—dry of course—and have tea . . .

[The Cooper] is just a wide expanse of perfectly dry river bed with thousands of dead trees standing in it . . . The mailman grabbed his axe and chopped down a dead tree and had a lovely fire going and the billy boiling in no time at all—but the Mungerannie truck had not turned up—so in we all had to pile again and go back and look for them—to find Mr Oldfield walking towards us with a torch some distance back—they had broken their front axle. This meant towing them from there on—a matter of 70 odd miles in the end.

We got them to the camp fire and then all sat round and enjoyed our tea. Billy tea is the best ever.

After this we set off again but the tow rope proved a nuisance and broke every few minutes—but with the patience of the bush, knowing that a job had to be done and the only way was to get to and fix it, the mailman climbed out again and again, sometimes only a few minutes break in between, and fixed the rope. The cars and trucks up here do not possess anything as superfluous as a horn, so the only signal they could give from behind was to switch on their lights and they came on all too often, believe me. The poor mailman, between trying to watch his track and keep an eye out for lights from behind, has a busy time. It was then decided to leave the Mungerannie truck at Mulka and pile them all on our truck somewhere as by this time Mrs Oldfield insisted that we spend the night with them.

By the time we got to Mulka however—here we left Mrs Staples and her daughter—the mailman decided he could fix the tow with an iron bar and chain and would finish the job and take their truck right home for them. We all went in to Mulka and had a cup of tea—something after 11 pm . . .

We left here about midnight and our next big obstacle was the Oorawillannie Sandhill [sic]—a perfect snorter if you have only just a car to get over it—you can imagine with an overladen truck plus another laden truck towed behind that the mailman had the job ahead of him. He seems to thrive on impossibilities however and he tackled it and by the aid of much digging out and iron plates we crept inch by inch taking almost an hour to go about 3 yards—however we got off it eventually—everyone by this time being beyond tired— none of us had had much, if any, sleep the night before—the Oldfields and the mailman having spent the night at a dance and I in the train not being able to sleep.

Oorawillannie Station [sic] was the next port of call— imagine your postman arriving at 1.45 am—but in the bush the mail arrives when it can and there is always someone up to greet it. The mail is the event of the fortnight and everything revolves around it. No one goes anywhere until the mail arrives—drovers wait round for days and nothing starts at all.

Mr Scobie was out in a shot to greet the mail but being

the early hours of the morning we didn't go in and have the usual cup of tea, but just pushed on for Mungerannie.

In between the breaks of the tow rope every so often and all too often our own front spring broke which kept locking the front wheel—this meant that we were now limping along with a vengeance and we crawled along, ticking the miles off mile by mile and being thankful as each one passed. At 4 am we arrived at Mungerannie a very tired party and Mrs Oldfield made me up a bed and we all crawled into our various beds without more ado . . .

The weather had been dull leaving Marree but this morning I woke to the most glorious hot sunshine, and after getting up and having breakfast Mrs O showed me round the station homestead. A delightful old place most suitable for the centre of Australia—square built of stone, very solid and limewashed—completely surrounded with very wide verandah, floored with burnt lime slabs, all done on the premises . . .

They have a lovely vegetable garden here all grown from the bore water. They do what they call 'air' it—it would not grow anything straight from the bore but they pump it up and then put it in huge containers, then use it after a few days and it will grow anything.

All along the track you see what they call 'bore drains'—and it is the bore water just airing on the surface—really they look like small natural creeks and often with rushes and small trees growing in it . . .

We had a cup of morning tea and then the mailman and I set off on the rest of our journey—220 miles.

Mirra Mitta was the first and last sign of human habitation from the time we left Mungerannie until we hit Birdsville . . .

for the next 200 miles or thereabouts we met neither man, beast nor bird, until about 18 miles off Birdsville when we met a few head of cattle.

We left Mirra Mitta about 1.15 pm and travelled on over miles and miles of gibber plains, flat as pancakes for as far as you could see east, south, north and west . . .

Some little distance further on the mailman decided we should eat—so pulled up near some dead trees, which are always necessary to a meal in the bush—grabbed his axe and went off and chopped himself a tree and had the fire going in no time and the billy boiling. This was a lovely spot—we had just seen a most lovely sunset—the sun had been shining brightly all day—and really this scene is hard to describe— just the mailman and I in the heart of Australia with the camp fire—it seemed that we were the only people in the world— we spread the rug and sat down on the gibbers round the fire and shared our respective tucker boxes and drank our billy tea with the wireless in the truck singing Holy Night—the night was starry, still and warm—and really it was the most perfect moment.

We went on again until about 9.30 pm when the mailman said he thought we would camp for the night—he was nearly exhausted from his two nights with practically no sleep and all the hard work he had been doing with the truck, and I myself was falling asleep on the seat and was afraid he might do so over the wheel—and the track was not the track for sleeping on believe me—two eyes were well needed for the job of driving—so about 9.30 pm we pulled up near a belt of trees, the few that we saw on the whole trip—and he made up my bed in front of the headlights on the road—said I might have the headlights on all night if I wished—and went off to his own swag at the back of the truck. I didn't want the headlights on of course—it was a moonlight night and so still it almost overwhelmed you—the still and quiet of the bush is unbelievable—but tired as I was or perhaps I was too tired, I couldn't sleep—the night was not cold, fortunately, as nights go, but I soon grew cold being used to hot water bags and what nots and the road was so jolly hard that I tossed and turned all night and of course began to wonder what I would do if a dingo came along and bit me and such like thoughts. Then properly got into my stride and began to wonder what I would do if the mailman suddenly died in the night and I was left there all alone—it seemed so entirely a world apart—we had not seen a soul from midday and did not see anyone at all until we arrived at Birdsville next day. However the mailman did not die in the night as was proved by his lusty shout from the back of the truck just before six, just when I had at last got comfortable and was settling in for a good sleep. Time to be on our way—so up I obediently got—and breakfastless, we set on our way.

He said the night before he could travel all night but it would be 4 am before we would arrive at Birdsville, if indeed we arrived then, and as the pedal wireless had warned us of rain that had fallen ahead he was afraid to tackle the canegrass swamps not knowing what to expect there—as to use his own expression they would 'bog a duck'. So before the sun was up and in heavy morning mists we once again set off and it was lovely indeed watching the mists gradually rise as the sun came up.

About 9 am we came to earth and had breakfast in Cartwheel Swamp—a little hollow spot in between two ranges of sandhills—a few shrubs and trees—boiled the billy once again and brought out the tucker boxes—but first of all of course had to have our morning wash and this was achieved with the greatest convenience—the mailman goes for a spade and digs a hole in the sand, then throws a groundsheet across the hole and fills it with water—and there you are, the most perfect basin—so down on our knees we go in turn and with plenty of soap, have a great morning wash—then did our hair—and sat down to breakfast with plenty of appetite. I then roamed the sandhills while he packed up, and picked wild flowers—the flowers are just coming and in some spots on the track are lovely.

Saturday night just about sundown we came to the prettiest spot on the whole journey—Kidman's swamp—a lovely little green oasis with trees and bushes—here we expected to meet a mob of cattle travelling to Clifton Hills Station and perhaps have tea with them but missed them somehow and so went on. From here on for miles the scent of the wildflowers was lovely in the sunset . . .

A little further on our way appears a post by the wayside with a few boxes and this is the Clifton Hills mail box—the mailman left here the mail, bag of vegetables and other requirements for the station . . .

We were now nearing Birdsville and see the first sign of life in a handful of cattle—the first living thing we had seen since midday the day before—almost if not quite 24 hours.

Here we struck boggy ground—as the mailman said, alright in the daylight while he could see what he was doing but a nightmare in the dark. We eventually got out of it by backing and going forward, go about a yard and back three quarters and so on until we got on to firmer ground.

We then came on the Queensland border—a thin

wirenetting fence that you just don't bother about but run straight over.

Then about 7 or 8 miles to Birdsville—we arrived about 1 pm . . .

Every morning just after 9 the news all goes round the town as the pedal wireless sets call each other about this time. My first experience of hearing them was at Mungerannie Station and it had me intrigued to hear all the call signs going over and then the various stations picking them up and chatting away . . . By these means the people know where the mail is and if anything has happened to it. For instance the mail left here on Monday but so far has not turned up anywhere—Clifton Hills should have been its first call, about 40 miles off but Clifton Hills reports they have not yet passed by—they are evidently marooned with the rain—so I think they will be going to look for them now on horses as although they have supplies on board they might be in difficulty . . .

The town is very busy preparing for its annual festivity, the annual race meeting—two days racing and two nights dancing and great preparations are afoot—people are coming from far and wide—they think nothing of coming from Marree, 320 miles away—but now I believe owing to excessive rain the meeting may have to be postponed . . .

Dorothy's married brother lives across the road and he comes across from time to time and lets us have the news as it comes over the pedal wireless—also across the road is the Australian Inland Mission . . . Sister Gordon is the matron at present and also the entire staff. At present she is there alone not having any customers. Her last patient was a young black gin having a baby—they are wonderful in this country, when a black gin is having a baby they send out one of the white men with a car to the camp for her and bring her in to the hospital where she receives the same attention as any white woman. Dorothy saw this last little baby when he was a few hours old, and she said, there he was wrapped in a little blue bunny rug as well cared for as if he was the most expensive white baby . . .

The Flying Doctor is a bit of a myth at present—the man who is allotted to this particular part is evidently not fond of flying and will not come except in most extreme cases and sometimes not even then. However they are not all like that and anyway Sister is pretty capable . . .

There are plenty of blacks here and every day you see them coming into the town—they do all the odd jobs round about—Jimmy arrived here this morning to chop some wood. As a matter of fact he is King Jimmy—Pussy the previous king having become tired of life crawled into the fire and died, having previously buried his worldly wealth, about 2 pounds 10—which seems to be the custom. There is now a lively interest amongst the blacks as to where this treasure lies hidden. Jimmy automatically took the throne and reported the fact to the local policeman who is their protector. The policeman, to please Jimmy, presented him with a chain and a little brass medal on it which, although Jimmy thinks it says King Jimmy, it actually says Queen Sally. However, he is quite happy and wears it proudly.

Tomorrow Dorissey, a young gin, is coming here to scrub the house out. They are very interesting in their customs, and it surprised me to learn that they have a pretty strict code of morals too. One young gin, Melva, was unmarried and about to have a baby and they were very disturbed and a husband had to be found for Melva before the baby arrived, so Tommy, who was working way out Durrie Station, was duly informed by pedal wireless that he had been married to Melva and please to send some money along for the baby—and Tommy, who was quite pleased with the arrangement, duly complied. The honour of their tribe is very dear to them and when the baby arrived it had a father—unfortunately the baby on arrival proved to be white ... But Tommy is quite pleased with it and very proud of his small son ...

Must close this letter now as the mail leaves in a week's time and the week that is ahead is to be a very busy one and will leave no time for letter writing.

The event of the year takes place week after next—racing carnival and dancing—two days racing and two night's dancing—and about 70 to 100 visitors are expected in the town. The men will start to arrive any day now with their horses and Dorothy will have friends coming here so we are to be busy preparing ...

Fond love to you all.

Florence

References

Copley Chronicle, Special Edition, Vol 1, Issue 3, September 1999.

Ding, Harry, *Thirty Years with Men: Recollections of the Pioneering Years of Transportation in the Deserts of 'Outback' Australia*, The Rotary Club of Walcha, Walcha, 1989.

Else, Eric, *John Heyer's Film, 'The Back of Beyond': A Study by Eric Else*, Longmans, London, 1968.

Farwell, George, *Land of Mirage: The Story of Men, Cattle and Camels on the Birdsville Track*, Cassell and Company, London, 1950.

Grove-Jones, Alex, *One Man to a Thousand: 50 Years in the Pastoral Industry, 1932–1982*, Omtat, Woodside, 1998.

Henry, Mona, *From City to the Sandhills of Birdsville*, Copyright Publishing, Brisbane, 1994.

Litchfield, Lois, *Marree and the Tracks Beyond in Black and White: Commemorating the Centenary of Marree, 1883–1983*, Lois Litchfield, Marree, 1983.

Maddock, John, *Mail for the Back of Beyond*, Kangaroo Press, Sydney, 1986.

Madigan, CT, *Crossing the Dead Heart*, Georgian House, Melbourne, 1946.

Ratcliffe, Francis, *Flying Fox and Drifting Sand: The Adventures of a Biologist in Australia*, Angus and Robertson, Sydney, 1947.

GET THE WHOLE STORY AT:

www.hachette.com.au